AF599327

life and limbs
Curated by Anna-Sophie Berger

Architecture and Design Series

SI

The gallery becomes a mouth. It has four pointy teeth and is an aged, even sickly, shade of off-white. The teeth are walls, and on them hang artworks selected by Austrian artist Anna-Sophie Berger for the exhibition *life and limbs*, Swiss Institute's fourth installment of its Architecture and Design Series. Berger's premise for the show considers the body an experimental testing ground for design, a living site that is both vulnerable and resilient. As the title implies, life and limbs exists in a world where the human body, unadorned, is at risk and often confronts threat with dark and knowing humor but also with grace. Across these works, which draw from speculative architectures, Surrealism, late twentieth-century fashion design, and Viennese Actionism, among many other subsects of modern visual culture, Berger's singular understanding of corporeal awareness unfolds. In the clutches of this jaw, bodies find ways to disappear, though some stretch, reach, and metamorphosize in attempts to escape themselves.

The book in your hands is a means to further explore Berger's thesis. Three remarkable essays, one by the artist herself, ponder the works that populate this wunderkammer and question design's transformative potential. In this catalogue's opening essay, Phillip Ekardt maps a close analysis of artist Birgit Jurgenssen's *Missing Limbs* to examine "the extent to which the concept behind *life and limbs*—and a certain artistic practice—can be seen as grounded in an understanding of forms as permanently changing," which is in "direct contact with the realm of looks, styles, and their persistent revision, which is called fashion." By analyzing this work, he concludes that "fashion makes itself felt profoundly as a force of metamorphosis, and a field soliciting a morphological view, which takes in forms and their shifts alike." In her essay "Body on the Edge of Crisis," Annie Godfrey Larmon declares: "Bodies are only determined if we are unwilling to see them otherwise." She examines the fluidity of corporality, linking it to Berger's curatorial position in which she bridges the personal (possessions of family members and a sculpture by Berger's boyfriend count among the works included) and the historical (the legacy of artist-curated exhibitions as a means of disrupting established understandings of forms). For Berger, design and the objects we place on our bodies are never singular. To draw from Henri Focillon, "Forms constitute an order of existence . . . this order has the motion and breath of life."[1] Godfrey Larmon gives depth to this assertion in her analysis of the temporalities (and politics) of group exhibitions, which in many ways replicate and perpetuate Berger's understanding of what designed objects can generate. Again, Focillon: "Plastic forms are subjected to the principle of metamorphoses, by which they are perpetually renewed, as well as to the principle of styles, by which their relationship is, although by no means with any regularity of recurrence, first tested, then made fast and finally disrupted . . . a work of art is motionless only in appearance."[2]

The book's final essay comes from Berger, who begins her text with an analysis of a photograph from her first communion. In it, Berger wears a white silk communion dress, while her mother emerges from the driver's seat of a car wearing the same red Moschino suit that hung from the ceiling in SI's gallery. It is embroidered with the phrase: Waist of Money. This embellishment becomes the title of Berger's essay, which deftly outlines the stakes of life and limbs, and serves as a treatise on the artist's relationship not only to garments and fashion but to Catholicism, class, and history. We behold the great mind of an artist at work, but bear witness to the messier, more complex instances and understandings that informed the philosophy that spawned the exhibition and subsequent publication. Reader, I leave you the pleasure of discovering Berger's world for yourself. While there are traditional installation views throughout these pages, there are also myriad snapshots, screengrabs, and pictures discovered on the internet by the artist; a foundation for the exhibition was a folder on Berger's desktop entitled "Art I Like." These discoveries and visual reminders imbue the book with the intimacy of a scrapbook or journal and demonstrate the impossibility of confining the themes of *life and limbs* to what is exhibited in the gallery.

Yet, the ideas put forth in this book are not always seen, or read or heard. They may also be ingested. On the afternoon of November 16, 2019,

SI hosted a small gathering in its second-floor gallery on the occasion of *life and limbs* entitled "A Pint of Tripe." Among café tables adorned with delicate flower arrangements, a chef prepared *motsunabe*, a popular Japanese stew made with tripe. On a flyer made for the event, Berger set a quote by Mikhail Bakhtin against a picture of beef tripe. "All these convexities and orifices," Bakhtin writes, "have a common characteristic; it is within them that the confines between bodies and between the body and the world are overcome; there is an interchange and an interorientation." From the cavities of SI's gallery to the stomach of a cow to the pleat of a blazer: in these folds, joints, and layers that accumulate within and on our bodies lie opportunities for transcendence. In *life and limbs*, Berger lends us her eyes in the hope that we might see them too.

1 Henri Focillon, *The Life of Forms in Art* (New York: Zone Books, 1992), 41.
2 Ibid.

Fig. 1 →

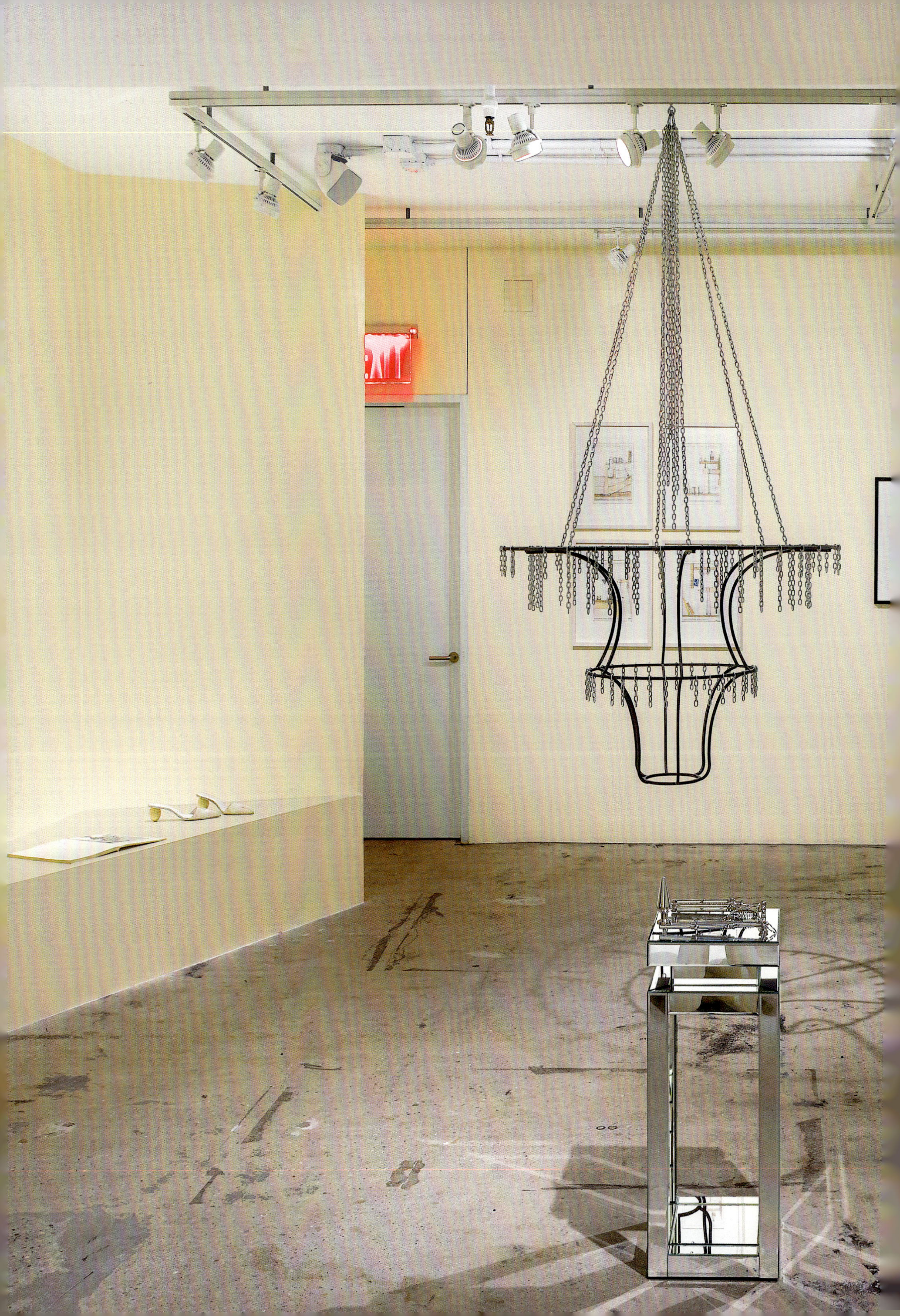

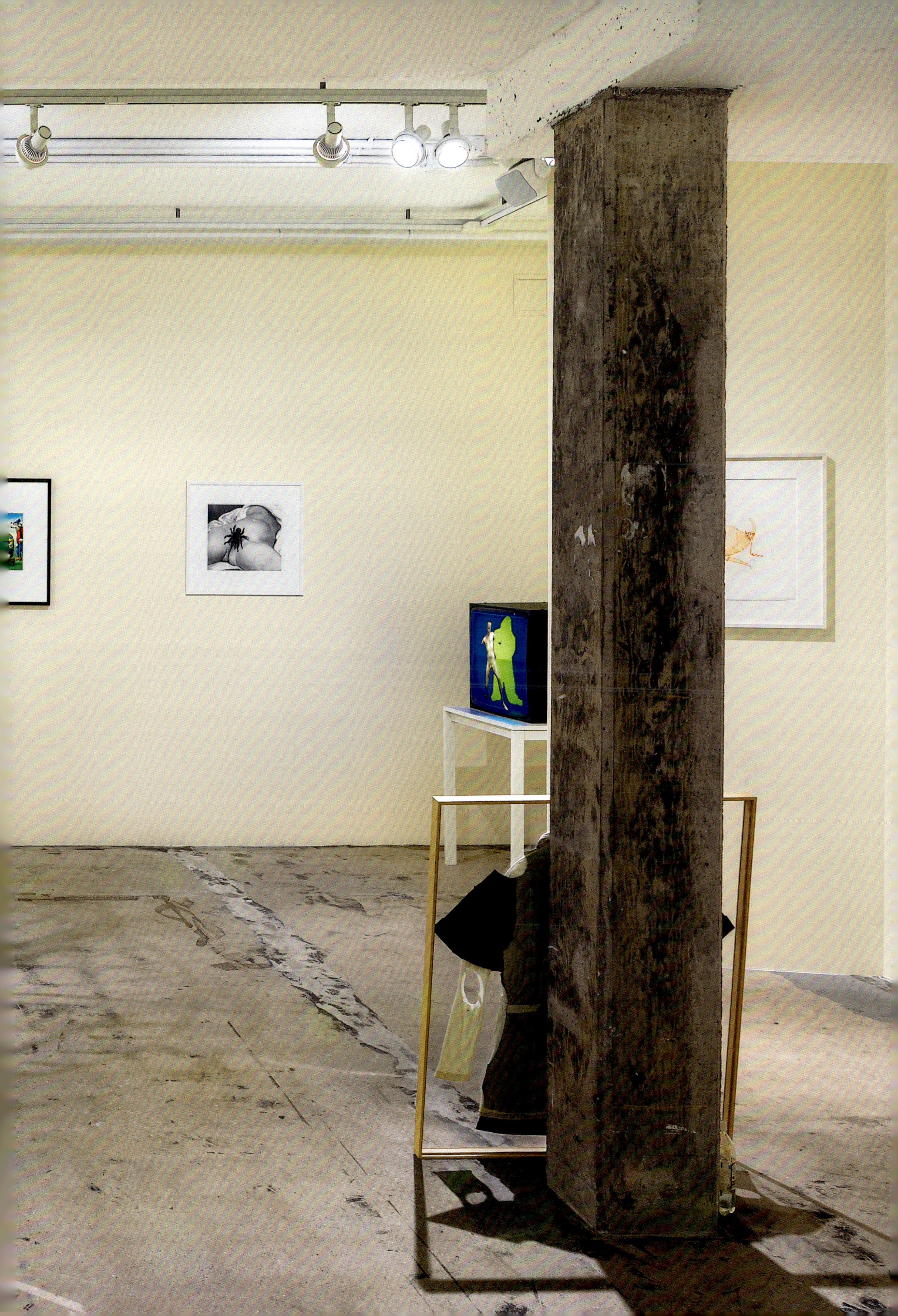

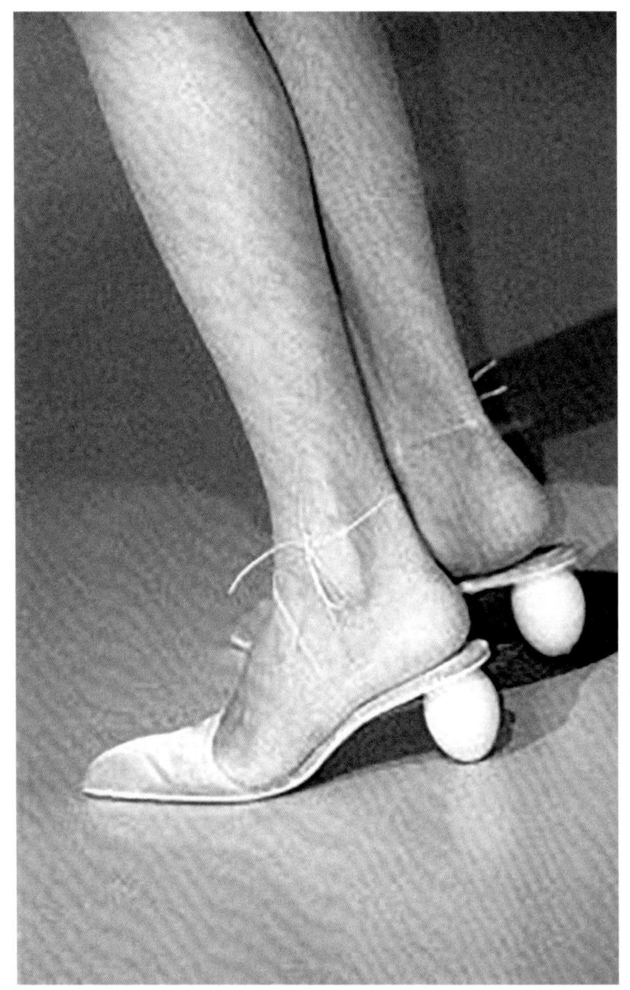

Fig. 2

Eggshell Slippers and a Calcified Cabinet

After descending the stairs into Swiss Institute's basement, the visitor to *life and limbs* entered an irregularly shaped wraparound display which framed the institute's lower-level gallery where the exhibition was shown. Constructed according to curating artist Anna-Sophie Berger's plans, its color—an unhealthy off-shade of cream—seemed prompted by a pair of elegant, and odd, mini-heeled slippers designed by Johnny Moke for Parisian couturier Adeline Andrée, in whose atelier Berger worked prior to embarking on her trajectory as an artist. Discreetly tucked away in a far corner of the cabinet, the slippers' dirtied shade of cream was picked up on the display architecture and walls, whose zigzagging protrusions and nook-forming shapes held associations of stained teeth, while also, strangely, harking back to the hospital-gown tones of Prada's early 2000s boutiques. Replacing the slender stems usually elevating the foot's back part by egglike shapes, these shoes set not just the color for the display, but also an overall tone for a show in which bodies were tethered and reassembled, dressed up and down, styled, and became participants in a game of wits: carefully, or not, treading—or trampling—on eggshells (another, if slightly euphemistic, linguistic prompt for naming the color of the downstairs walls and floor).

This calcified scenario housed reverberations of Surrealism's various fragmentations and distortions of the body. For instance, by member of the original movement Meret Oppenheim, by whom a small-scale 1935 drawing for a jewelry design displayed a horseshoe-shaped pair of bodiless legs, presumably a girl's, finished with feet in bright-blue socks and patent leather shoes. Wrapping around a woman's neck from behind, in a manner in which one would wear a foulard, the image evokes the uncanny specter of a missing child *not* sat on these shoulders. There was Kajode Oyo's 2018 work *I'm Fine*, a polished mirror and metal pedestal displaying an assortment of instruments, triggering medical or—resonating with the dungeonlike basement situation—S&M-related associations: all sorts of shiny contraptions for forcefully impacting the limbs of the body and its orifices. The subject of penetration and perforation, and the flesh-pretzels of intertwining bodies, were also deftly presented in one of Ebecho Muslimova's fatly drawn graphics of her alter ego *Fatebe*, who here joyfully tunneled a toy train through a hole in her left thigh. Walter Pichler's *Fingerspanner*, a series of three photographs, displayed decorative yet crooked ortheses strapped around fingers: nasty yet somehow cool corsets for the digits, harking back to android armors as seen in Fritz Lang's *Metropolis*, and anticipating later Mugler pieces. Facing these was Lyle Ashton Harris's 1994 work *Venus Hottentot 2000*, made in collaboration with artist Renee Cox, departing from her performance *HOTTENTOT*, and the documentation thereof, in which the artist supplied herself with a double set of bulging prosthetics, breasts and buttocks, which she strapped around her waist and chest, to visibly amplify the shapes of her respective body parts. Returning to the life of Sara Baartman, a Khoikhoi woman born in 1789 in what is nowadays South Africa, Harris and Cox here re-imag(in)e her appearance, and body parts which became flashpoints of a racist, racializing European discourse that marked non-"whites" as the site of a spectacle of "primitive sexuality," exhibiting and enslaving Baartman on the stages of a continent that would later pride itself for birthing the Enlightenment at the historical moment in question.

Jürgenssen's "Missing Limbs"

Included in this panorama was also a work which, if studied a little more closely, gives us cues as to what might be considered one of the general propositions of the entire show. This is not to say that the image in question stood "at the beginning" of Anna-Sophie Berger's conception of the exhibition. Such an idea—that a larger project, be it a show, a group of works, perhaps a text, should be derived from a single source image—would also seem at odds with Berger's declared preference for working from a gradually assembled set of images, a folder, a grouping together, a cluster. In this, Berger's approach seems—to an extent—informed by production modes that depart from image collections, rather than from individual prompts. This is reminiscent of standard practices in the visual arts and fashion alike, where these image aggregations appear, for example, in the

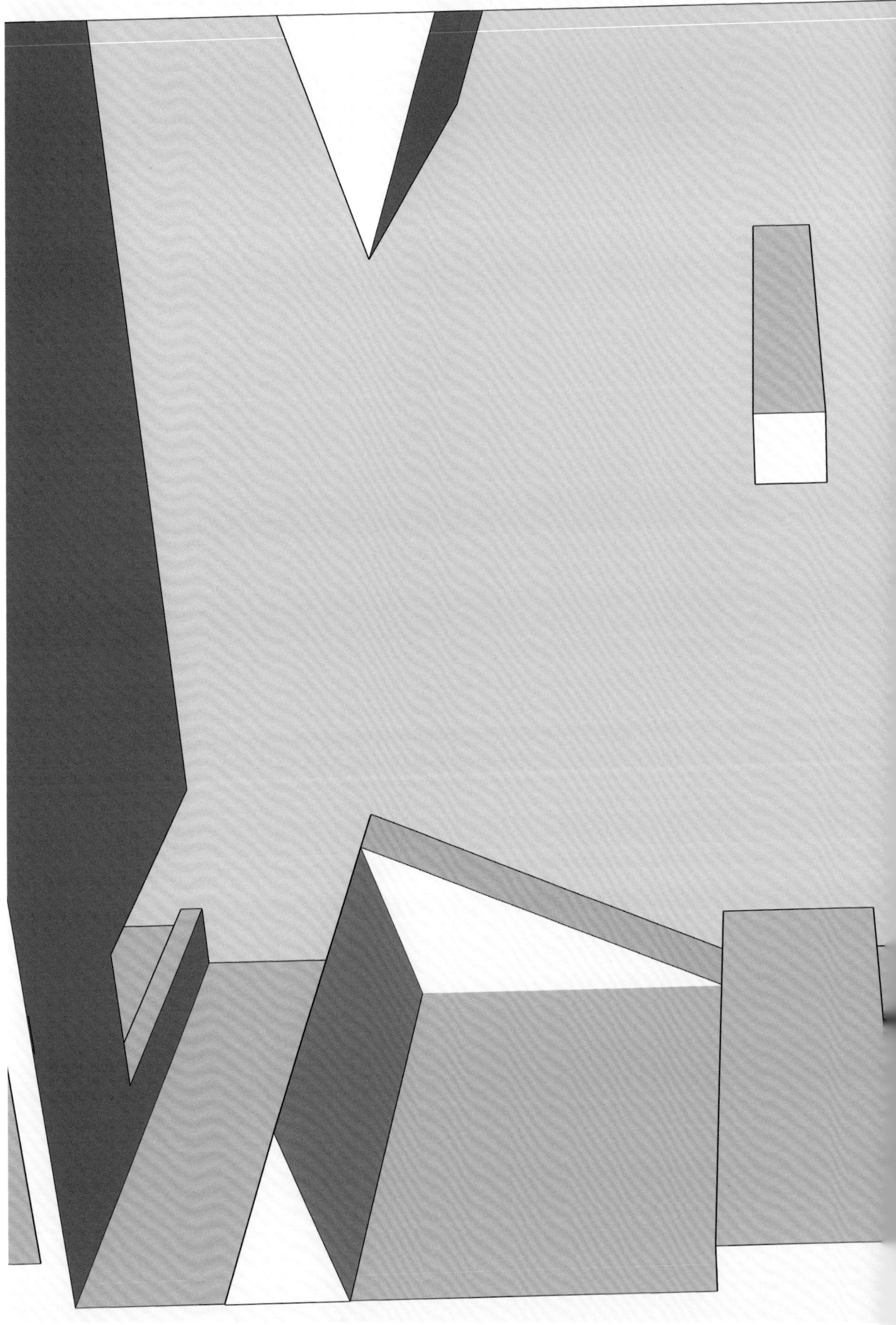

Fig. 3

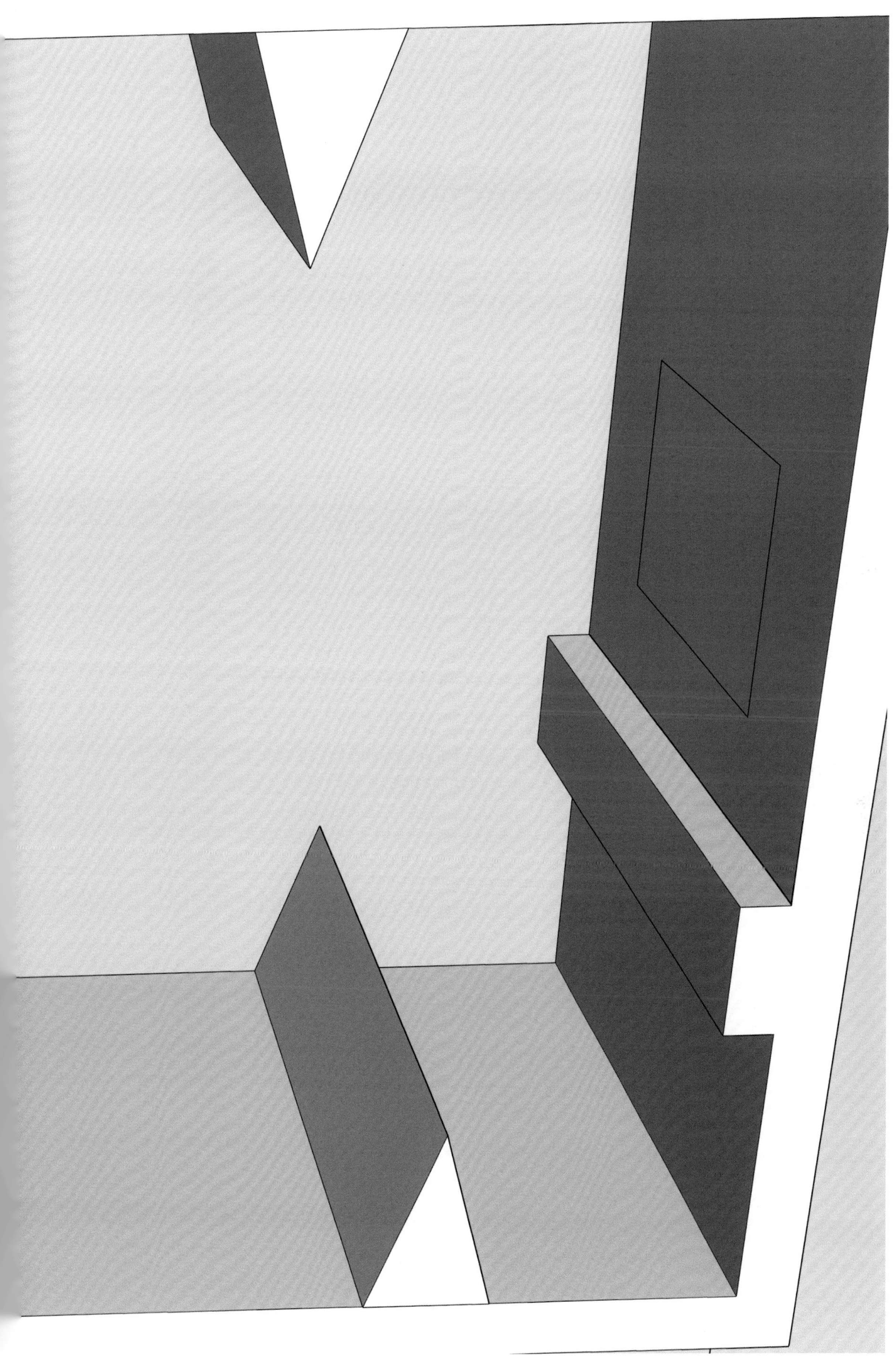

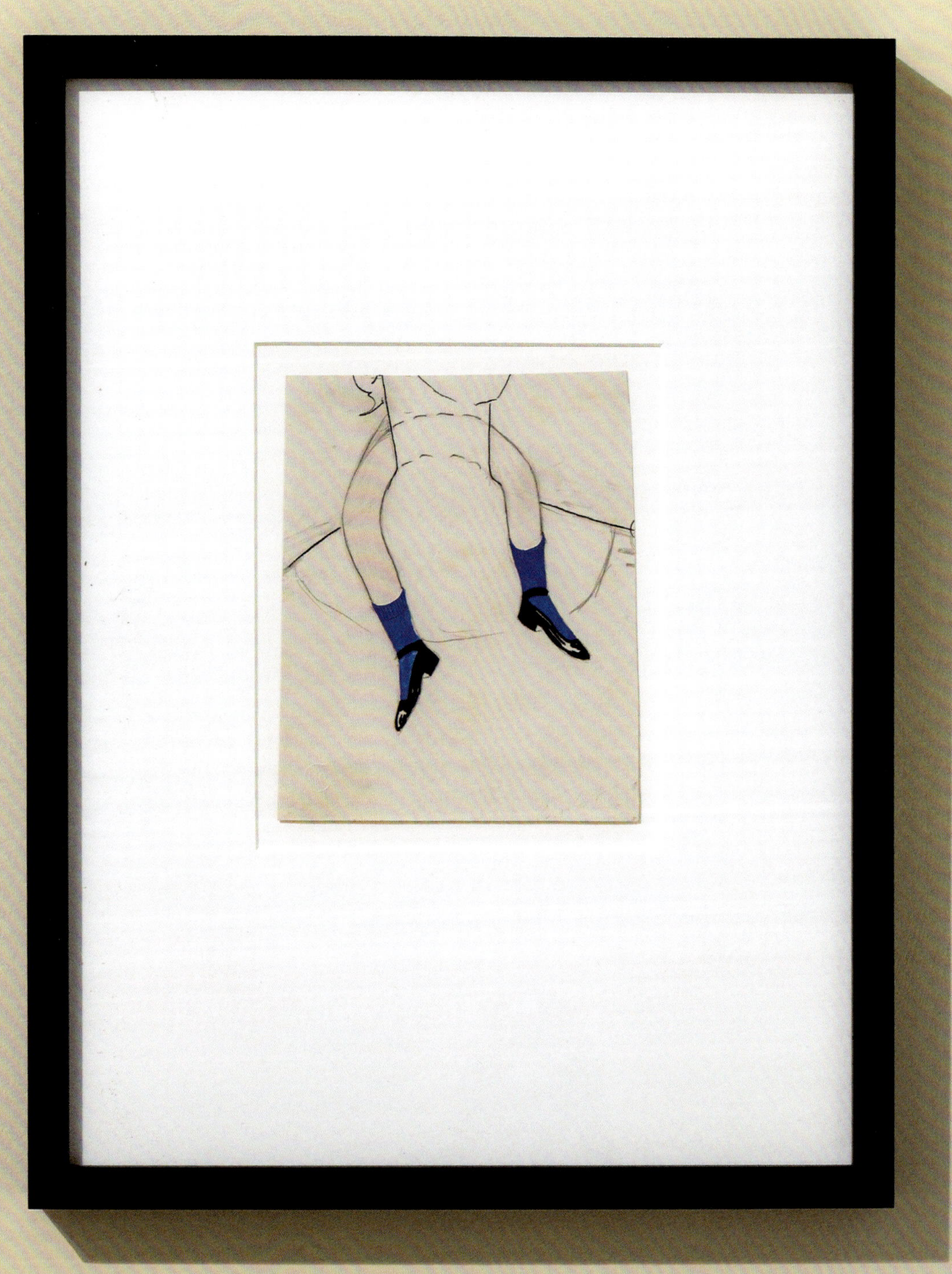

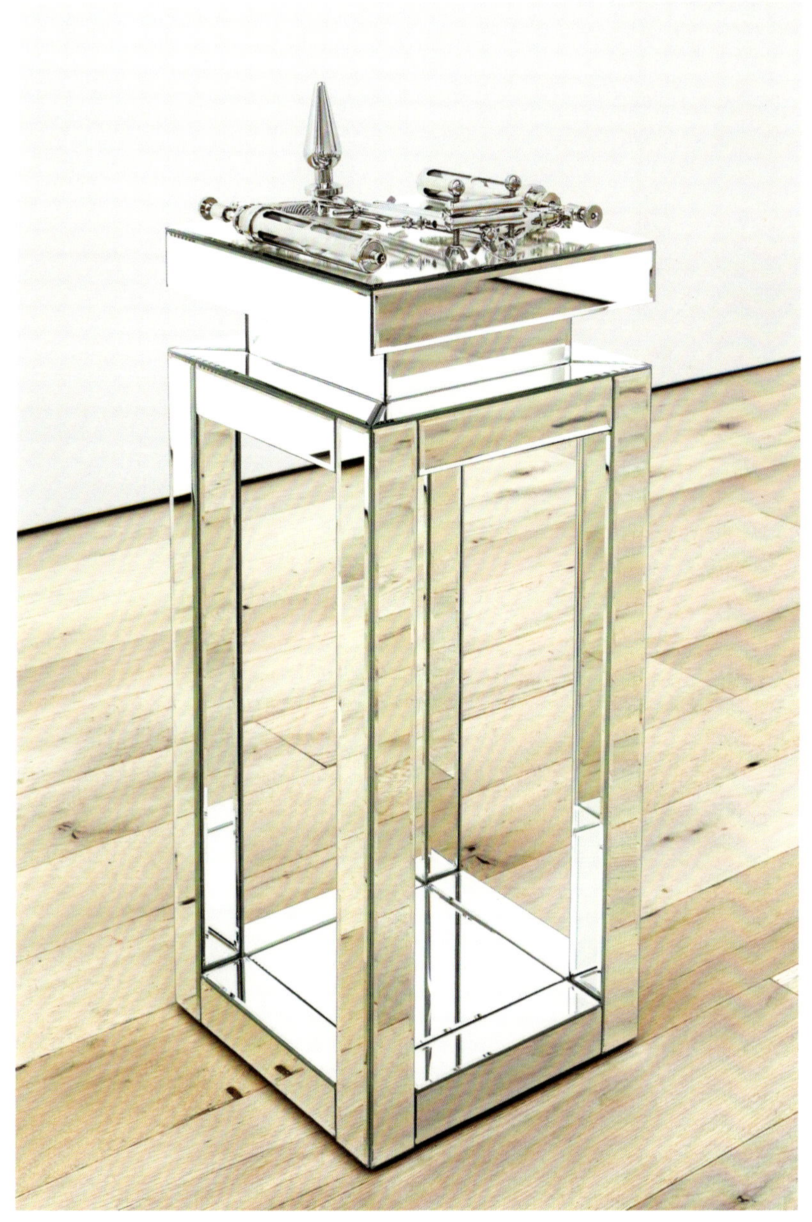

Figs. 4, 5

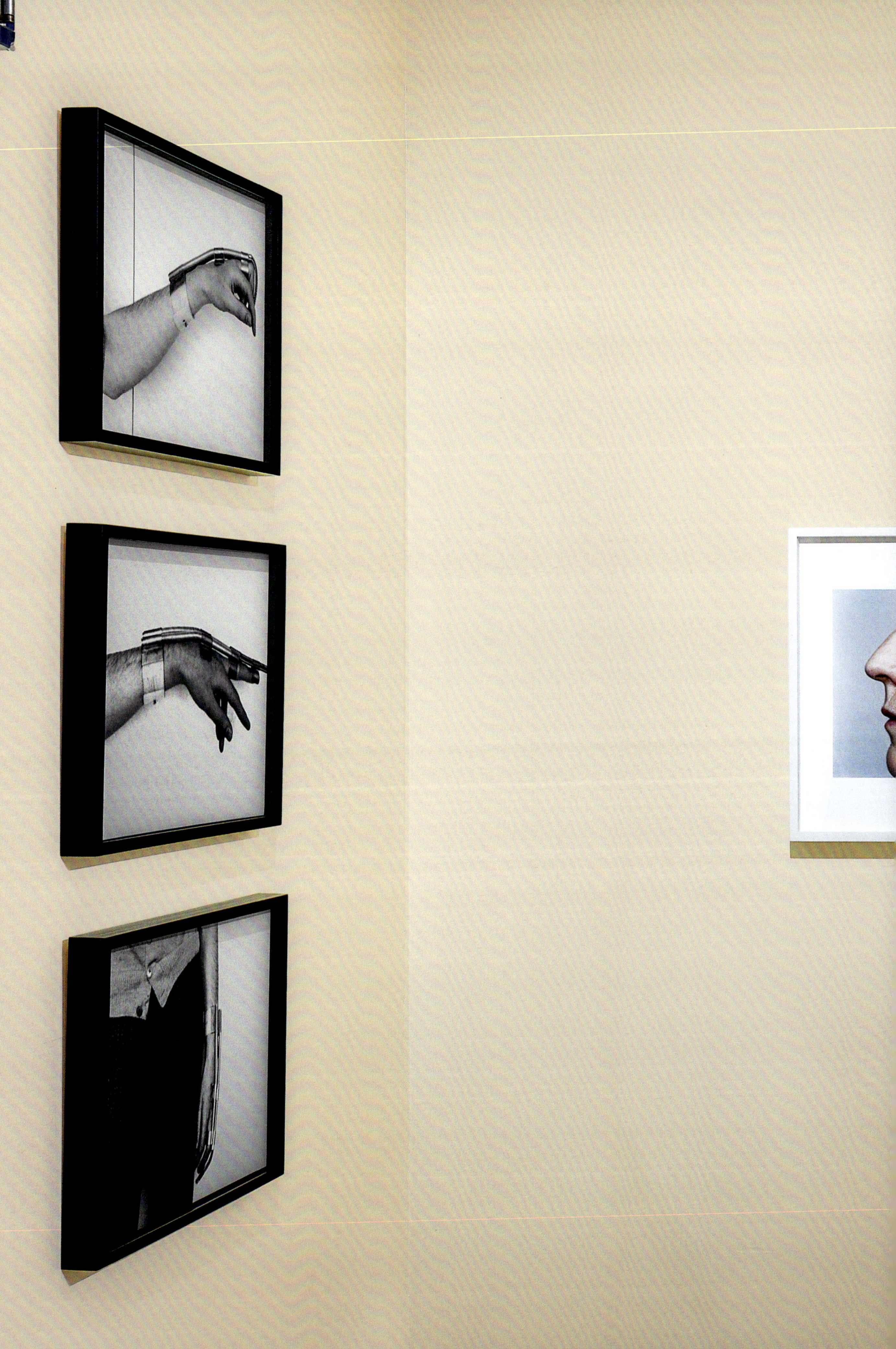

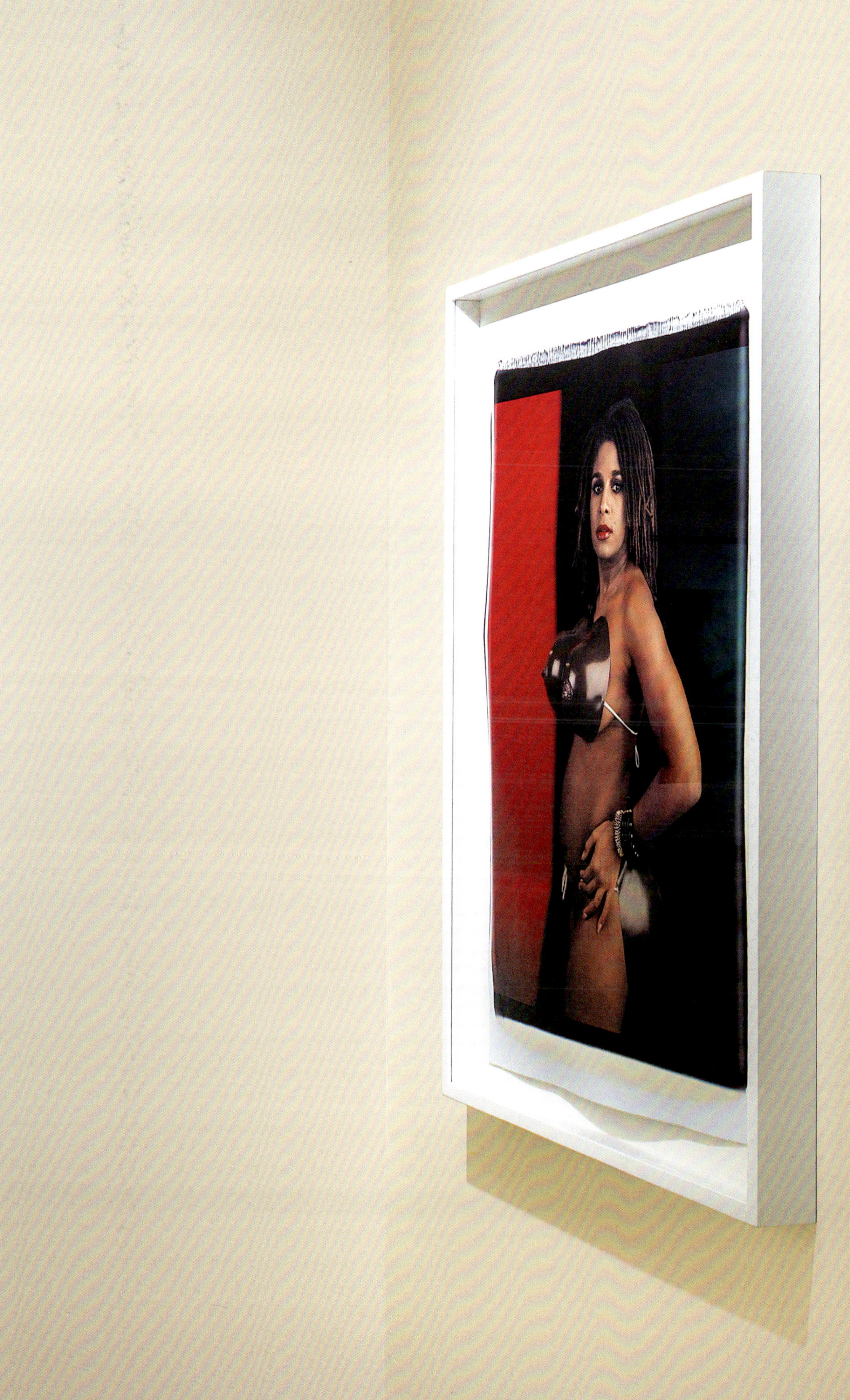

form of so-called mood boards. It is also a practice that is particularly well suited to our digital and networked condition, in which the possibilities of sourcing image material have increased exponentially; a principle on which Berger also relies in editing the extended image flows of iPhone footage that make up her digital film *Duel* (2020).

The following is not to say that other works in the show wouldn't qualify for comparable scrutiny and wouldn't prove valid positions for addressing such vaster trajectories. Yet the picture in question seems to hold the key to something special here. It is a work that, ultimately, will help us understand the extent to which the concept behind *life and limbs*—and a certain artistic practice—can be seen as grounded in an understanding of forms as permanently changing. Just such a concept underlies the twisting and shaping of bodies and members that were on display at Swiss Institute. And although this may at first sound like a very philosophical approach, the mentioned practice is in direct contact with the realm of looks, styles, and their persistent revision, which is called fashion. The work in question is Austrian artist Birgit Jürgenssen's 1971 colored drawing *Missing Limbs*, or *Fehlende Glieder* in the original German. Its particular proximity to the show's overall title and concept is double. First, there is the mention of "limbs" (as in *life and limbs*), which, in the title of Jürgenssen's drawing, are designated as absent. The formulation "missing limbs" thus evokes scenarios of incompleteness: perhaps at first, the image of a body bereft of legs and arms. Or, a representation of these limbs, as severed from the body from which they have become untethered. Dismemberment, either in the form of the truncated body, or the truncated limbs themselves. However, Jürgenssen's drawing shows us something different: in a variety of ways, the left-hand side of the depicted male figure passes over into an array of limbs and other extensions, most of which, although not all, seem to belong to a lobster. We see its feet, its claws, its antennae; also, sprouting from the figure's head, an assortment of extremities that might not be entirely animal, but rather para-mineral: the branches of a coral, perhaps, or some sort of underwater flora. The finely drawn boundary between human figure and its nonhuman limbs is occasionally permeated, at other spots distinctly marked. At several points the marine animal segment seems to emerge from the man's outfit, at others directly from his body, hence establishing a peculiar three-way relationship between the anatomies of crustacean, man, and the latter's dress. It is also not quite clear whether the lobster extremities, the coral arms, have been attached to the human figure, as if to prosthetically make up for some absence, or whether they are an outgrowth of it. It is clear, however, that, contradicting the drawing's title, the depicted figure is, if somewhat heterogeneous, quite complete. Things and limbs may differ from what—or how—we expect them to be; yet there they are, and quite prominent at that.

Jokes and Mixed Creations

In the face of this palpable contradiction, it is clear that the title of Jürgenssen's drawing operates on the level of irony; it is, perhaps, in the terminology of her and Berger's Vienna compatriot Freud, a joke, a *Witz*. Freud described one of its techniques as condensation, the production of *Mischgebilde*—composite structures, i.e., hybrids. We could also translate Freud's term more literally as "mixed creations," akin to the one we're seeing in Jürgenssen's drawing. Freud also speaks of "mixed words" (*Mischworte*) such as *anecdotage*—comprised of *anecdote* and *dotage*—the act of oversharing anecdotes; or *alcoholidays* (no explanation necessary). These, Freud continues to explain, function as a concise substitute for an otherwise longwinded description.[1] Through playing on a linguistic aspect, Jürgenssen's work would also chime in with the show's overall title: although there were quite a number of limbs and other body parts to be contemplated in the exhibition, Berger's *life and limbs* alludes to "life and limb," a saying which describes a state in which, intentionally or not, everything is put on the line, sometimes at the risk of harm: to risk life and limb, as if there's no tomorrow.

Returning to the moment of the joke, Jürgenssen's title could also be read as an ironic commentary from a feminist standpoint.[2] For there is of course also that one inevitable joke here: the German *Glied* (for limb) is a (technical, even medico-anatomical) moniker for not just any member, but *the* member, i.e., the cock. (A cock which, although invisible, could have been conspicuously elided as well as alluded to in Jürgenssen's drawing, given the rather carefully

← Fig. 6

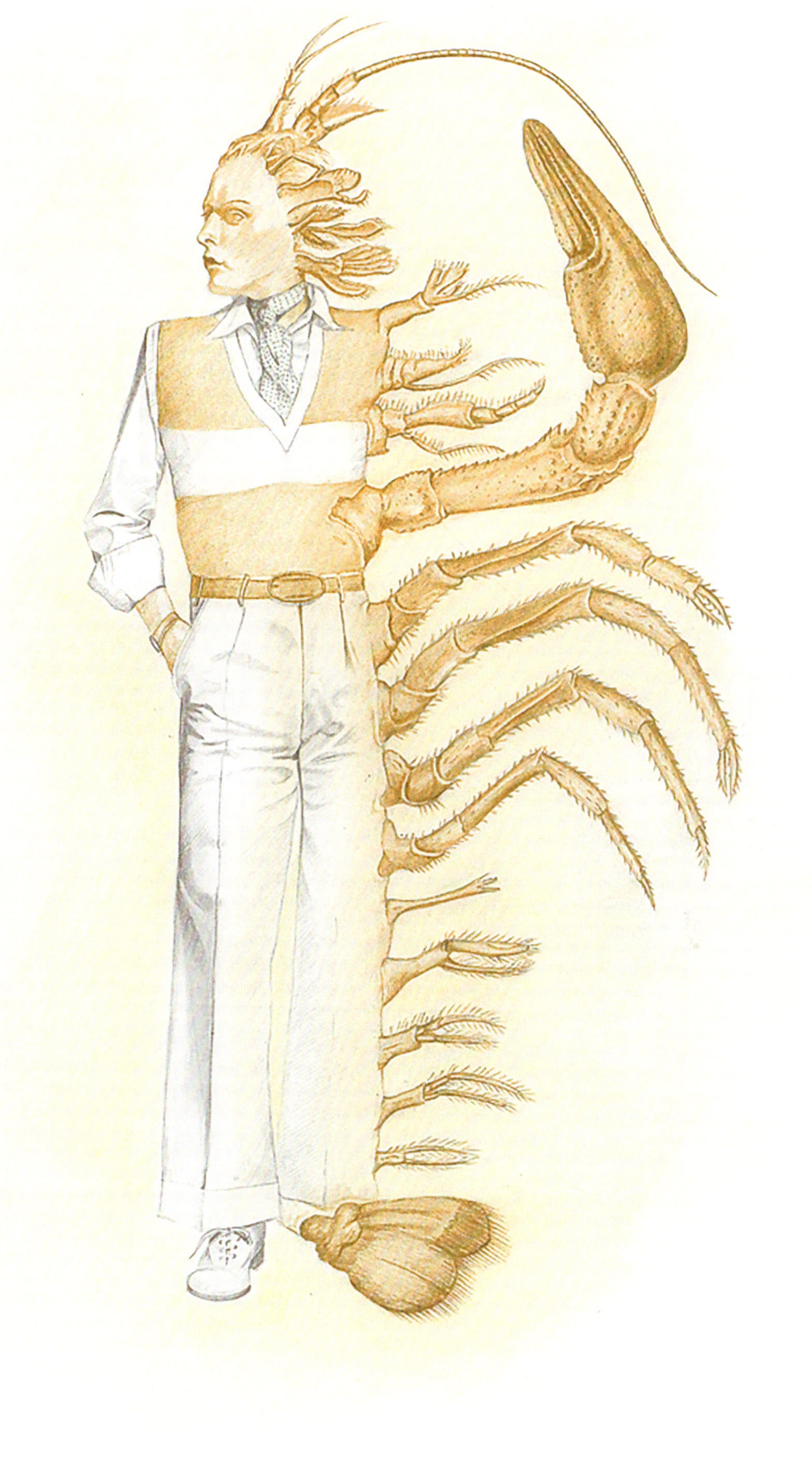

Fig. 7

modeled relief of creases that settle around the drawn figure's crotch; while these distinctly do *not* display a visible penis line, the figure's demonstratively occluded right hand would seem perfectly placed for a game of what is sometimes referred to as "pocket billiards.") Reiterating the tired yet unfortunately still powerful assumption that woman's position is, in relation to man's, understood via the absence of said member, a third leg, or limb, *Missing Limbs* could, in a strange plural, even refer to a multitude of women, or women artists.[3] Or, perhaps Jürgenssen ensnares the potentially "masc" viewer in a game of—pardon the pun—one-up*man*ship, pointing to all those excess members that are on display here. Boy, consider *this* lobster...

Exquisite Corpse, Sideways (Metamorphoses and Surrealism)

Given this operativity of the linguistic dimension, the references to sexuality, and the overall strange opacity of the depicted subject (on what grounds do man and lobster meet?), Jürgenssen's work ever so finely touches on the medium of the rebus, the riddle picture—a staple procedure of Surrealism, the avant-garde movement to which Jürgenssen herself ascribed a significant influence on her production.[4] The figure's mixed status between human and animal, human and vegetal, and even human and mineral that we are seeing in *Missing Limbs* might point us in the direction of Surrealism as well, where, as part of a wide strand of artistic and scientific discourses, the spectrum between the animate and inanimate, states of living and matter, and between species was being explored.

Spyros Papapetros has recently drawn our attention to the elaborations of the Daphne motif, for instance, in the work of Dalí; Daphne, as the story goes, chased by Apollo, would rather be turned into a bush of laurel than succumb to her persecutor.[5] We could also think of Claude Cahun's ca. 1931 photograph *Je tends mes bras* (I Extend My Arms), a picture in which a human figure, perhaps the artist themselves, appears to either inhabit or have their body replaced by a rather massive rock; their arms, poking out on each side, forming what seems like a potential embrace.[6] Note not only the parallel to Jürgenssen's play on human/animal/mineral substitutes here, but also the reappearance of the limbs.

Looking at the slightly monstrous side-by-side of left and right, man and lobster, Jürgenssen's drawing might even, for a moment, strike us as a lateralized version of a *cadavre exquis*, an "exquisite corpse." This was the title for a game by which the members of the Surrealist avant-garde liked to entertain themselves: each participant begins a drawing of a figure at the top of a sheet, then folds this upper section backward, hiding their work but for the narrowest indication of where to continue. The paper is passed on to a fellow player who draws a torso section, and so on, until the group has achieved a series of fantastically hybrid creatures whose production was fostered by structured chance procedures.

In appearance, *Missing Limbs* carries traces of these pieces, but, apart from relegating production from a group endeavor to the activity of a single artist, it also rotates the orientation of the segmentation axis along which the hybridization of the figure occurs from the horizontal to the vertical. What, with the Surrealists, was a model of a top-to-bottom striated hybridity is now flipped by ninety degrees and reduced to two sections. In the act of joining the disparate halves, *Missing Limbs* also undoes bilateral symmetry—a morphological property otherwise common to human *and* lobster. An avant-garde experiment turned sideways.

Species Shifts and Missing Links

Jürgenssen has explored species transitions like the one between *Homo sapiens* and crustacean on several other occasions, including a number of photographic self-portraits, among them the well-known *Selbst mit Fellchen* (Self with Little Fur) (1974), in which she poses with animal props such as fox fur attached to her body and face.[7] In these the camera fuses human and animal elements into pictures of creatures of more than one species. Jürgenssen develops the merging of human and animal forms further in a number of works from her series *Körperprojektionen* (Body Projections), all photographic self-portraits again, for which she captures various surfaces and angles of her body and face onto which are projected shapes and patterns, among them animal anatomies, and skins.[8] In these occurs a quite literal superimposition of differently speciated morphologies, which, in the reception of Jürgenssen's work, has been

Fig. 8

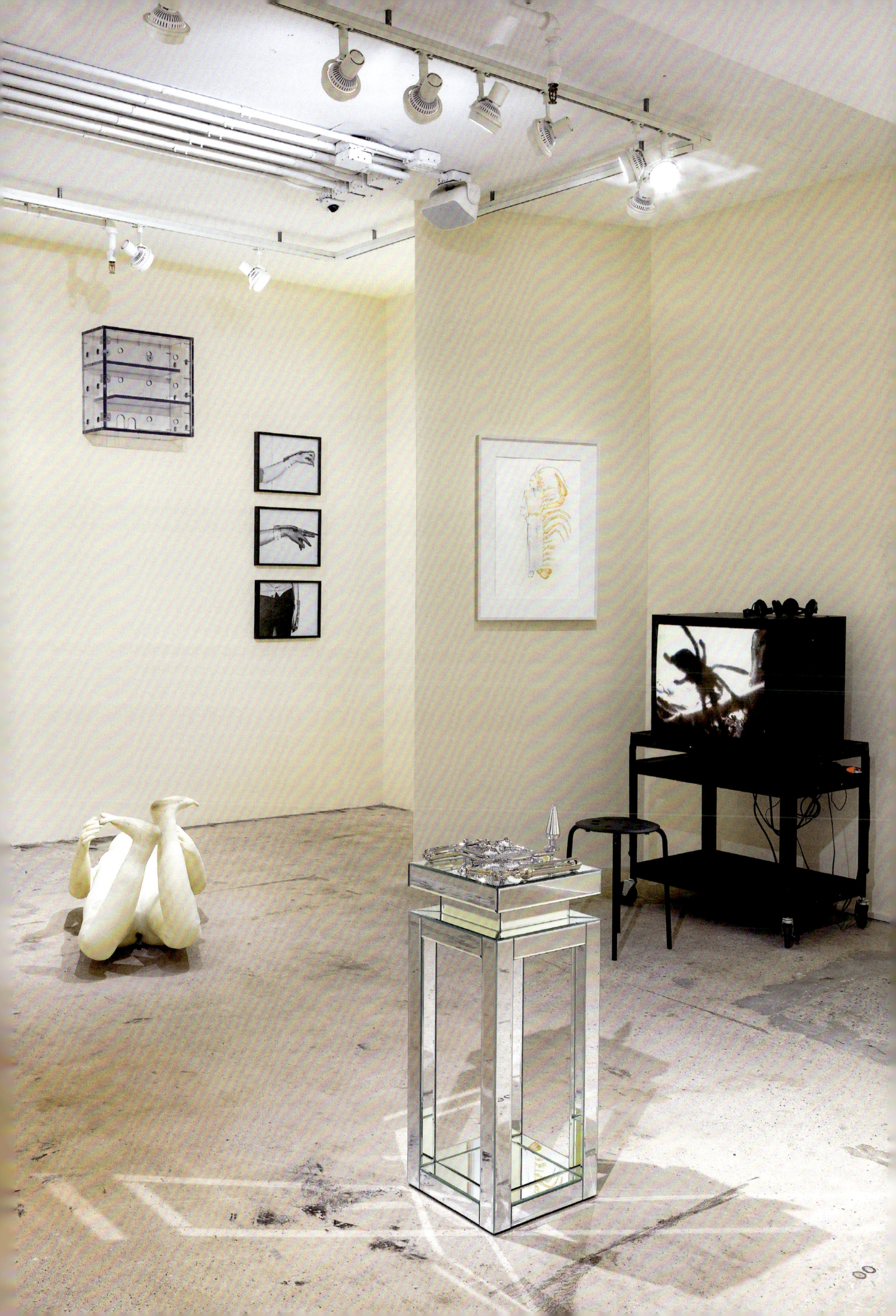

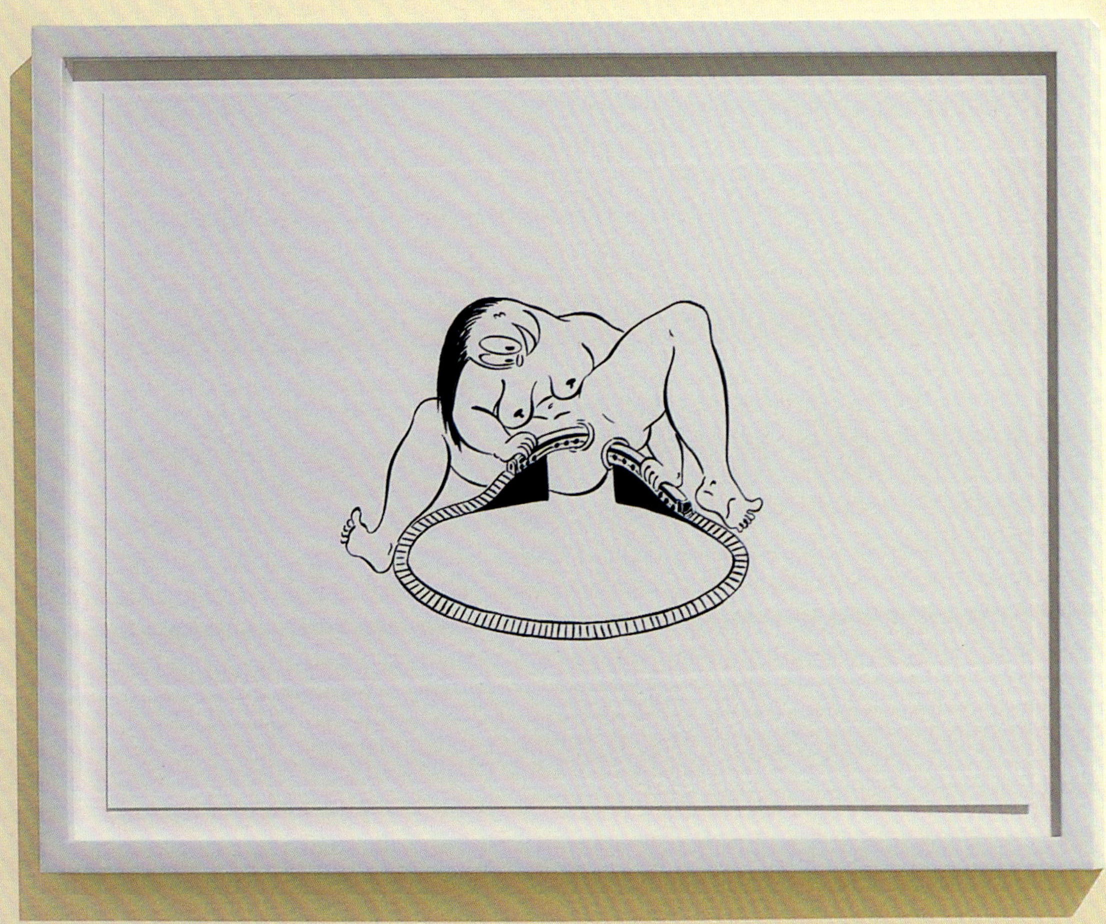

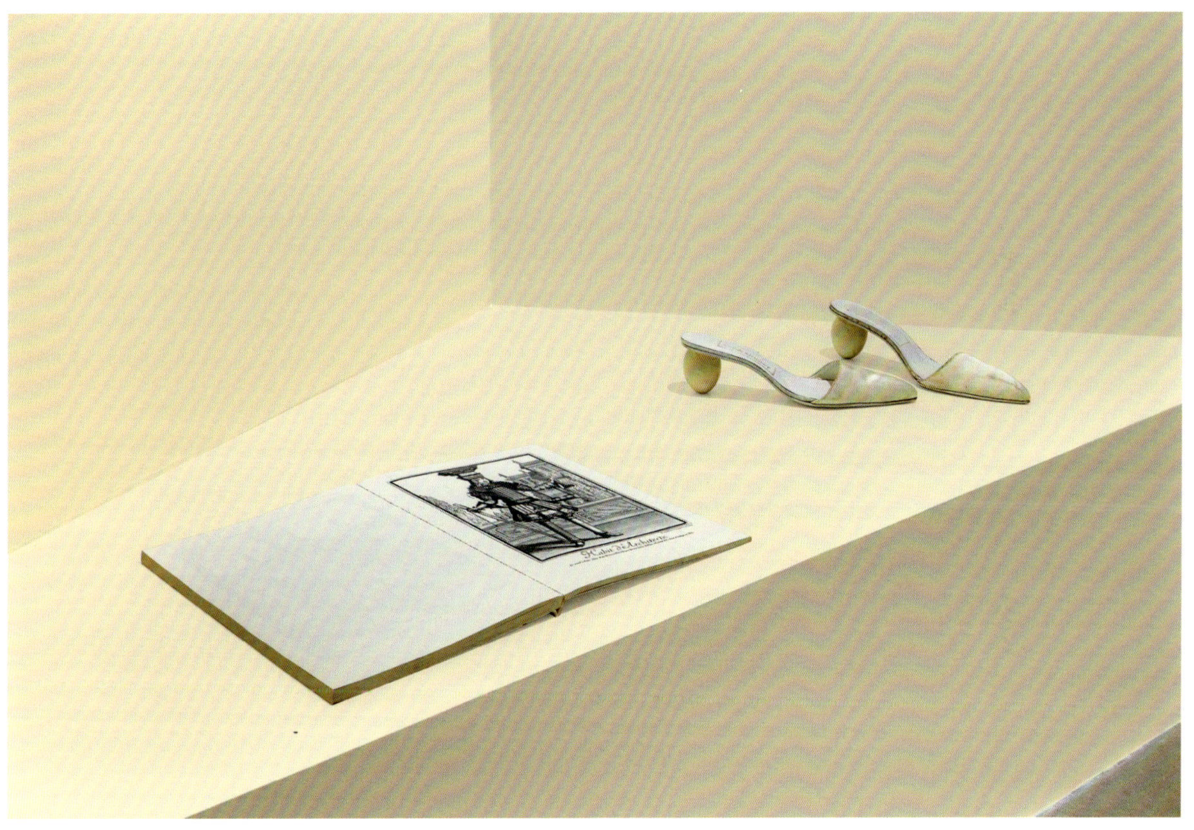

understood as relating metaphorically to representations of the precarious position of femininity under patriarchy, and attempts at constructing artistic escape routes from the fixities of the concurring image norms.[9]

While these are evidently not the concerns pursued in *Missing Limbs*, the themes elaborated in this drawing—an encounter or metamorphosis between species within a single figure—overlap with female human/animal superimpositions in other pieces. There is an untitled 1978 drawing depicting a furry female individual of humanoid shape, shown in profile moving on all fours. Three—unfurry—hands reaching from above and both sides into the picture align and direct the creature's movements.[10] The work has been connected to evolutionary theories of the emergence of the upright gait, which are here blended into a thematization of the quite literal "suppression" of woman (another of Jürgenssen's word games, as one of the hands is literally pressing the creature downward).[11] We might consider as related works the 1975 drawing *Der Wettlauf* (The Race), in which the artist superimposes the semitransparent figures of a man in a running outfit and a gorilla, racing in parallel to the picture plane, thus producing an ironic variation of the common graphic representations of the evolutionary transition from primate to humanoid, as well as the emergence of the upright gait, rendered as a frieze-like procession of specimens of evolutionary successive species.[12] Or *Elsa*, a laconic 1973 drawing which places a muscular lioness side by side with an extremely hirsute, undressed female individual, who, captured in sexy contrapposto, is casually leaning against the backrest of a folding chair familiar from film sets and soundstages, its cloth spelling out ELSA in capital letters, as if reserved for some star known by her first name only.[13]

In the face of these species shifts and superimpositions yet another layer of meaning to Jürgenssen's strange encounter of man and lobster within a single figure comes to mind; another joke, if you will. *Fehlende Glieder* might not just translate as "missing limbs." What is missing here—the *Glied* in question—and what we might at the same time be looking at could also be a "link" in a chain (in German: *ein Glied der Kette*); more specifically: a link in that one great chain of speciation which we have come to call evolution. More plainly put: the *fehlendes Glied* might be that famous *missing link* by which evolutionary theory designates a yet undiscovered but hypothetically posited intermediate step between two recorded species. Jürgenssen's punch line here being that, rather than adhering to the deep-time, gradual shifts from species to species, two of them are smashed together in front of our eyes.

Fashion Form and Lobster Legs—Toward a Morphology of Looks and Limbs

Yet in the case of *Missing Limbs* it is quite clear that Jürgenssen's visual interest goes beyond and cannot be reduced to the construction of a picture that in some form executes the logic of a pun or finds a pictorial form for a joke; and it is also clear that her point is not to merely extend a few select traits of the Surrealist project, about thirty to forty years after its heyday; to merely set an art historical reference. Nor is the aim to produce an ever-so-punning artistic elaboration of trans-speciation.

In Jürgenssen's drawing there is, to begin with, quite simply rather too much interest in just how the depicted figure looks. And not just "how" as in a descriptive assessment. This "how" is also an evaluative question, which solicits an evaluative answer: How does he look? Good? Or not? His slacks with their slight bell-bottoms are the epitome of 1970s casual sharpness; the trousers' high waist is held up by a thin belt; the sleeveless sweater, tucked into the pants, displays a two-way color-blocked field, reminiscent of sports jerseys; and the foulard or cravat is twisted into an elegant knot: were it not for the sprouting lobster side, the figure would have a distinct dandy flair about it; a match, for instance, for David Hockney's slick rendering of the dress styles of British designers Ossie Clark and Celia Birtwell in his 1971 canvas *Mr and Mrs Clark and Percy*—contemporary to *Missing Limbs* down to the year. And while not exactly a running theme, there are other examples of Jürgenssen turning her attention to the subject of period fashions, if not those of her own historical moment. In a 1977 self-portrait she draws herself outfitted with a post–World War I cloche hat and a characteristic bow of the same period around her neck—vestimentary emblems of the 1920s emancipated *Neue Frau* (New Woman).[14] Jürgenssen's attention to the stylish and her engaging with looks as a medium for artistic work are also amply demonstrated by her coproductions with fellow members of legendary artists group *Die Damen* (The Ladies) Ona B., Evelyne Eggerer, Ingeborg Strobl, and occasionally Lawrence Weiner; not just a pioneering feminist formation, but also conceptual arbiters of "the look," to match and anticipate other players on this field, such as General Idea and Artclub 2000, or, more recently, DIS.[15]

It is on this level, through Jürgenssen's engagement with the realm of looks and styles, that another connection to Surrealism, and another connection to the play of shifting forms, can be established. This connection is routed via the territory of fashion—a territory which, let's remember, was also one of the points of departure for Anna-Sophie Berger's curatorial work on *life and limbs*. The point of connection lies in the frequent superimposition of fashionable forms and the morphological repertoire of evolutionary thinking that can already be found in Darwin's work, and still prevails among the Surrealists and their contemporaries.

Not only did Charles Darwin in his 1871 *The Descent of Man and Selection in Relation to Sex* directly compare the morphological shifts between members of an individual species and their gradual development through mutation into other species, to "caprices of fashion" which, in his own Victorian moment, he would have witnessed in rather extravagant forms indeed. His son George, in an article titled "Development in Dress," published a year later, went on to understand fashion's formal transformations as descendants of (and, to an extent, analogues to) evolutionary morphological shifts. The idea persisted in the fashion discourse of 1920s and 1930s Paris—period and place of Surrealism's most intense activity—and was espoused, in various permutations, by Paris-based German fashion critic Helen Grund and Dadaist writer Tristan Tzara, among others. It was also here and then that the designs of Elsa Schiaparelli forcefully implemented it in the realm of couture. Consider, for instance, Schiaparelli's 1938 so-called Tree Dress, which displayed a faux bois-print, imitating the veined pattern of cut wood; or her usage of so-called tree-bark crepe for a skirt that extended way up beyond the wearer's waist. Both designs visually transformed the wearer into a vegetal, silvan figure. On the animal front, think of Schiaparelli's ample usage of monkey fur outfitting harnesses, jackets, hats, and, particularly effective, trimming a set of ankle boots; think of the beret displaying a cheetah's facial features and fur, sported by the designer herself; or, finally, think of the transformation of hands into paws effectuated by a set of claws applied to the tips of the fingers of a pair of gloves.[16]

Beyond the mere tracing of historical anticipation, or of describing Jürgenssen's work as developing "under the influence" of Surrealism, there is, then, a more important genuine *structural parallel* between *one segment* of the Surrealist program, and what is at stake in Jürgenssen's drawing (and, perhaps, also a valid indicator concerning the general argument of *life and limbs*). *Missing Limbs* seems to be a flashpoint for this connection. We could track this parallel along a motif—considering that the lobster marks out one of the iconic engagements with the creaturely in Surrealism—think of Dalí's lobster phone, or Schiaparelli's lobster dress, made in response to it. What matters more than the reiteration of the motif, however, is a similarity between such Surrealist projects and Jürgenssen's combined interest in a chimeric creature and her dedication to the stylish, or even the fashionable. For Schiaparelli, the idea of fashion was not to create looks that adhere to an imaginary standard of beauty. This is also the case in more recent positions in fashion history, such as the work of Alexander McQueen, who, famously in his last two collections, sent out designs that engaged formally with Darwin's ideas of evolution and that emblematically defined the creation of fashionable outfits which shifted the shapes of the wearer into those of a semi-imaginary animal realm. The guiding thought was that, at the heart of fashion, lies a trans-formative agenda; that it changes, alters, and modifies bodies and their shapes. (There are moments in Rei Kawakubo's work that move along a similar proposition. Think, for instance, of the 1997–98 Body Meets Dress, Dress Meets Body collection; or her visual flattening of the body into the planar dimension in the 2012 summer collection.)

Such examples mark a general truth: fashion is a genuinely morphological practice; and by morphology we mean a science of forms, a concept initially coined by Goethe and the physician Karl

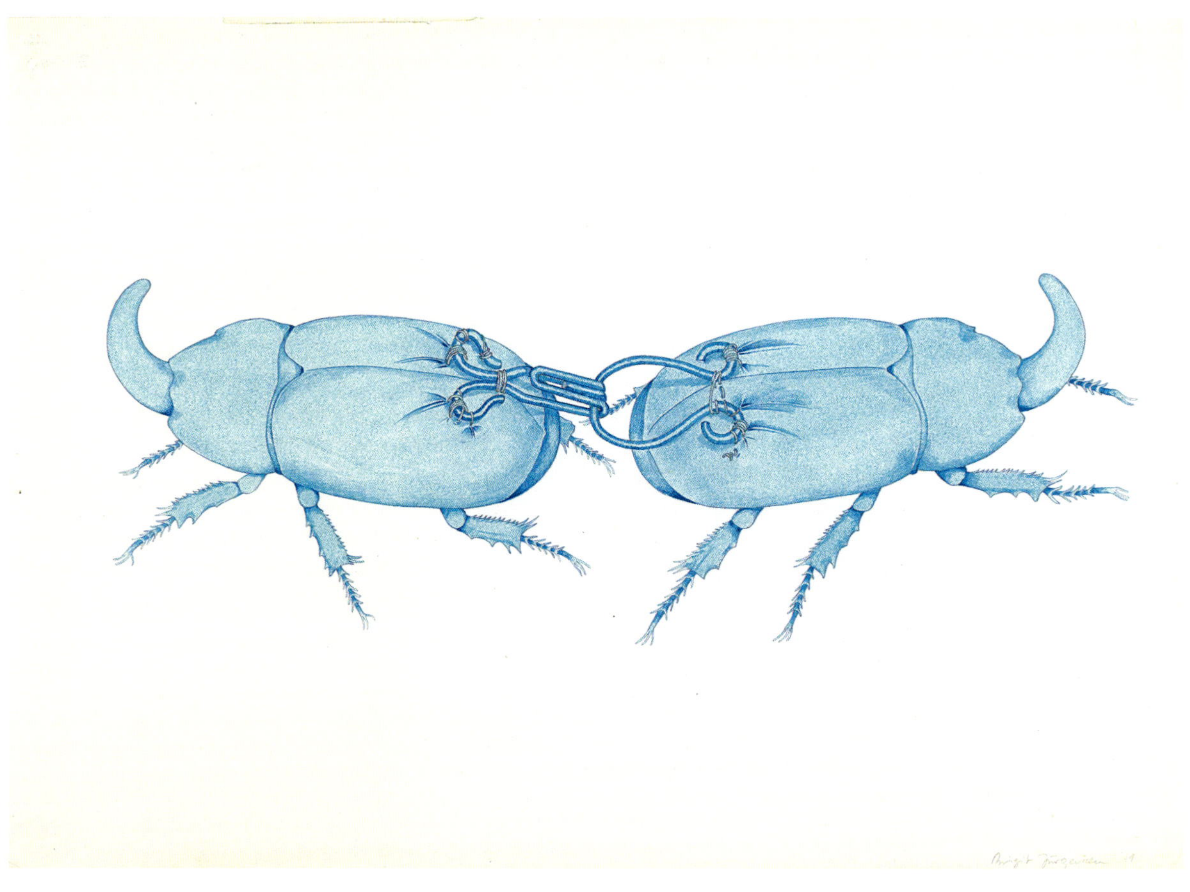

Fig. 11

Friedrich Burdach in late eighteenth-century Germany, which, from the very beginning, accounts for forms as trans-formational.[17] Morphology's ur-narrative in the Western tradition is perhaps Ovid's *Metamorphoses* (from which, of course, the earlier mentioned example of Daphne turning into a bush of laurel also derives).[18] As French art historian Henri Focillon, Parisian contemporary of the Surrealists, put it in his treatise *The Life of Forms in Art*, fashion is one of the imponderables that transforms everything it touches—it creates a new humanity, experimenting with the creaturely, even the heraldic, the chimeric.[19] This trans-formation, it bears repeating, is not what is usually considered to be fashion's heartbeat, namely, the consumption-driven, capitalistically amplified diktat by which one collection follows another, by which one batch of garments hits the racks, for another to be thrown out. These processes are, of course, an integral part of fashion under capitalism. But, as everything is touched by capital in our current condition, these examples would seem to mark what fashion has in common with other non-necessity-driven consumption patterns, rather than exemplifying what is specific to it. In fact, what the fashion *industry*, including retail and all its branches, has done here is to piggyback on a dynamic that precedes its own currents, and exploit it very effectively.

Fashion, as a Surrealist couturier such as Schiaparelli, as well as Jürgenssen, knew, is doubly chimeric. It deals in appearances, projections, intangibles, perhaps the phantasmatic. Yet, just as Jürgenssen in *Missing Limbs* depicts the transition of man and lobster, the dandyesque and the freakish, this double—the stylish and the transformative—might just sit at the heart of fashion itself. And, by implication, the work perhaps also speaks to a set of concerns informing the panorama of body-politics (or body politic-s?) presented in the context of *life and limbs*. Rather than monumentally propping up "liberated" bodies, these provide models for how to twist the omnipresent ties from within, as it were; and, in these twists, how to escape, while never naively pretending to have been fully freed. As well as how to project looks in the process, and how to ride them. The ruses of fashion, indeed. In the calcified cabinet furnished by Anna-Sophie Berger, Jürgenssen's *Missing Limbs*, then, marks the point at which fashion makes itself felt profoundly as a force of metamorphosis, and a field soliciting a morphological view, which takes in forms and their shifts alike.

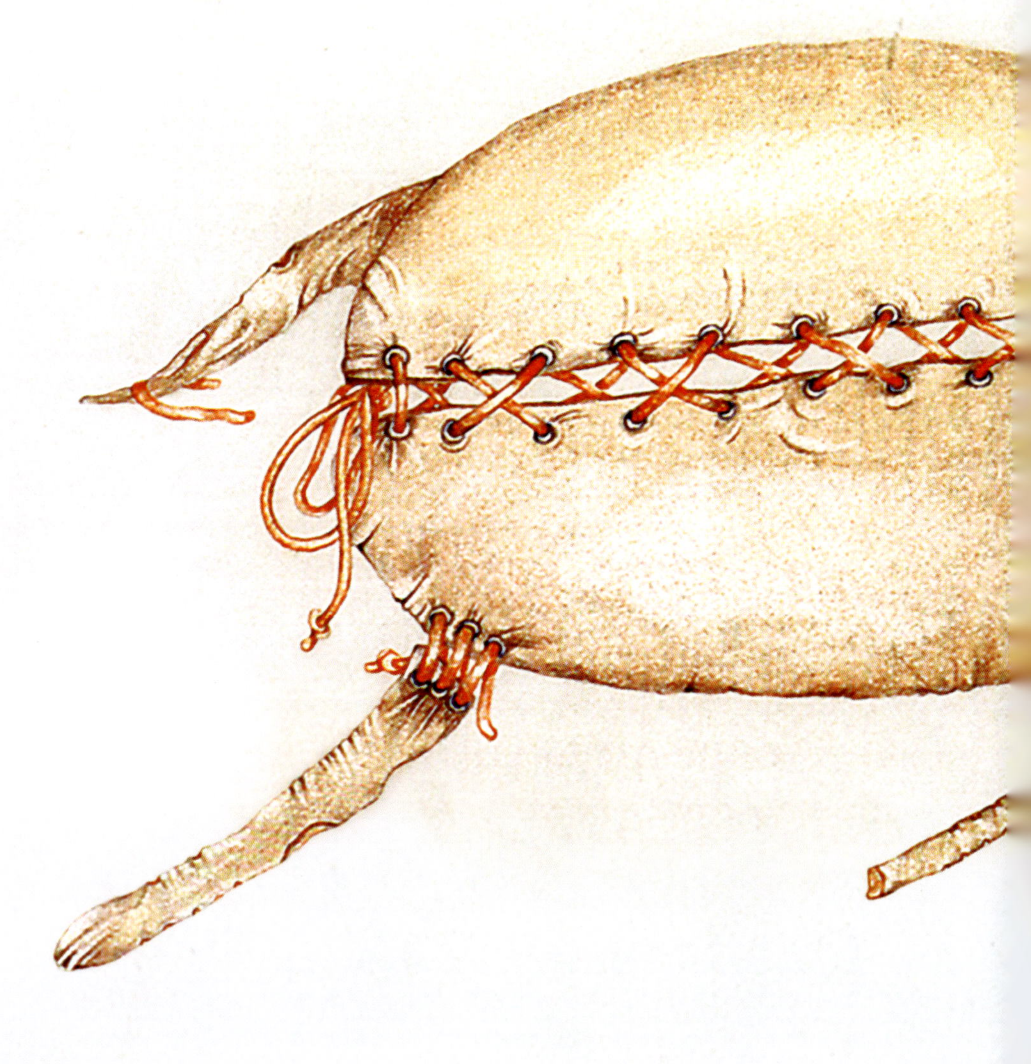

Fig. 12

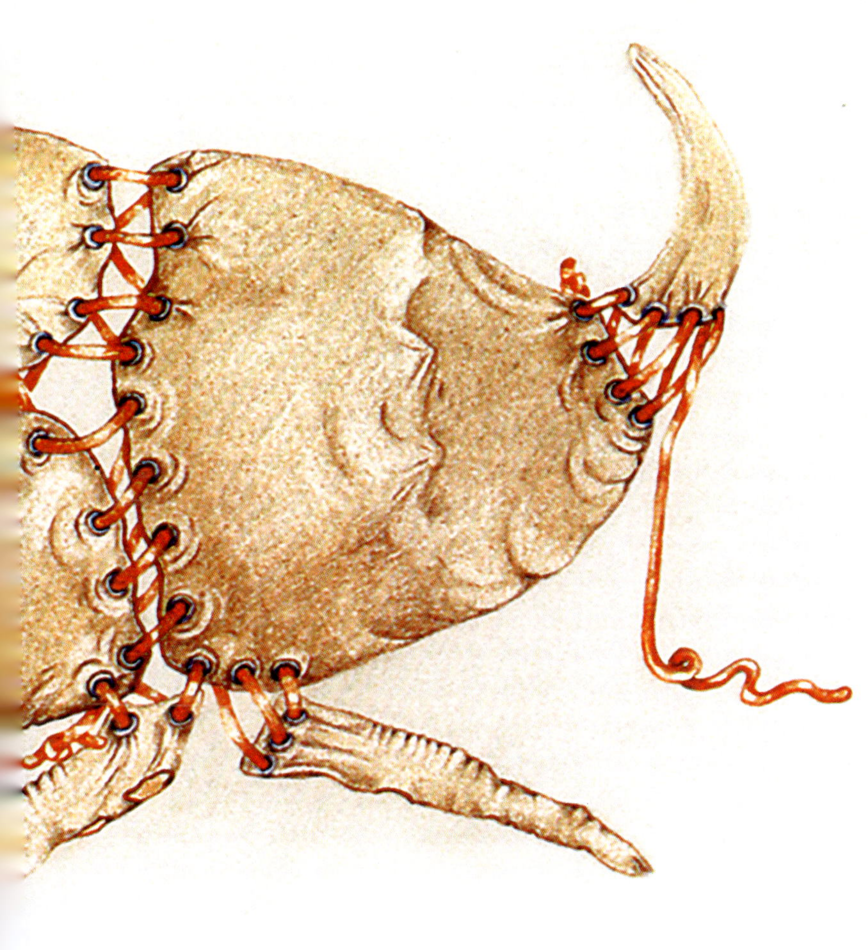

Notes

1 Sigmund Freud, *Jokes and Their Relation to the Unconscious*, vol. VIII of *The Standard Edition*, ed. James Strachey et al. (London: Hogarth Press), 1960.

2 Jürgenssen's work is committedly feminist, and a number of scholars, critics, and curators have produced fundamental analyses of it from this vantage point, including Gabriele Schor, Silvia Eibelmayr, Heike Eipeldauer, Abigail Solomon-Godeau, Katharina Sykora, and Giovanna Zapperi, some of whose texts I quote from. Gabriele Schor has also made a strong art historiographical case for including Jürgenssen's production among a group of oeuvres that she has called the feminist avant-garde, spanning a wide range of practices developed by women artists in North America and (mostly Western) Europe during the 1970s. See Gabriele Schor, ed., *Feminist Avant-Garde: Art of the 1970s in the Verbund Collection, Vienna*, rev. ed. (Munich: Prestel, forthcoming 2022). See also Schor's article "Birgit Jürgenssen's Poetic Surrealist Feminism," in *Intersections: Women Artists/Surrealism/Modernism*, ed. Patricia Allmer (Manchester: Manchester University Press, 2016), 241–56, in particular on Jürgenssen's employment of wit, word games, and puns, 244, 249–50.

3 In her article Schor also describes what could be regarded as a precedent to *Missing Limbs*, namely, Jürgenssen's diploma work at the Vienna Academy of Applied Arts, titled *zipfeln* (approximately translated as "tails"), a collection of faux-naïf drawings depicting such "*zipfel*": the tails of hoods and cushions; hair coiffed into tails; or tails marking the ends of soft abstract volumes. The point here being that *Zipfel* in colloquial Austrian German also refers to the penis: a defining trait of the members of the academy's faculty, who were all male. See ibid., 245.

4 Schor explains that during Jürgenssen's formative years this French historical avant-garde also functioned as a point of orientation for her that provided an alternative to the theatrical, extrovert, and frequently scandal-seeking paradigms of Actionism that dominated Vienna's contemporary art scene at the time. See ibid., 242–43.

5 Spyros Papapetros, *On the Animation of the Inorganic: Art, Architecture, and the Extension of Life* (Chicago: University of Chicago Press, 2012), 263–318.

6 Peter Weibel has generally described Jürgenssen's work as the "postmodern echo" of Cahun's oeuvre, the French Surrealist thus figuring as Jürgenssen's antecedent. The case that I am making in this essay does not rely on this periodization, and neither do I base my argument on the psychoanalytically grounded theory of subjectivity that informs Weibel's approach. See Peter Weibel, "Birgit Jürgenssen and the Night of Psychoanalysis," in *Birgit Jürgenssen*, exh. cat., ed. Gabriele Schor and Heike Eipeldauer (Munich: Prestel, 2010), 111–23, here 117–18, available at https://birgitjuergenssen.com/en/bibliography/texts-essays-interviews/weibel2010. The connection I am establishing between Freud's theory of the *Witz* and the logic of Jürgenssen's drawing relies purely on Freud's linguistic and semantic analysis of the mechanism of jokes. In my view, Jürgenssen and Freud—as well as the Surrealists' rebus pictures—share a rhetoric of the image, not a view of subjectivity. It is in this sense that I also understand Jürgenssen's ironic statement concerning her ongoing "tryst with art on Freud's couch." See Schor, "Jürgenssen's Poetic Surrealist Feminism," 243. And if I have pointed to potential connections between *Missing Limbs* and what could in short be called the "castration complex," I haven't done so to suggest that Jürgenssen's work is based on this theory (and I myself couldn't be any farther from endorsing it). Rather, Jürgenssen's drawing seems to refer to it as a discourse, which it in fact mocks. If at all present, it is subjected to her joking, rather than the subject of her work. The logic of *Missing Limbs*, including its connections to Surrealism, thus seems to be related

to (modernist) joke-work, in particular surrounding the groups of Paris Dada and Surrealism, as analyzed by David Joselit in his "Jokes and Their Relation to Modern Art: Picabia's Painting," in *Francis Picabia: Our Heads Are Round So Our Thoughts Can Change Direction*, exh. cat., ed. Anne Umland and Cathérine Hug (New York: Museum of Modern Art; Zurich: Kunsthaus Zürich, 2016), 284–92.

7 Jürgenssen gifted and dedicated a print of *Self with Little Fur* to Meret Oppenheim, whom she repeatedly singled out among her Surrealist peers, alongside Louise Bourgeois, as having held particular importance for her. See Giovanna Zapperi, "Formen von Weiblichkeit. Birgit Jürgenssens Metamorphosen," in *Birgit Jürgenssen*, ed. Schor and Eipeldauer, 79–91, here 80. See also Birgit Jürgenssen, "'Wie erfährt man sich im Anderen, das Andere in sich?' Ein Gespräch mit Rainer Metzger," in ibid., 273–79, here 276.

8 Heike Eipeldauer discusses the body projections in "'Wie erfährt man sich im Anderen, das Andere in sich?' Aspekte des (Un)Heimlichen im Werk von Birgit Jürgenssen, " in ibid., 29–43, here 33–35.

9 See ibid. and Zapperi, "Formen von Weiblichkeit," 85–91. For a wider discussion of representations of animality—and human/animal transitions—in Jürgenssen's work, including a nod to the recent scholarly field of animal studies, see Abigail Solomon-Godeau, "Birgit Jürgenssen, betrachtet durch das Brennglas des Anthropozäns," in *Birgit Jürgenssen. I am.*, exh. cat., ed. Natascha Burger and Nicole Fritz (Munich: Prestel, 2018), 189–200.

10 Reproduced in *Birgit Jürgenssen*, ed. Schor and Eipeldauer, 201.

11 See Eipeldauer, "Aspekte des (Un)heimlichen," 34.

12 Reproduced in *Birgit Jürgenssen. I am.*, ed. Burger and Fritz, 142.

13 Solomon-Godeau mentions both *Race* and *Elsa* in "Jürgenssen, betrachtet durch das Brennglas des Anthropozäns," 189, 198. The above discussion of metamorphoses in Jürgenssen's work is necessarily incomplete. Natascha Burger also discusses Jürgenssen's late works *Zebra 1* and *Zebra 2* (2001) as examples of such metamorphoses: a set of digitally manipulated photographs in which the artist portrays herself conventionally by wearing a mask as the titular zebra, but further breaks down the image into a staggered and stashed field of undulating geometrical elements, which emulate a zebra-like pattern. See Natascha Burger, "Birgit Jürgenssen. Ich weiß nicht," in *Birgit Jürgenssen. I am.*, ed. Burger and Fritz, 21–42, here 23–24. The connection between these and the earlier works implicitly raises an important question: To what extent does our understanding of transformative shifts such as the ones that Jürgenssen depicts rely on their respective media-technological basis? In other words: Does our understanding of metamorphoses change substantially in the age of the (digital) morph? Burger also mentions Jürgenssen's engagement with a whole set of (imaging) technologies which would eventually lead her, in her capacity as an instructor at the Vienna Academy of Fine Arts, to establishing the school's first photography class and later to teaching on its media course. In a wider perspective, we could also begin to think of Jürgenssen's deliberately trans-medial practice as another example of a morphological, trans-formative approach, in which forms are developed and shifted across photography, drawings, and objects. See Jürgenssen's remarks on her work across media in Jürgenssen, "Ein Gespräch mit Rainer Metzger," 274.

14 Reproduced in *Birgit Jürgenssen*, ed. Schor and Eipeldauer, 78, and mentioned in Zapperi, "Formen von Weiblichkeit," 81.

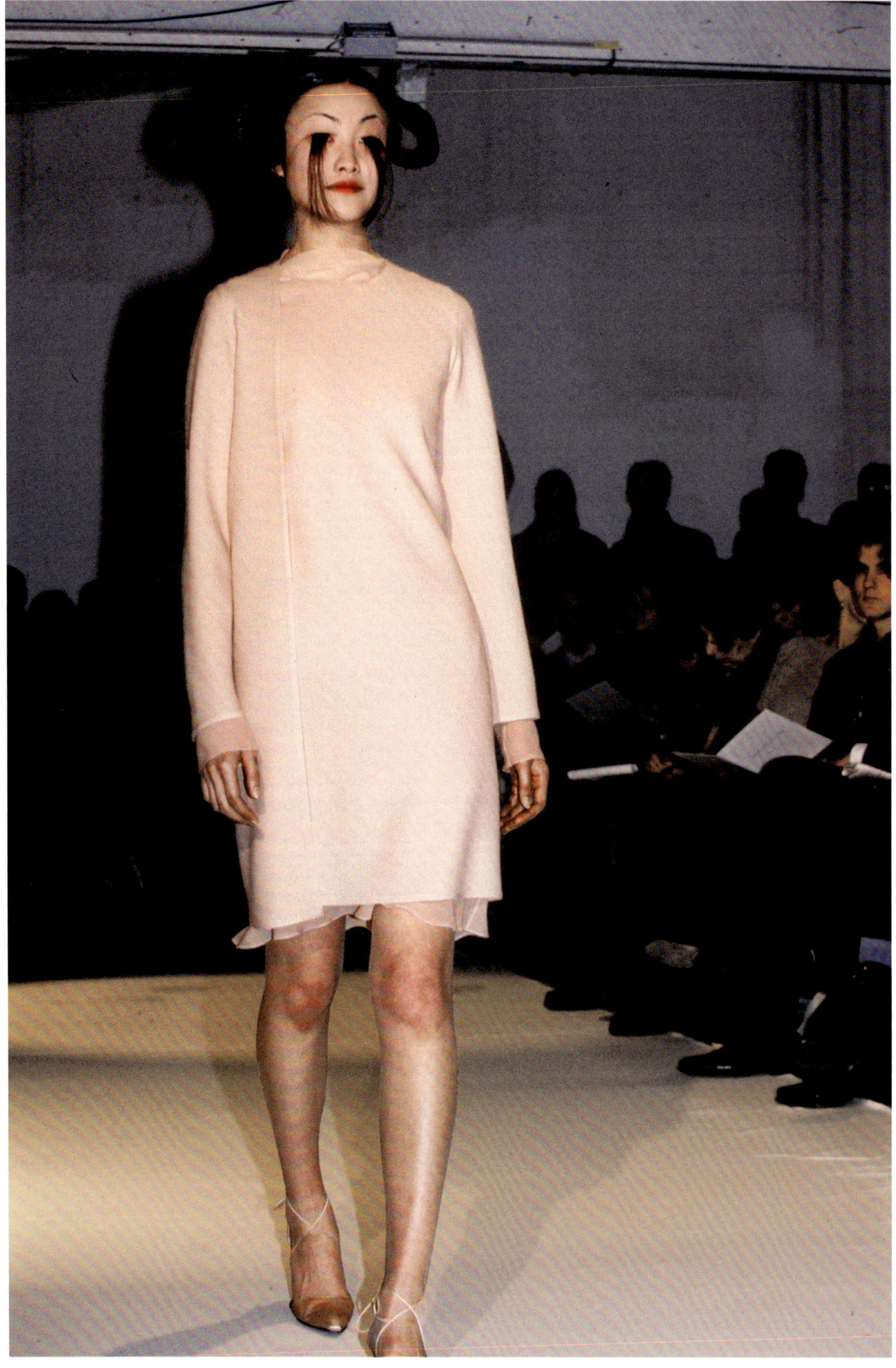

Fig. 13

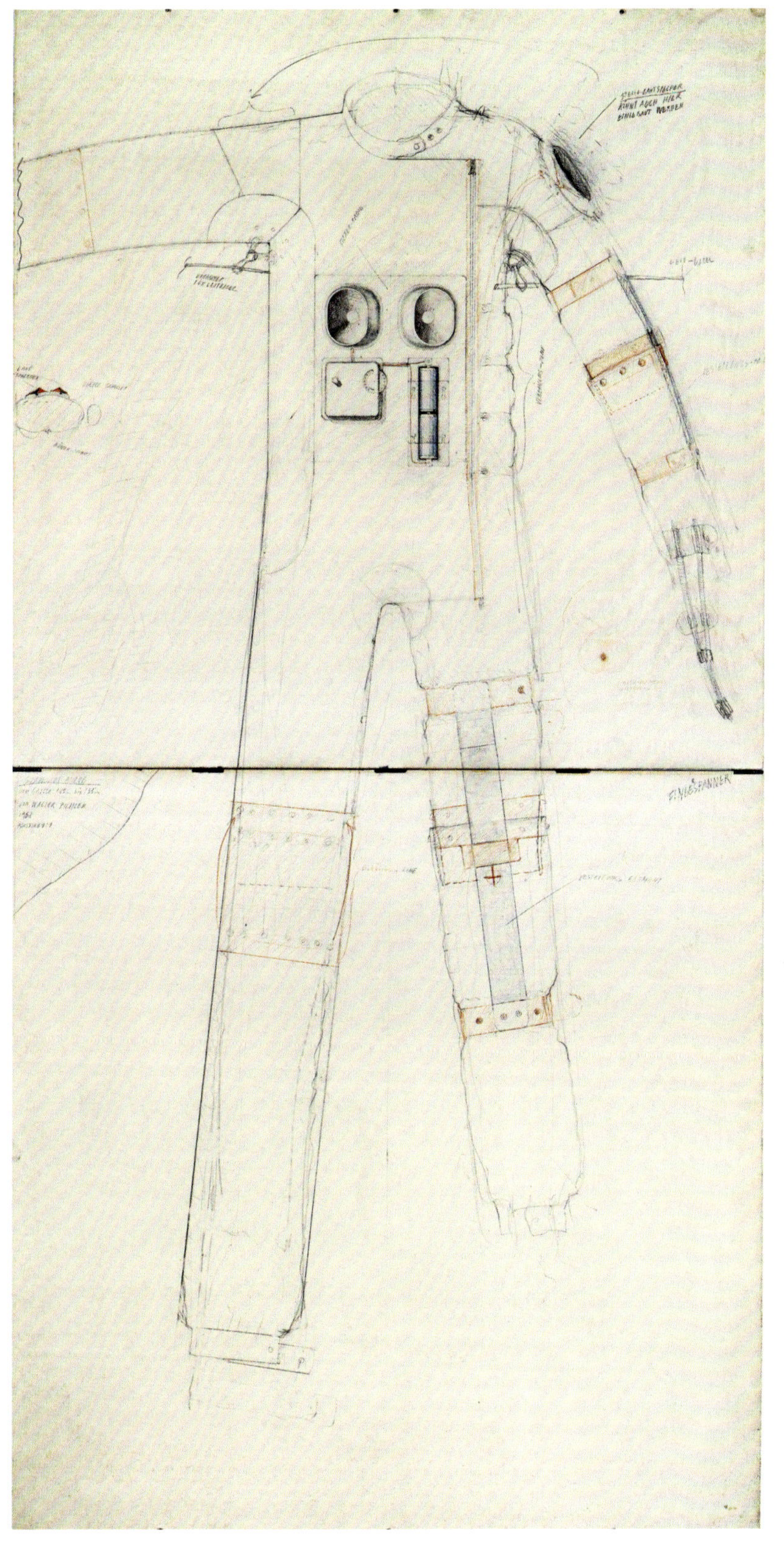

Fig. 14

15 For an overview of their work, see *Die Damen. Ona B., Evelyne Egerer, Birgit Jürgenssen, Ingeborg Strobl, Lawrence Weiner,* exh. cat. (Nuremberg: Verlag für moderne Kunst, 2013). Jürgenssen has stated that General Idea, in particular the group's *FILE Megazine*, did indeed serve as an important point of orientation for her own work. See Jürgenssen, "Ein Gespräch mit Rainer Metzger," 277. She also included a catalog of the Canadian collective's work in the exhibition *Die schwangere Muse* (The Pregnant Muse), which she co-curated at the Vienna Academy of Fine Arts in 1992, as well as soliciting a brief statement from General Idea for an artists' questionnaire for this occasion. See *Die schwangere Muse*, exh. cat. (Vienna: Akademie der bildenden Künste, 1992), 29, 37. This overall proposition, to understand Jürgenssen's production at least partly through its engagement with the realm of fashion, shares certain affinities with Maurizio Cattelan and Marta Papini's recent joint exhibition of Jürgenssen's art with works by radical Italian designer Cinzia Ruggeri at Galerie Hubert Winter in Vienna.

16 For an elaboration of the evolutionary unconscious of late 1920s and 1930s Paris fashion discourse, for Schiaparelli's designs, and for Darwin's connections between evolution and fashion, see my *Benjamin on Fashion* (London: Bloomsbury, 2020), chapter 2.

17 See ibid.

18 In his brief discussion of Jürgenssen's 1991 object *Narziß und Echo* (Narcissus and Echo), Jasper Sharp also suggests a connection to Ovid's *Metamorphoses*, from which the story of the beautiful man turned flower derives. See Jasper Sharp, "Narziß und Echo," in *Birgit Jürgenssen: I am.*, ed. Burger and Fritz, 275. Zapperi relates Jürgenssen's metamorphoses and their displacement of the human figure into the realm of other species and even objects to the problem of fetishism and its implications for the negotiations of (heterosexual) gender roles. See Zapperi, "Formen von Weiblichkeit," 85–91. This approach is supported by the artist's stated interest in the subject of fetishism; see Jürgenssen, "Ein Gespräch mit Rainer Metzger," 275. My take on Jürgenssen's work is situated at an angle to and complements these approaches: whereas a well-traveled interpretative road certainly connects the shape-shifts of fashion (including the transitions of the human form into those of animals or things) to the problem of sexual and commodity fetishism, my analysis is grounded in a morphology of art (and fashion) which emphasizes its form-altering activity, rather than anchoring it in the assumed target-objects of its transformations ("things," "animals"). One could also ponder whether the interpretations of Jürgenssen's art that connect its human/animal and human/object transitions to the question of fetishism are truly reliant on the formal moment of the shape-shift. A provisional survey would seem to indicate that those works which are seen to be connected to the problem of the fetish tend to be those in which the artist turns to shoes or fur. It is certainly no coincidence that these two motifs emerge directly from the canonical (Viennese) literature on sexual fetishism, namely Freud's work on the subject and Leopold von Sacher-Masoch's 1870 novella *Venus in Furs*. The mentioned approaches to Jürgenssen's work thus seem to imply more of an *iconography* of the fetish, rather than an attempt at understanding the transition between forms. One work that would, in a strange manner, lend itself to a triangulation between species transitions, fetishism, and fashion questions is the 1974 drawing *Gemeinsames Joch tragen* (Wearing a Common Yoke). In this double portrait of a female and a male head, both caught in transition between bovine and human features and executed in clear reference to French Baroque painter and art theorist Charles LeBrun, a contraption yokes together both heads and, in its strangely architectural, angular, and linear quality, performs an effect that treads the fine line between fetish—here, a harness—and fashion, in its modification of a body(part)'s appearance. An effect, by the way, reminiscent of Pichler's *Fingerspanner* briefly touched on at the beginning of the present essay and included in *life and limbs*. Abigail Solomon-Godeau mentions *Gemeinsames Joch tragen* and its connection to LeBrun. However, whereas she points to

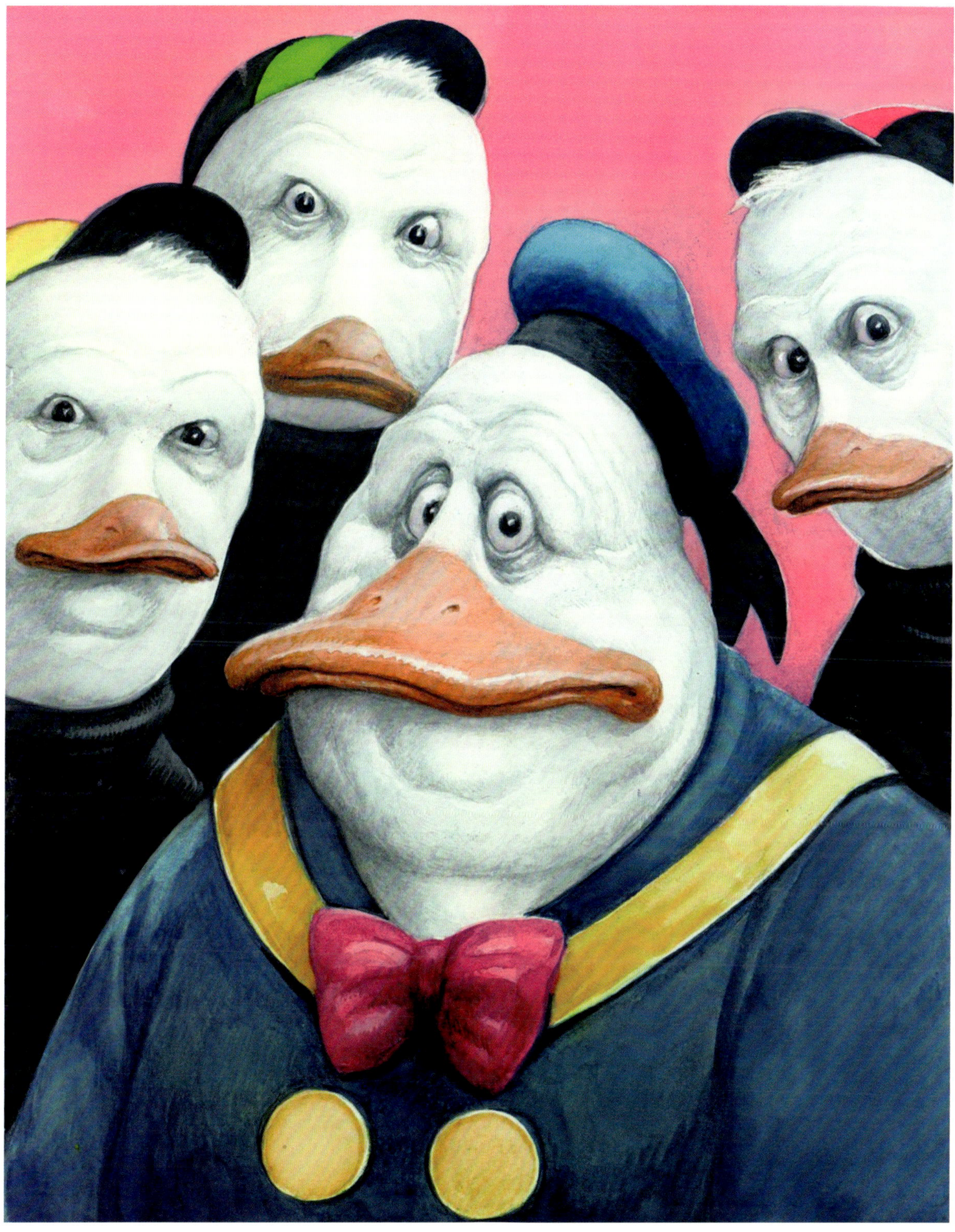

Fig. 15

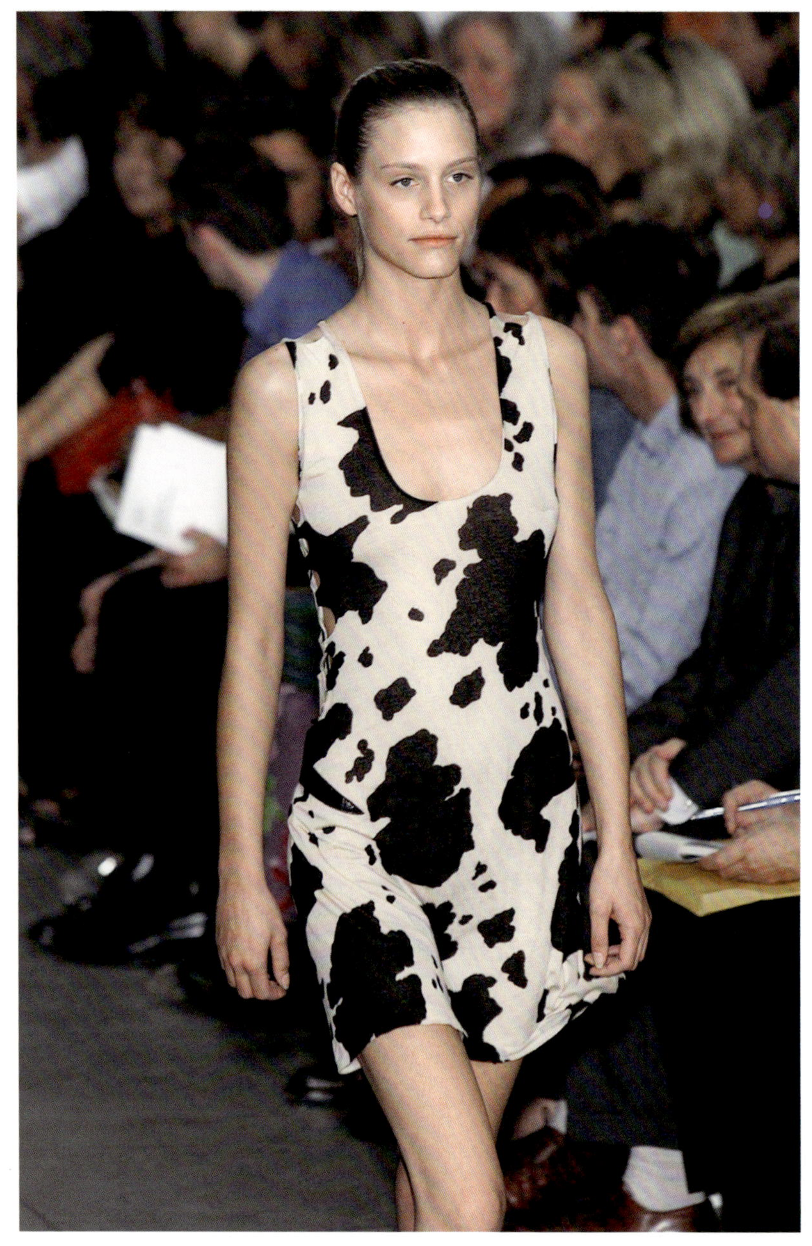

Fig. 16

LeBrun's treatise on the expression of the passions as its point of reference, Jürgenssen must be aiming here for LeBrun's lectures on physiognomy, the illustrations for which comprise the human/animal transition charts. See Abigail Solomon-Godeau, "Birgit Jürgenssen, von Linien begrenzt, über Grenzen hinweg," in *Birgit Jürgenssen*, ed. Gabriele Schor and Abigail Solomon-Godeau (Ostfildern: Hatje Cantz, 2009), 107–44, here 114.

19 Henri Focillon, *The Life of Forms in Art* (New York: Zone Books, 1989), 154.

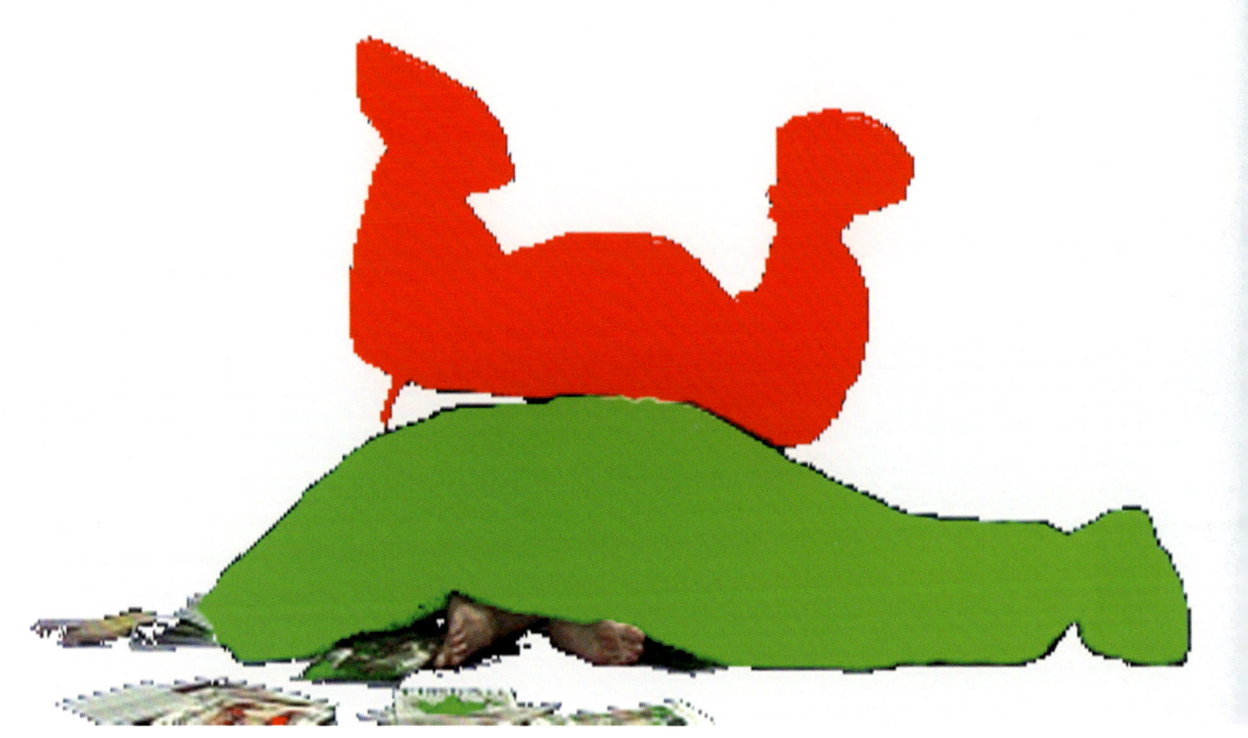

Fig. 17

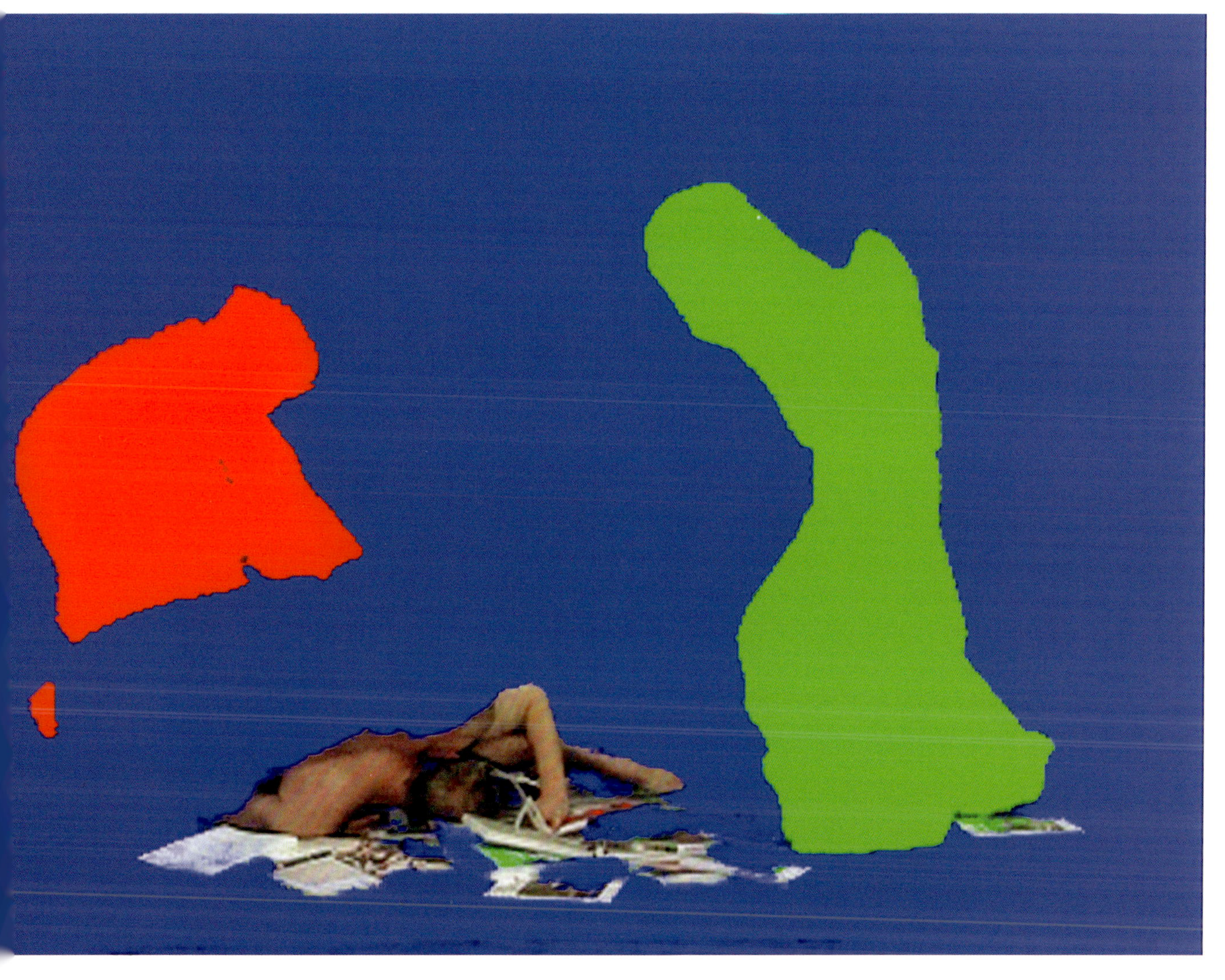

Fig. 18

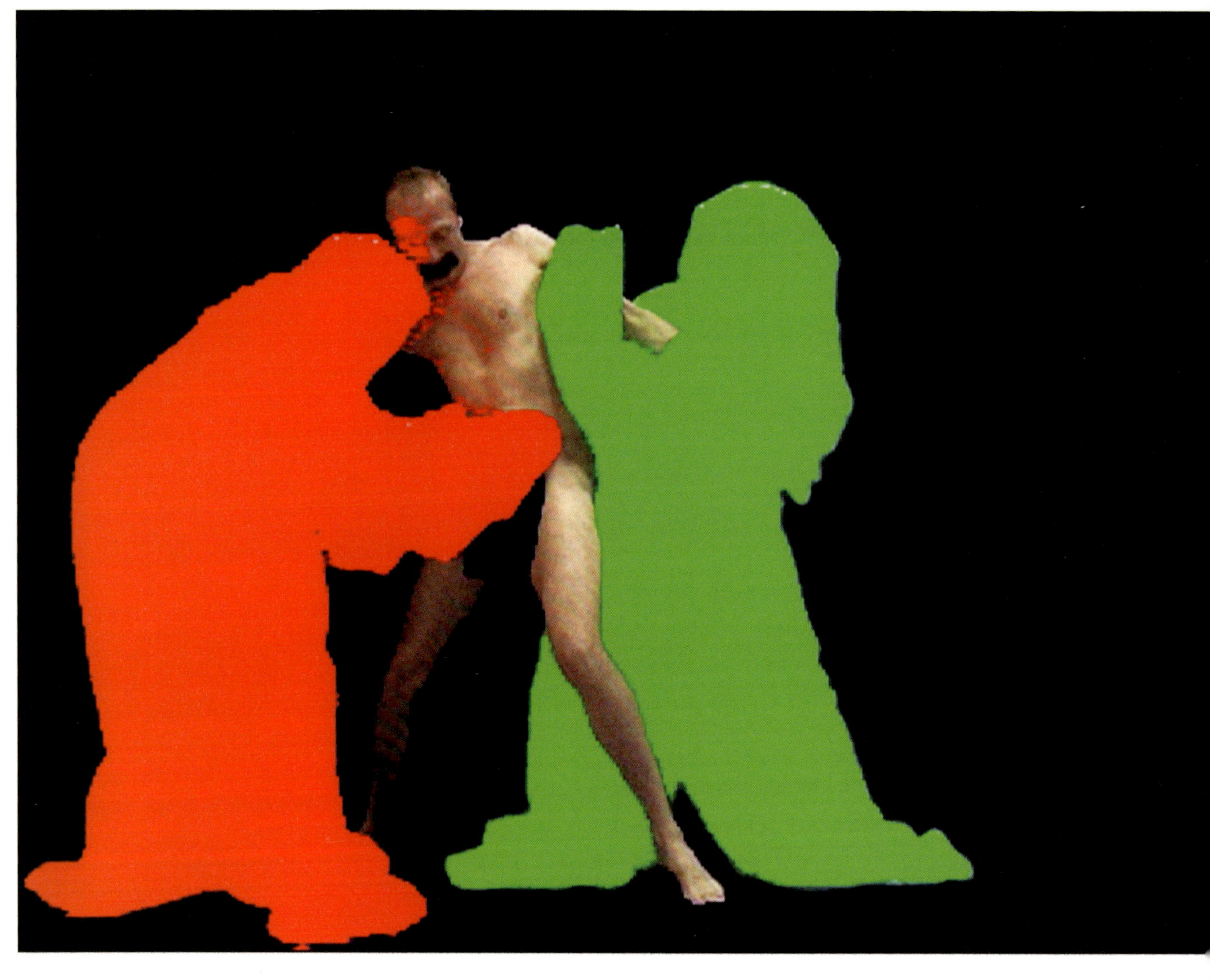

Fig. 19

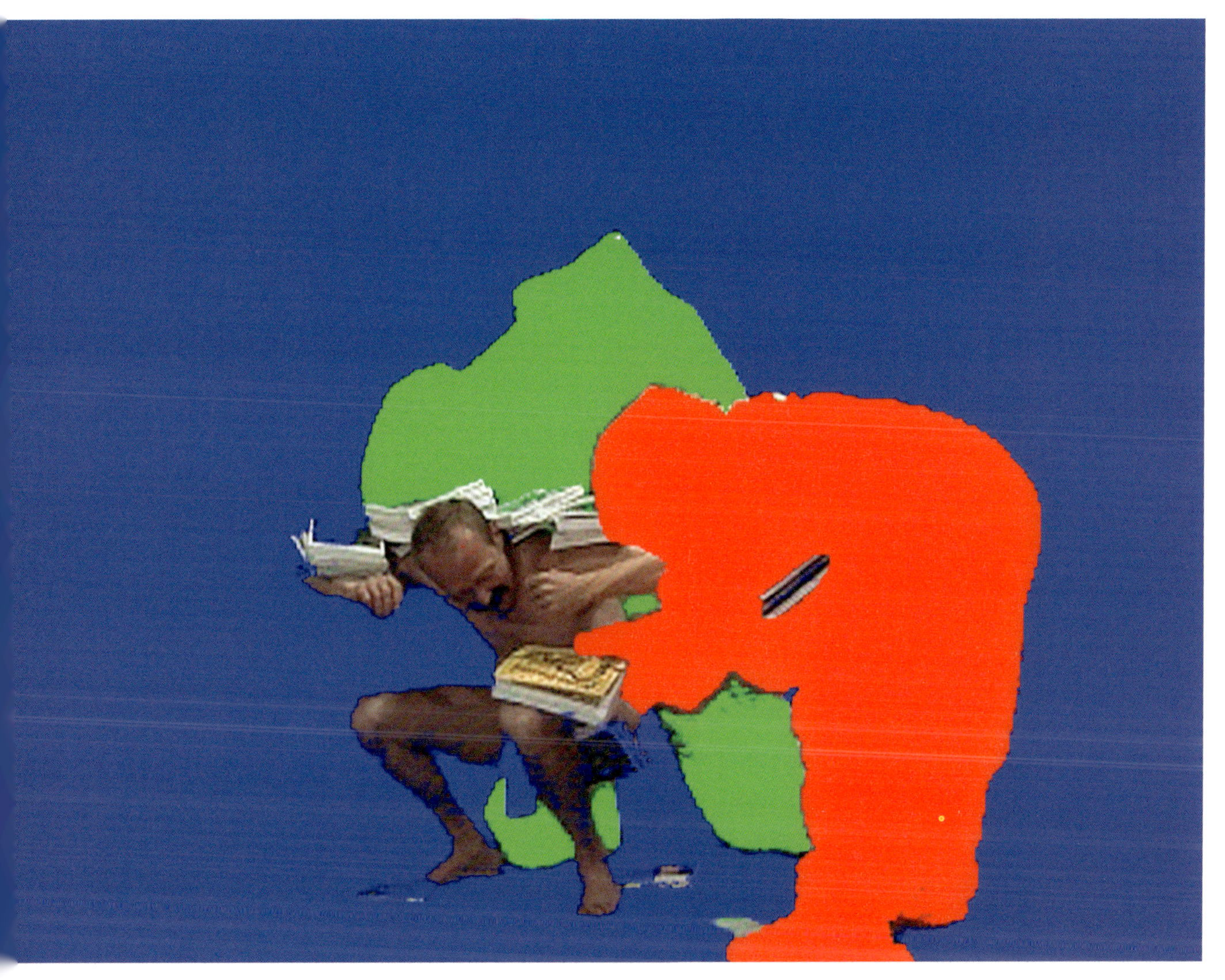

Fig. 20

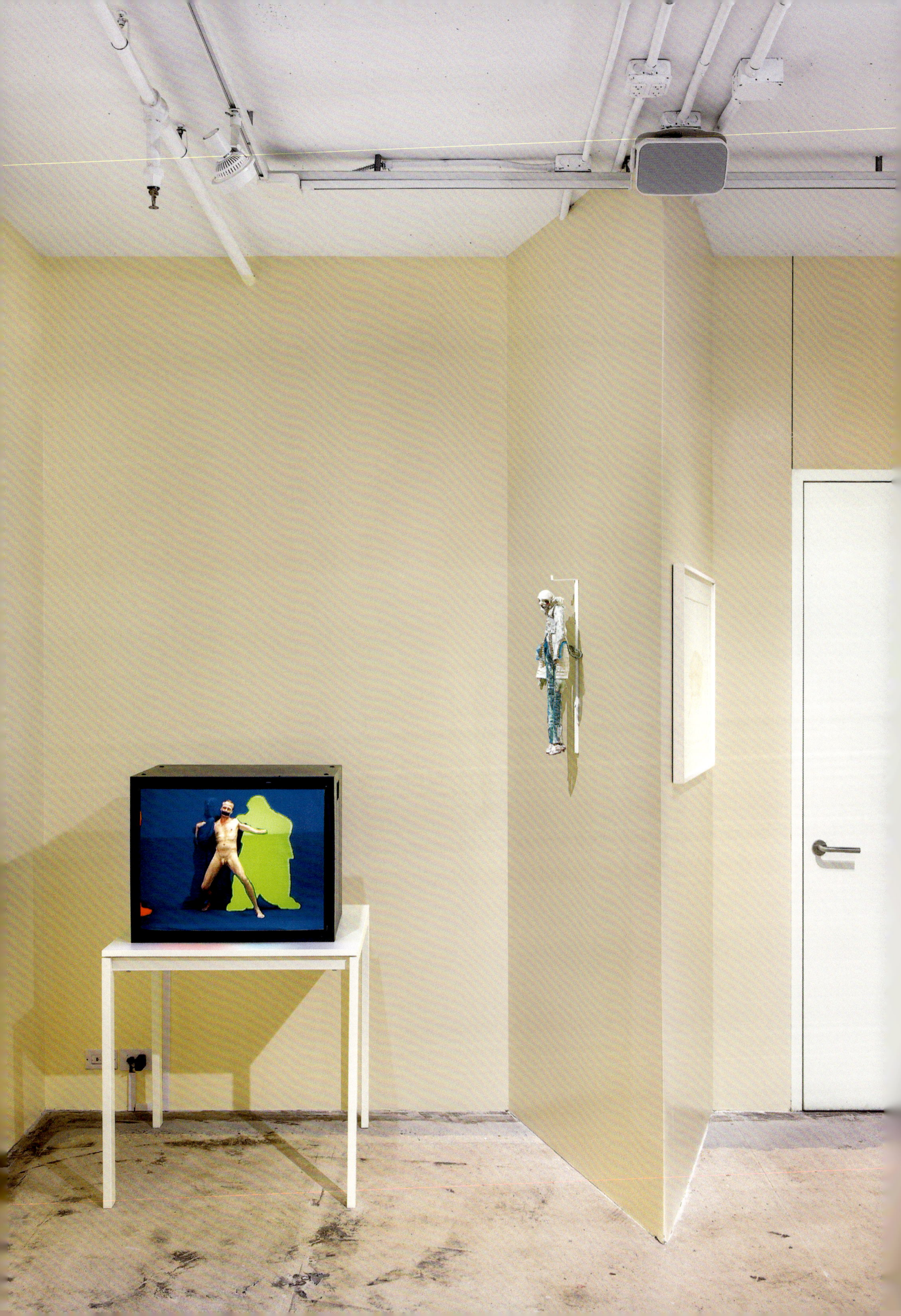

Fig. 21

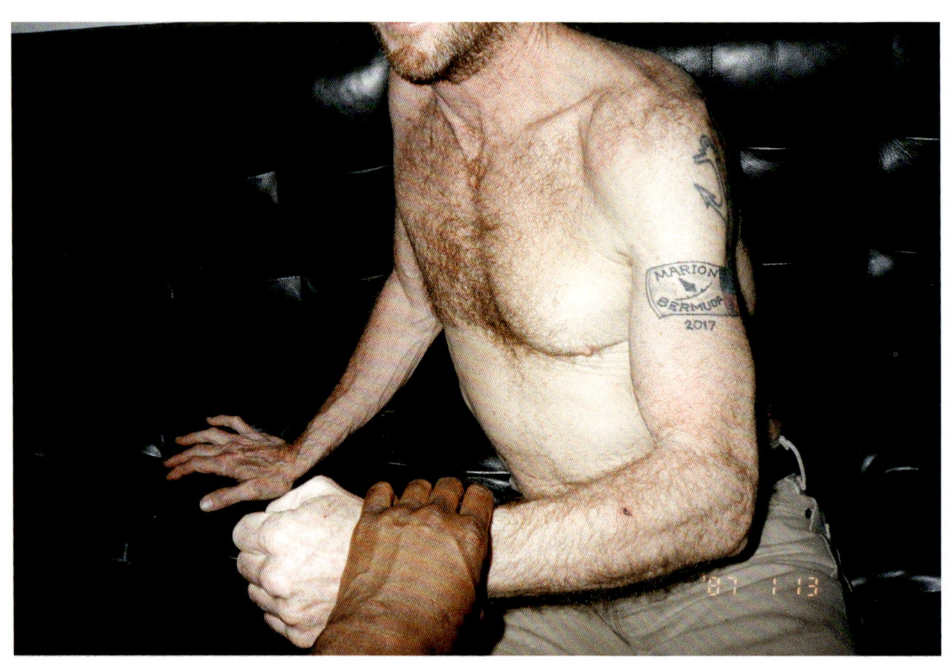
MARION
BERMUDA
2017

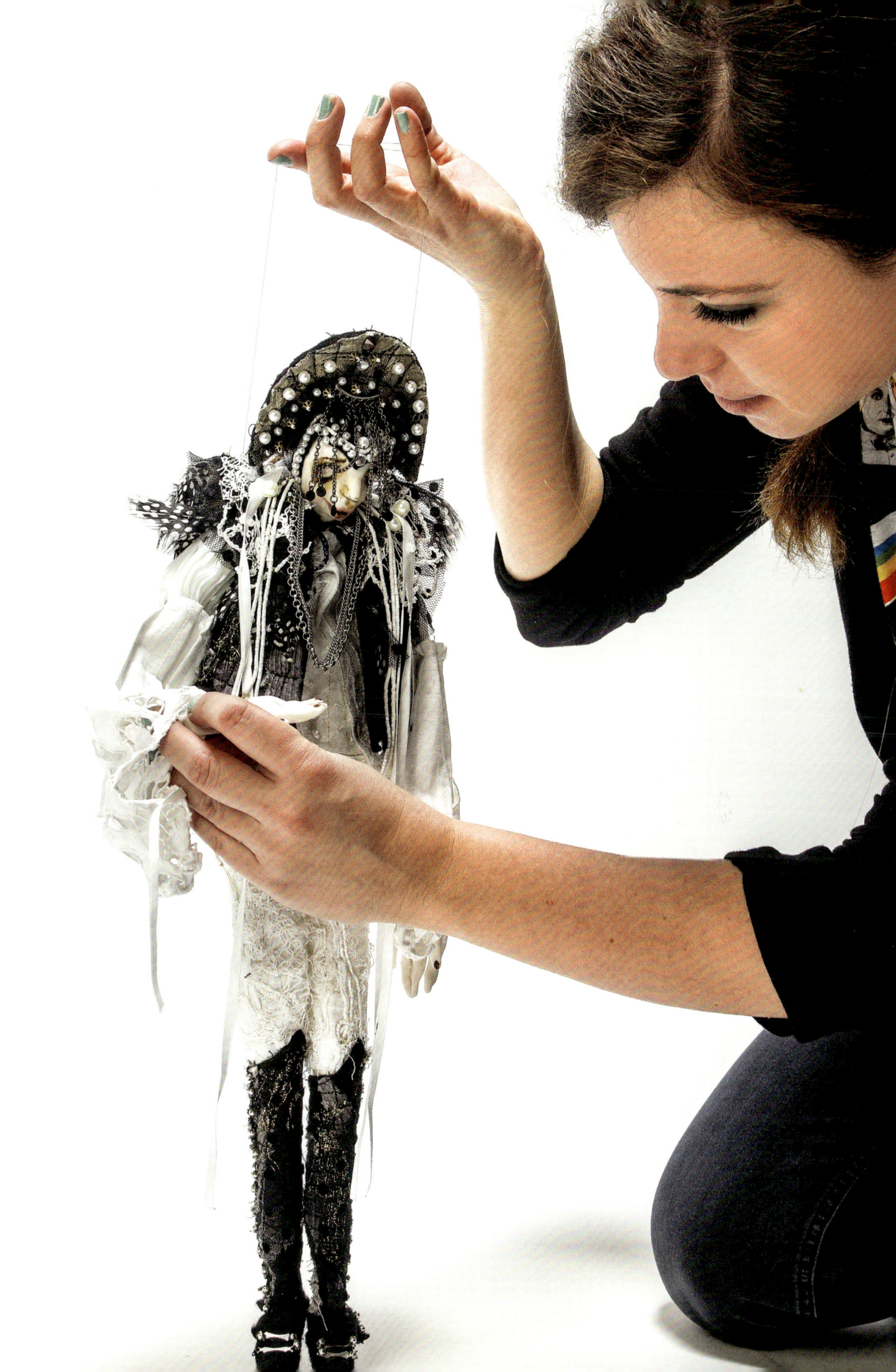

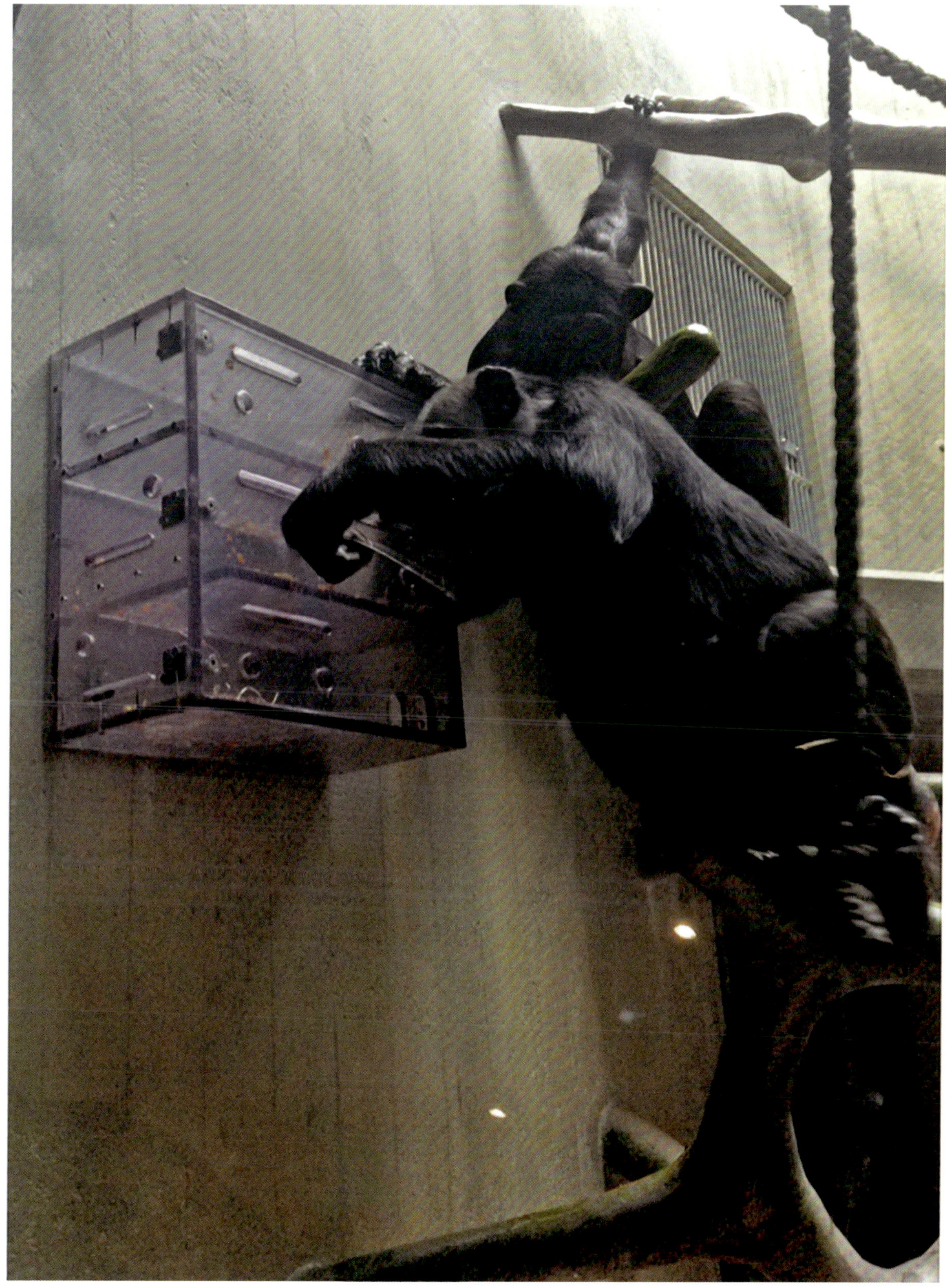

Fig. 24

Fig. 25

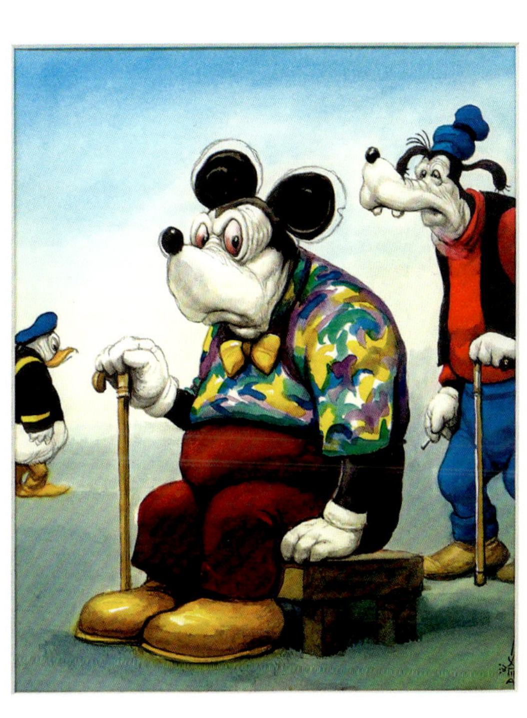

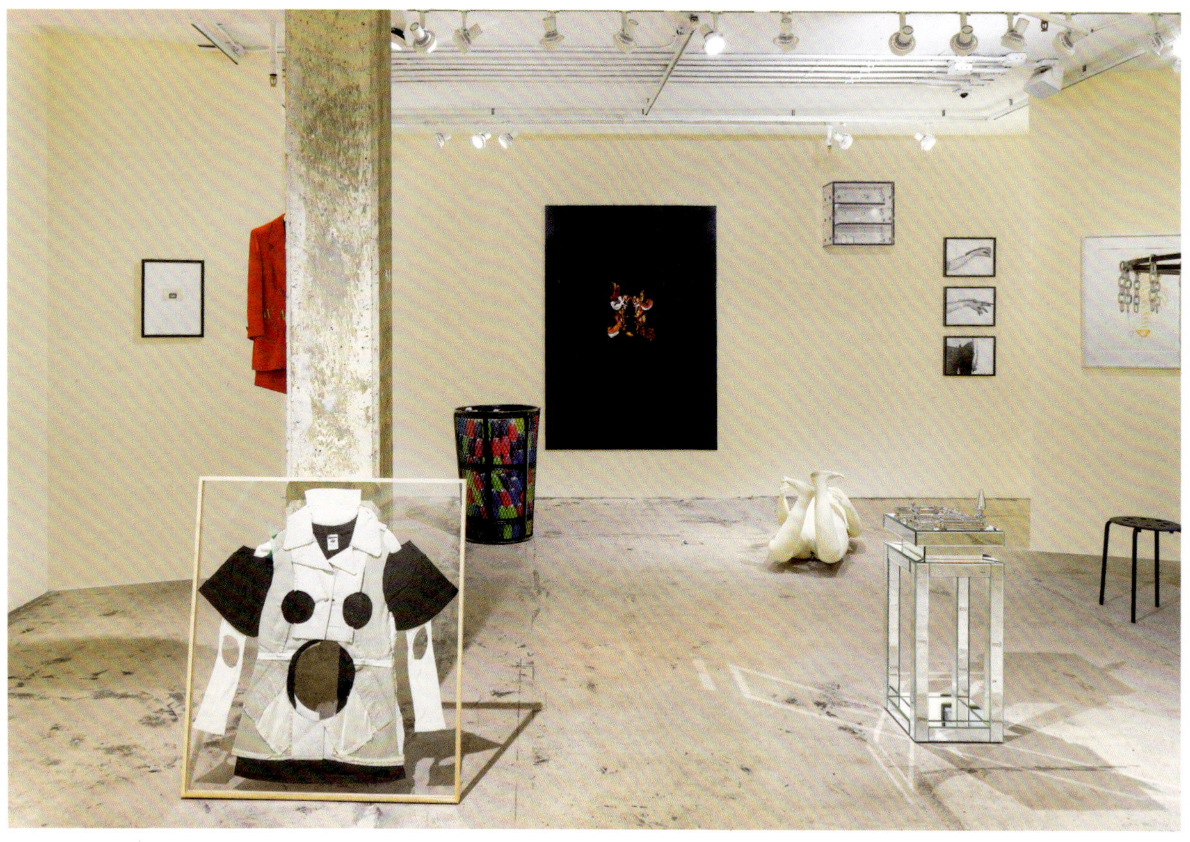

Fig. 26

I.

Our dog was killed by a felled tree. For months after, we didn't sweep the floor in order to preserve the tangles of his hair. As though, like tumbleweeds, the hair was evidence of a root structure that thrived elsewhere. As though it were part of an eddying, diasporic body. This was magical thinking.

This moment returned to me when I visited *life and limbs*, the fourth exhibition in Swiss Institute's Architecture and Design Series, organized by the artist Anna-Sophie Berger. Its thirty-two works engaged the ways in which design informs and is informed by the body, the potential for each to reconceive the other. Here, we saw bodies work with or against objects to perform Übermensch feats, act out fantasies of desublimation, exceed their bounds, and communicate their failures. Spanning nearly a century—the earliest works are drawings of lewd anthropomorphized jewelry by Meret Oppenheim from 1936—the exhibition didn't so much tell us about the contemporary body, stultified by screens and stretched thin by gigging, as it did evince the *longue durée*, from Ovid to bodies without organs, of frustration with the body's capacity to align with and accommodate the labors and desires of its subject. It told us about our willfulness to believe things might be otherwise.

Some works were visionary: Madeline Gins and Arakawa's 2004–6 photomontages of speculative architecture introduce instability as a prompt for the reorganization of the spirit and body alike. Others were recuperative: in Lyle Ashton Harris's 1994 collaborative photos with artist-activist Renee Cox, Cox dons armorlike prosthetics to reappropriate the image of Sara Baartman, the "Hottentot Venus" of nineteenth-century freak shows. Still others offer caricatures of toxic masculinity: Günter Brus's 1971 series of drawings in which a lily-white penis must sustain an erection to prevent Rube Goldberg contraptions from slaughtering a guinea pig. There were ecstatic odes to transformation: Birgit Jürgenssen's 1974 drawing imagines a dandy mid metamorphosis into a lobster and Ebecho Muslimova's 2015 drawing pictures the contorting figure Fatebe, whose vagina is a portal for ludic transhuman experience.

Berger built out the walls of the gallery so that four toothlike partitions jutted unevenly into the space, a misaligned grin. These structures imposed irregular sight lines, such that the relationships among the works were always punctured. Depending on where the viewer stood, one work would protrude into the space of another, or the angled walls would lend the illusion of a frame not being level. To some extent, the exhibition design enacted the very acrobatics and hybridities explored in the works themselves, bucking the purist in pursuit of autonomous objects. If this exhibition were a body, it would be a grotesque one.

In many ways, the gathered works constellate the inquiries of Berger's own project. Her 2016 work *Parabolic Reflector*, for example, features a pair of found concrete acoustic mirrors sourced from a Vienna playground near the artist's former home. These structures allow the voice, even in intimate registers, to be thrown great distances, resulting in an uncanny displacement of the body's effects.

Berger studied fashion design at the University of Applied Arts in Vienna, and she deploys elements of fashion for its uncomplicated, conspicuous consumerism in an art context that isn't as comfortable with admitting its financialization and fetishism. The incorporation makes vivid what both contexts have done to alienate the subject from authentic desire and need. Take her 2019 sculpture *The Wearer of Clothes*, a hybrid between a high-performance camping tent and a health-goth crinoline, intermixing forms that at once recall elemental structures of protection and aesthetic symbols of excess.

Fashion is explicit in its rhetoric of euphoria—in its proposition of a frictionless, uterine flow between desire and fulfillment. But there is a double bind in its promise of self-expression and its requirement of constant update. The machine of fashion, like a living body, depends on regular disposal. Disposal that isn't acknowledged, rendering process itself vulgar. Berger made the point graphic with her 2019 sculpture *time that breath cannot corrupt*: three polyester lace coats soaked in shitlike mud and thrown against the wall, left to harden where they fell on the floor. In *life and limbs*, Berger included Moyra Davey's 1990/2017 film *Hell Notes*, which Davey narrates from a toilet in a public

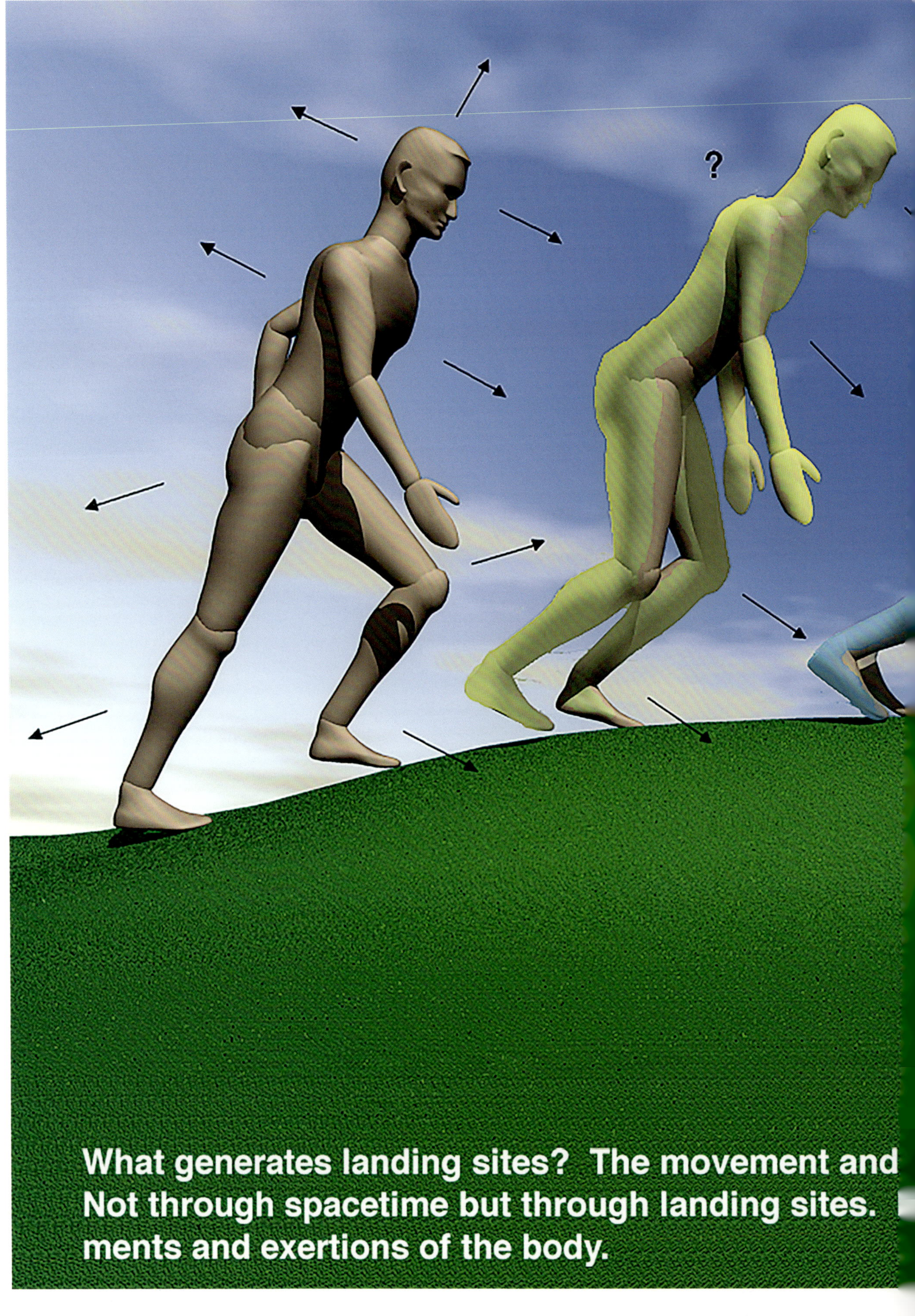
?
What generates landing sites? The movement and
Not through spacetime but through landing sites.
ments and exertions of the body.

Fig. 27

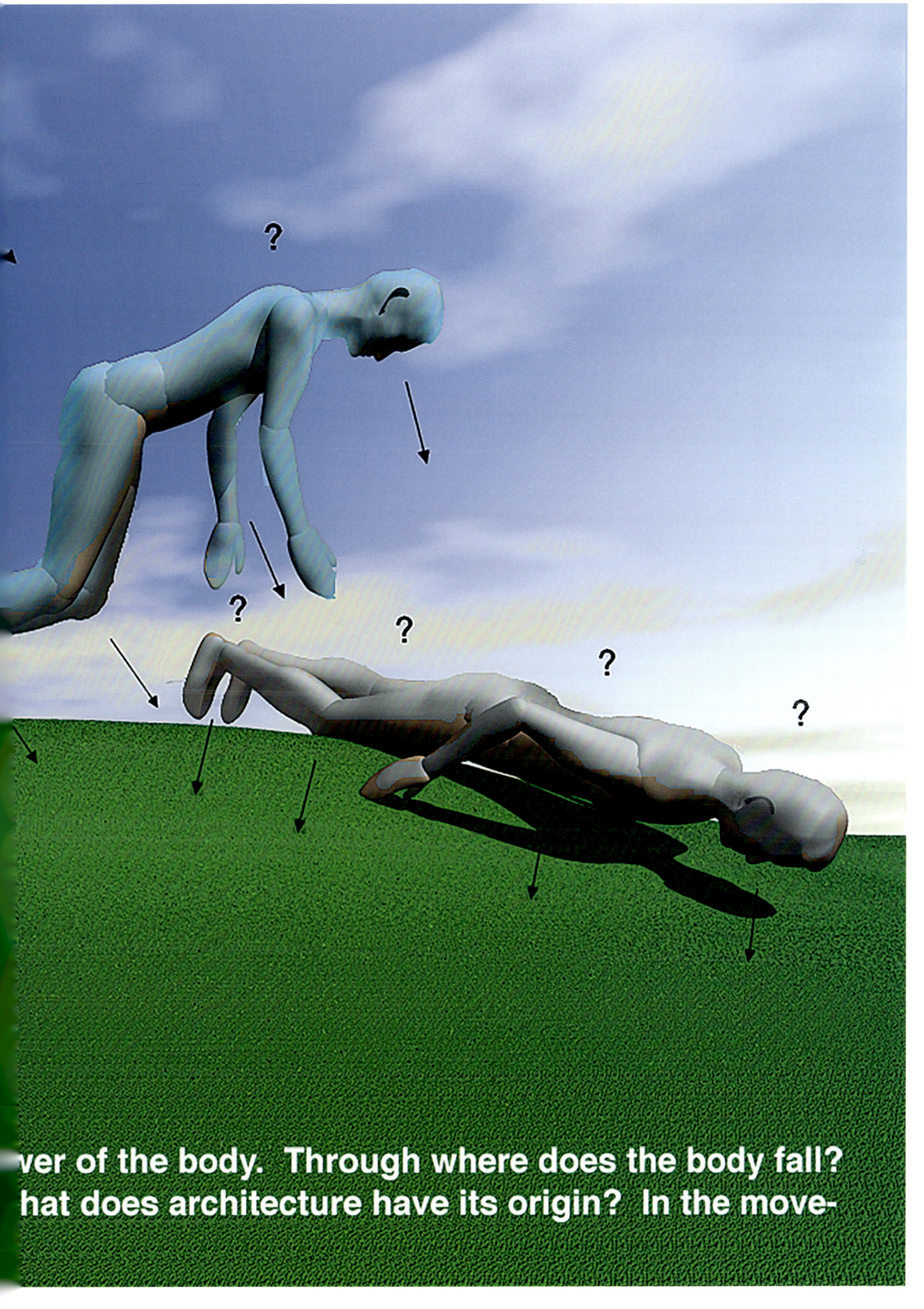
?
?
?
?
?
ver of the body. Through where does the body fall?
hat does architecture have its origin? In the move-

Fig. 28 →

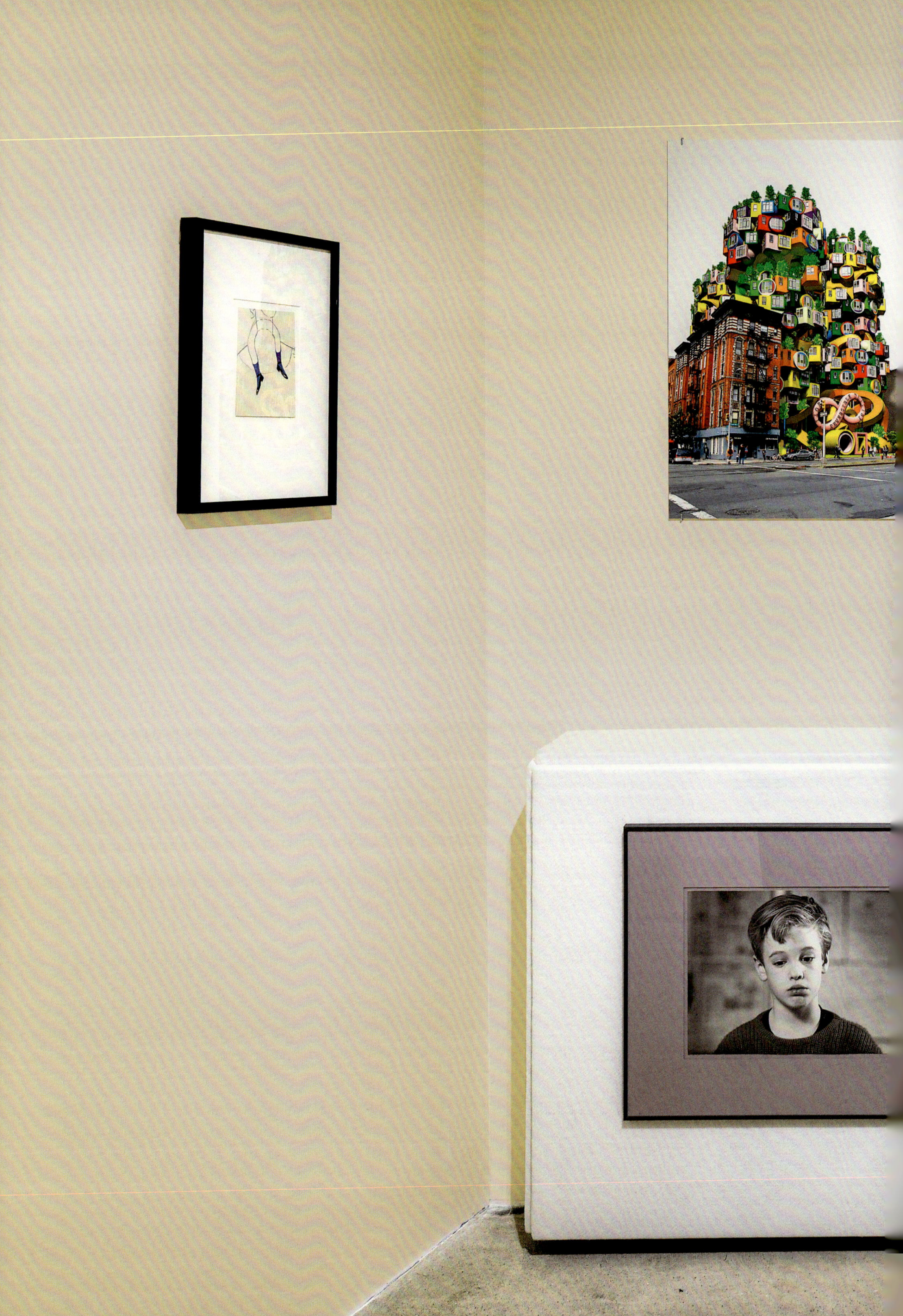

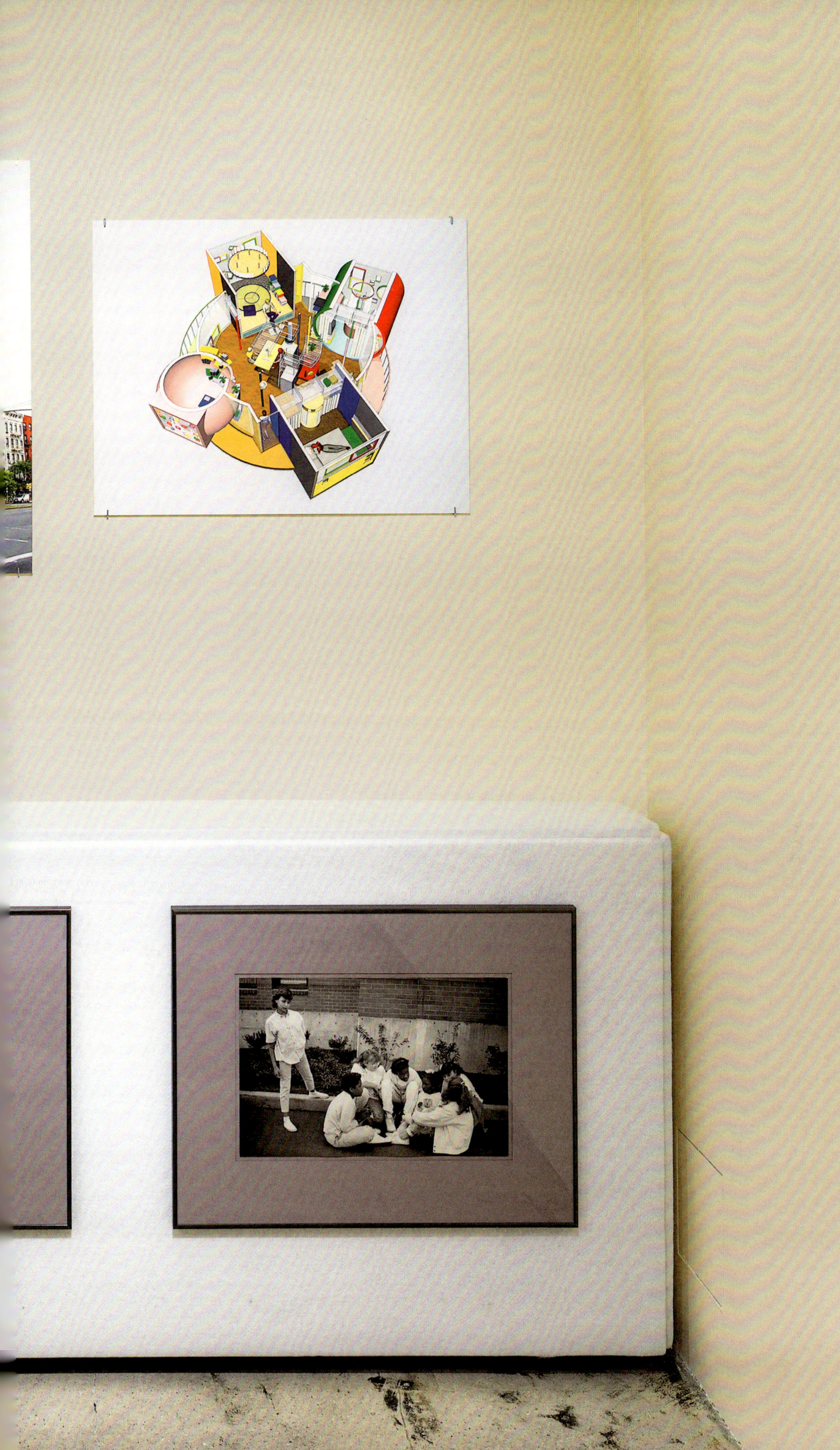

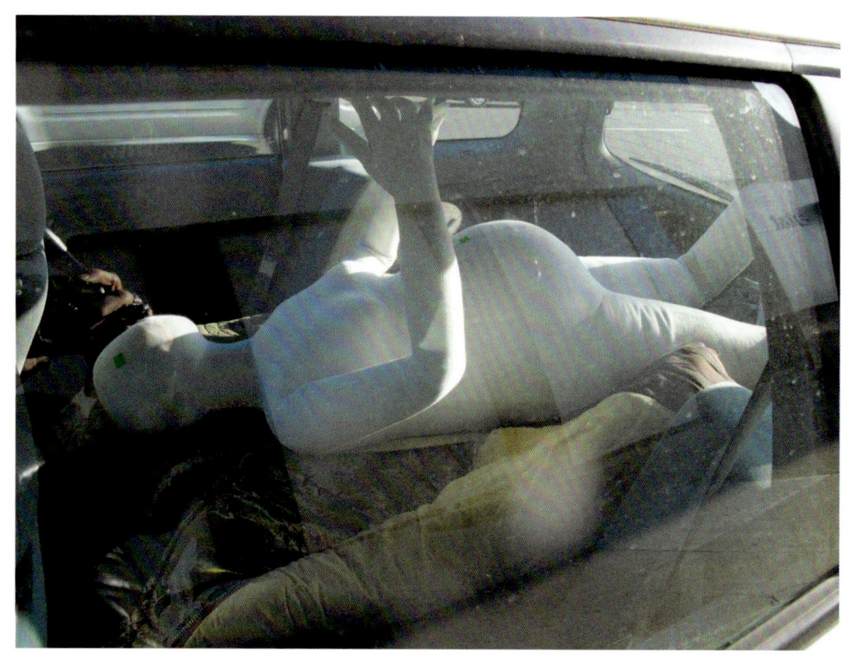

Figs. 29, 30

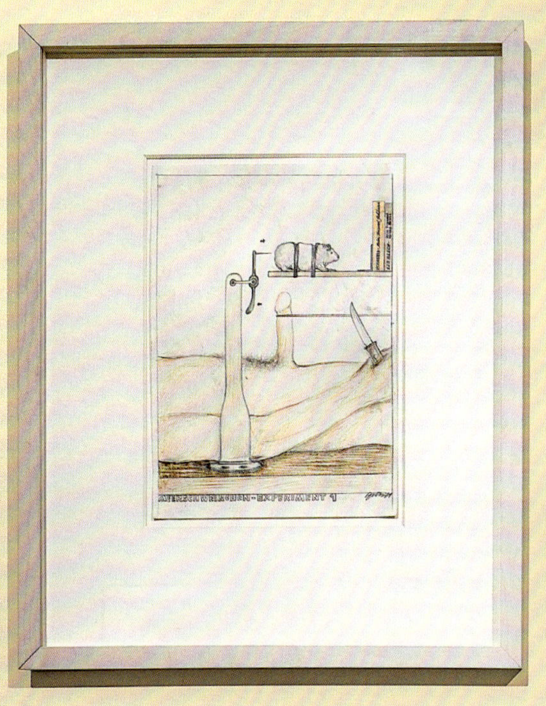
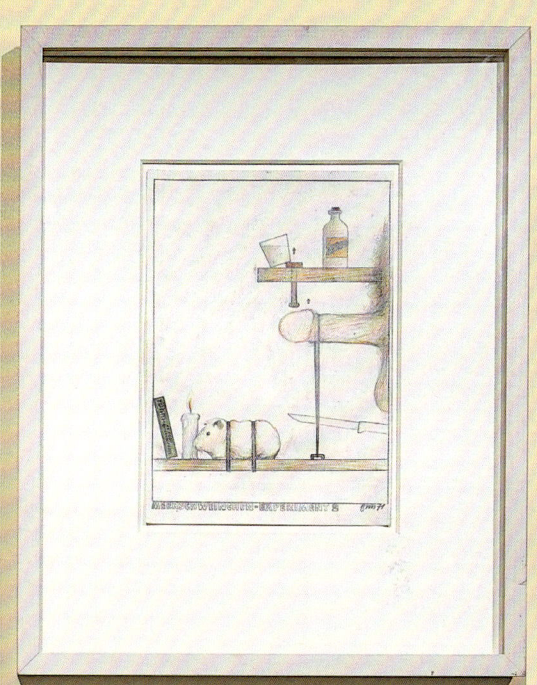
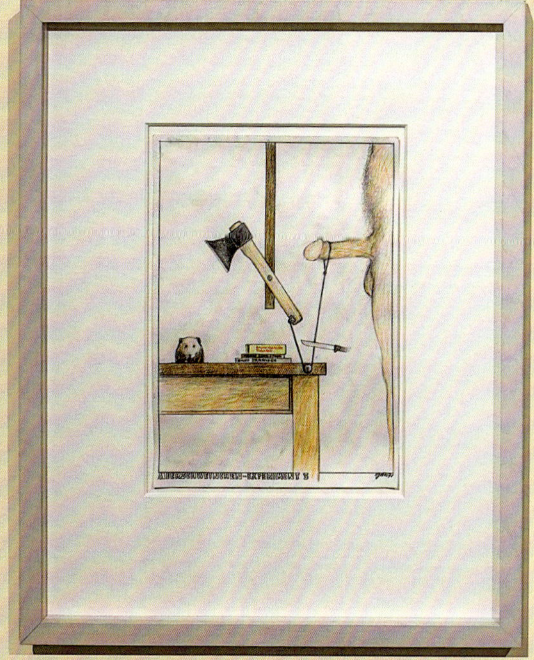
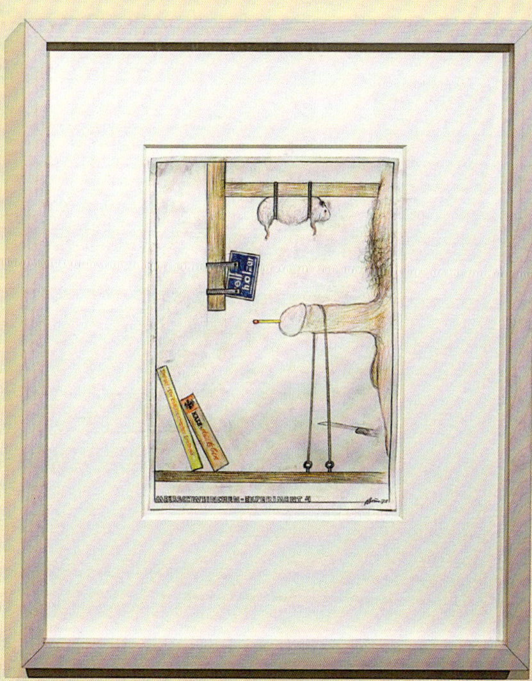

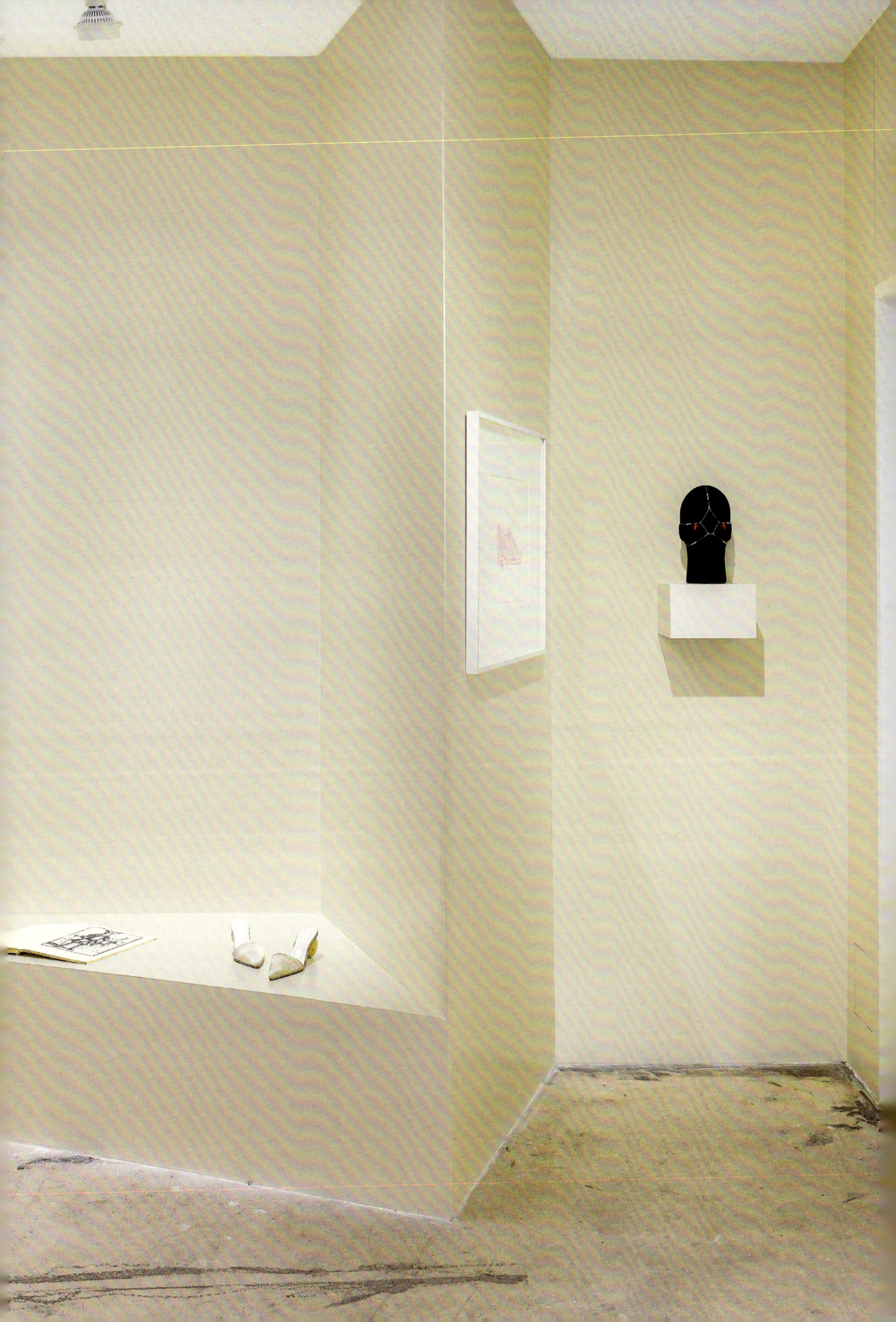

restroom. The sound of trickling piss underscores a description of the bedrock of Manhattan and an exegesis on money, property, and shit: "If money were shit which then became food, then it would fully gratify the infantile desire." For Freud, the scatological is the original creation, a tool mobilized by children to challenge authority.

In 2016, Berger wrote about making her own mess. "Recently I keep the kiwi, apple or pear juice on my hands after eating. That wholly unpleasant feeling gluing together fingers in the most uncomfortable way. I keep it because I like to keep it and watch it naturally fade. I leave it on my sweater's worn out cuffs, on my face scratching my cheeks and eyes, I leave it on the countless handles."[1] Her attraction to disorder isn't so much excrementally inventive as it is passively curious about time and resolution. It's a curiosity about the shapes, and then the one shape, of entropy. Before it dissembles into its surround, the tacky residue indexes her patterns of movement, marks the expanded ecologies in which she participates. On an iPhone screen, the film interrupts alienated images with wayward, tactile biology. On her sweater, it makes interchangeable fashion unexchangeable. "As is." If, as Roland Barthes observes, fashion reserves "the luxury of connotation for the world, for the garment's elsewhere,"[2] stains and smudges short-circuit that connotation, insisting on the here and now.

It's not only melancholy that motivates people to save unsavory things. Or compulsiveness. Sometimes, it's to build a semiotics of shame. Mary Kelly's dirty nappies. Mike Kelley's stuffies. The shoulder of Pelops. Sometimes, it's to step out of euphoria and return to the here and now of things. It's to reckon with a bad object.

II.

Berger's conception of *life and limbs* developed based on images she had collected over four or five years in a folder on her desktop labeled "Art I Like." The images therein represented an unmitigated reflection of ad hoc research; not destined for public display or geared toward a particular aim, they rather offered a landscape from which the artist operated. It was only in reviewing the folder that categories, discourses, and resonances cohered. One might call this curating through association or affinity; one might call it curating through kinship.

Here are Berger's friends, family (her mother's 1991 *Waist of Money* Moschino blazer), her boyfriend (Benjamin Hirte's 2019 *Ghost*), but also the artists who arrived in Google searches, scrolls, and on the pages of books. This kind of curating has drawn criticism for narcissism or nepotism, for not having "stakes," or the critical distance from which to take a position. On the one hand, this umbrage comes from the modernist tradition of privileging a cohesive avant-garde with a prescriptive message. On the other, it draws from the liberal notion that an exhibition must present some disinterested, utopian pluralism for pluralism's sake.[3] But the artist-curated exhibition, from Courbet's 1855 sendup of the Salon in Paris to Andy Warhol's 1969 *Raid the Icebox I* (1969) and *Burton on Brancusi* (1989) on to Fred Wilson's *Mining the Museum* (1992), is poised to challenge the ways in which art is historicized and valued.

We could think of Berger's curatorial approach as following the "beside itself" logic of the developments in painting that David Joselit and Martin Kippenberger identified in 2009, when work made in Cologne in the 1990s began to visualize the context in which it circulated. These artists developed practices that entangle the viewer in "extra-perceptual social networks rather than merely situating them in a phenomenological relationship of individual perception."[4] Against the sheer accumulation of content and the "semiotic aporias" of the digital world, making the paths and nodes of circulation visible was made significant itself.

The network Berger presents is not one limited to the terms of an art world validated by specific institutions or striated by discipline. Neither is it one that merely imprints a social body, if the social body is conceived as those who care for each other, or share assistants or galleries or lovers, or transact or convene. The network Berger presents here acknowledges a scope of distributed relationships that together create meaning. This social network reveals threads of influence in its many degrees: immediate and ahistorical, intellectual, empathic, and reproductive. To disrobe the network is to reveal even its vulgar processes and habits, to perhaps discover what it carries unwittingly.

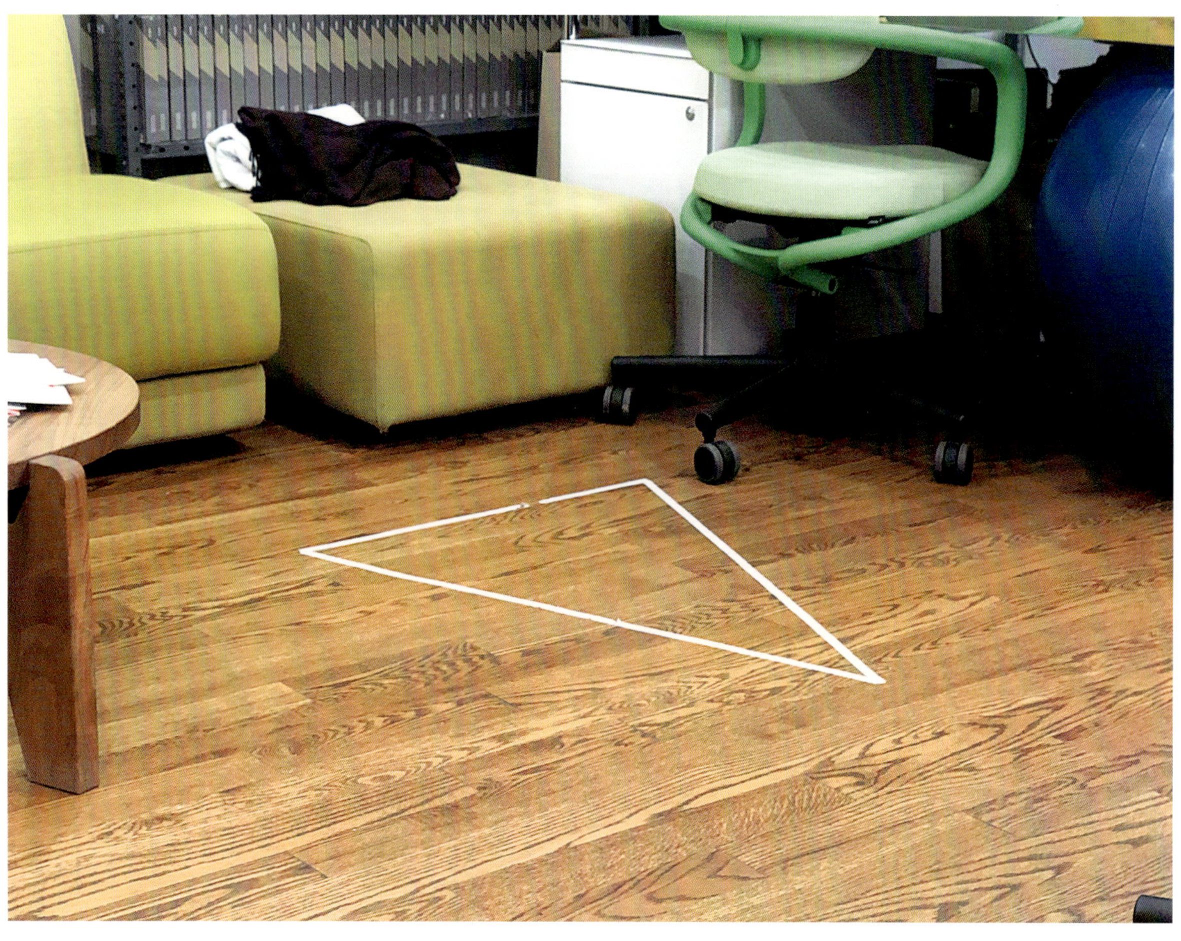

Fig. 32

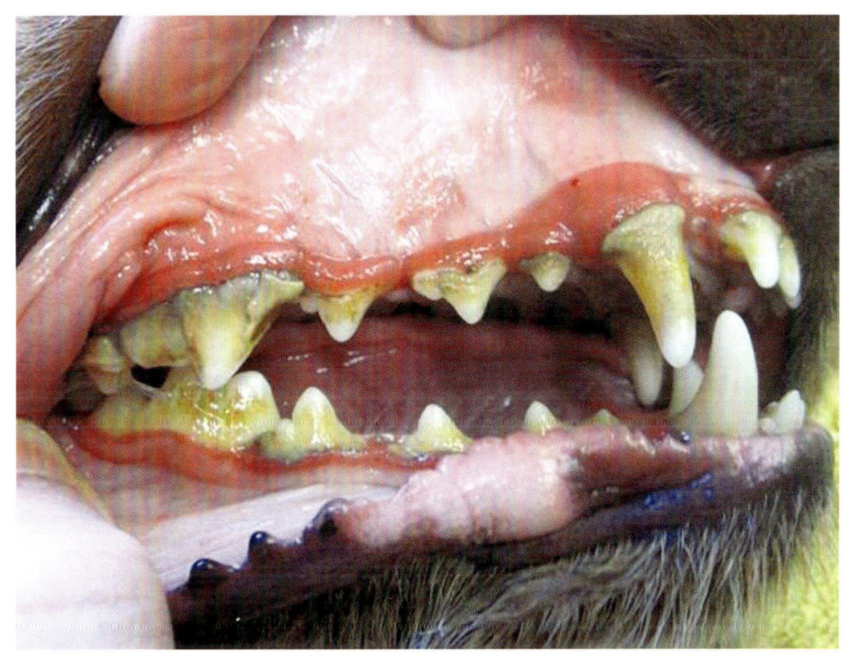

Fig. 33

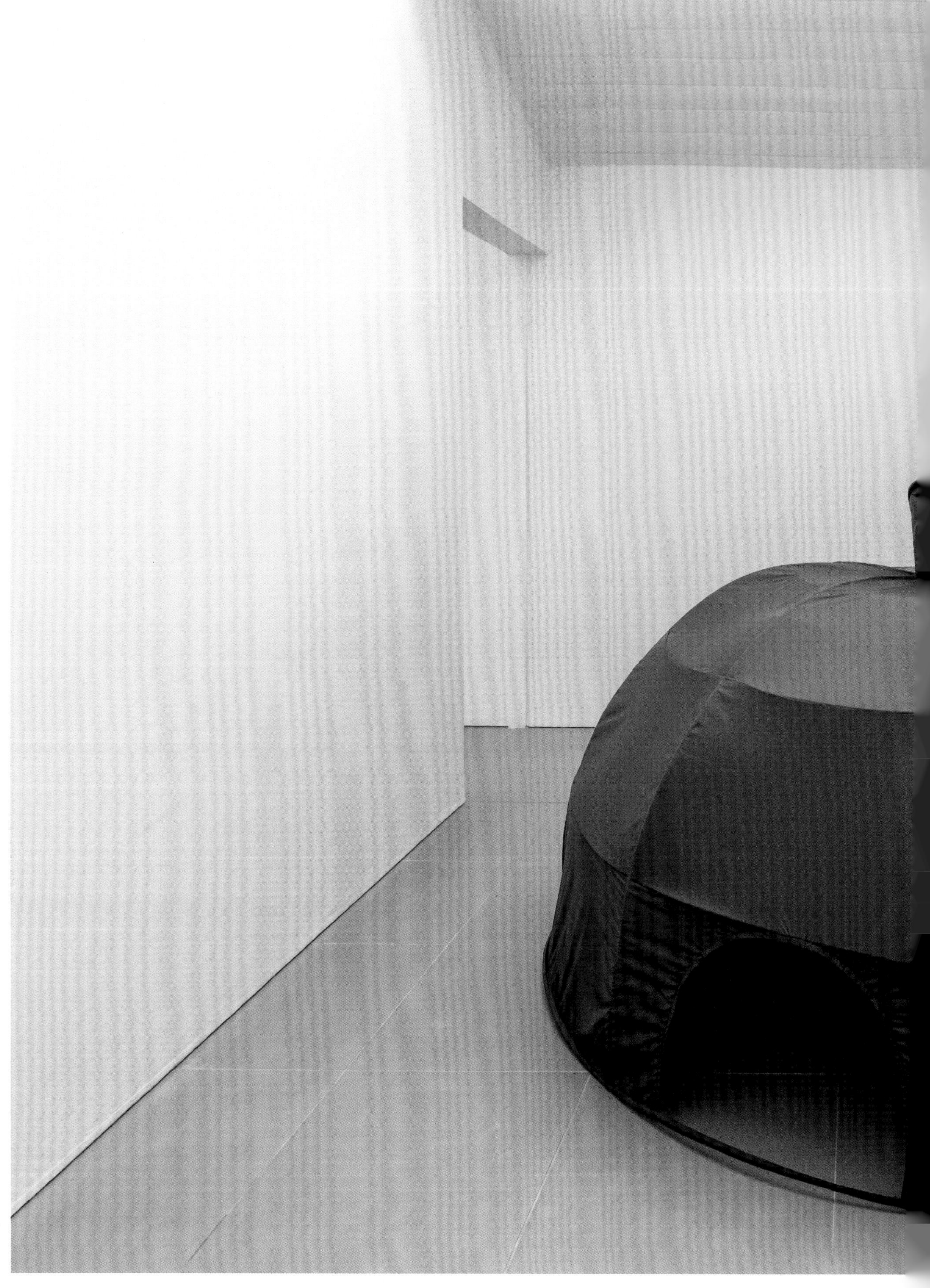

Fig. 34

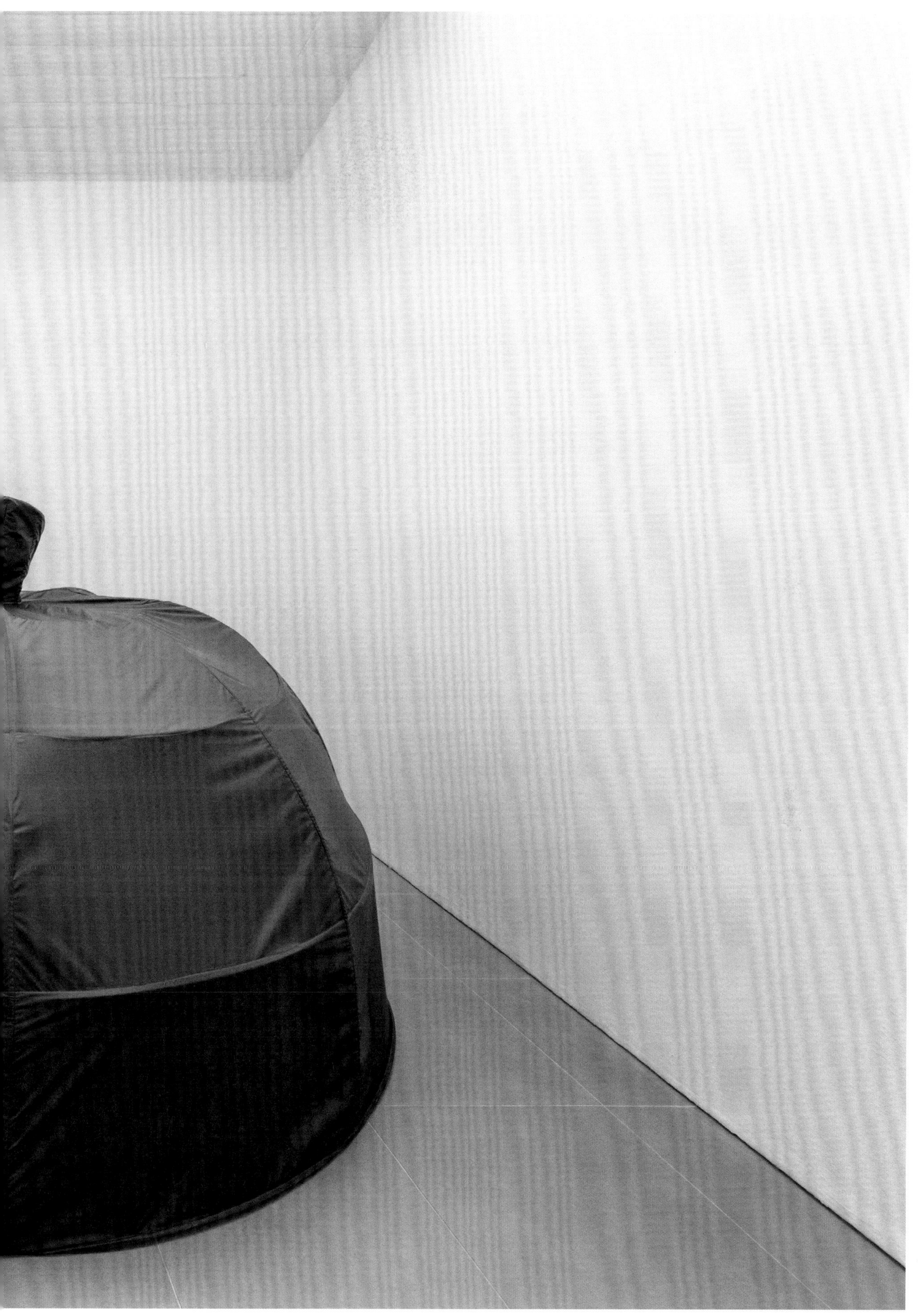

Fig. 35

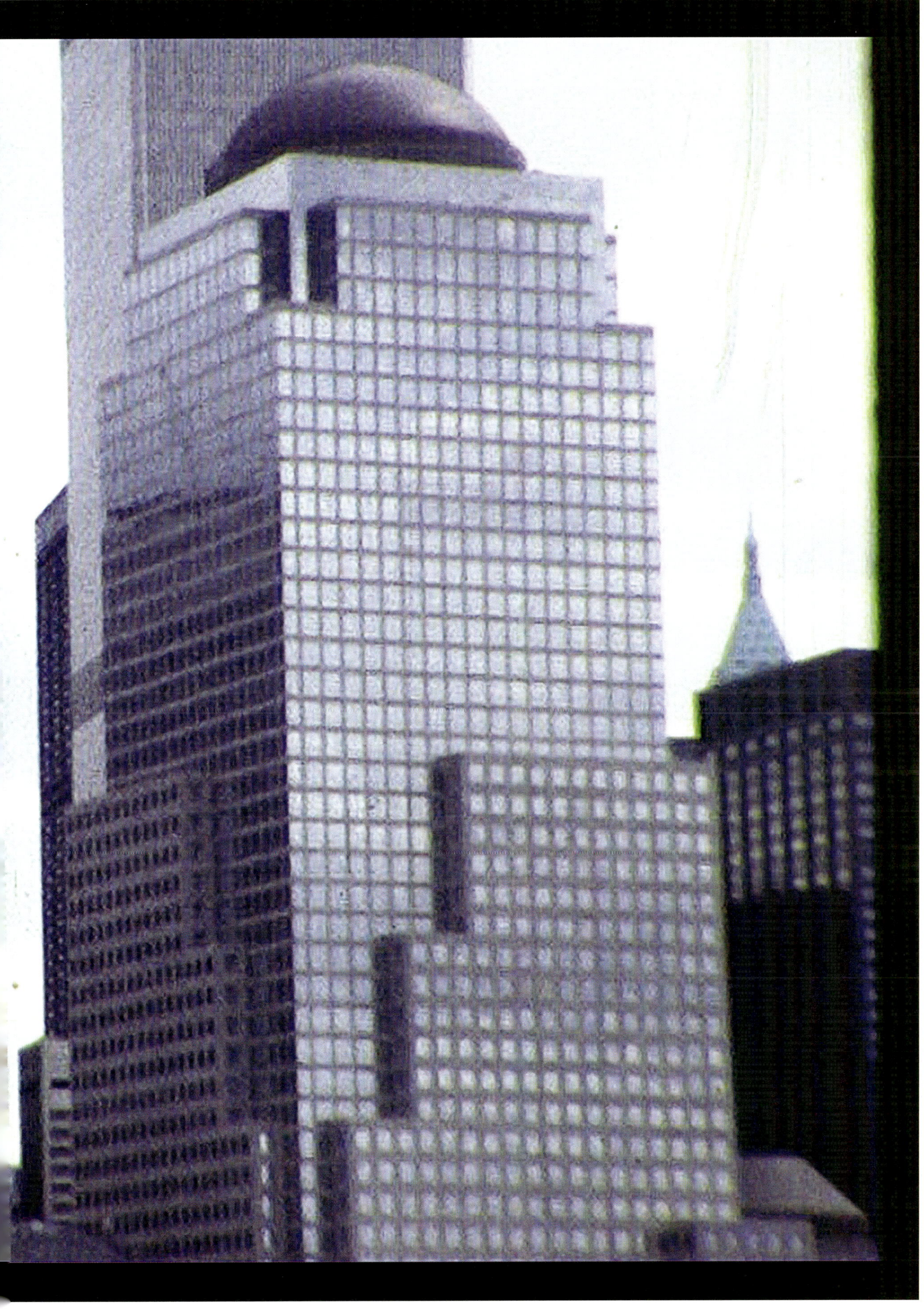

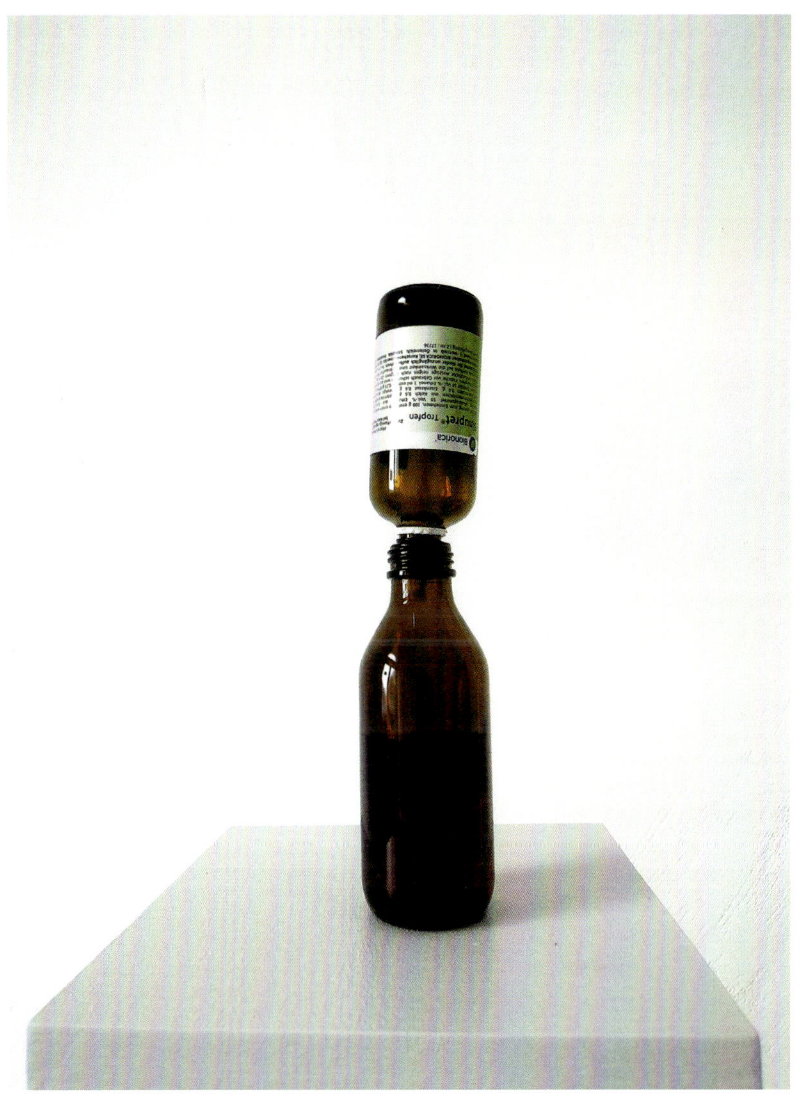

Fig. 36

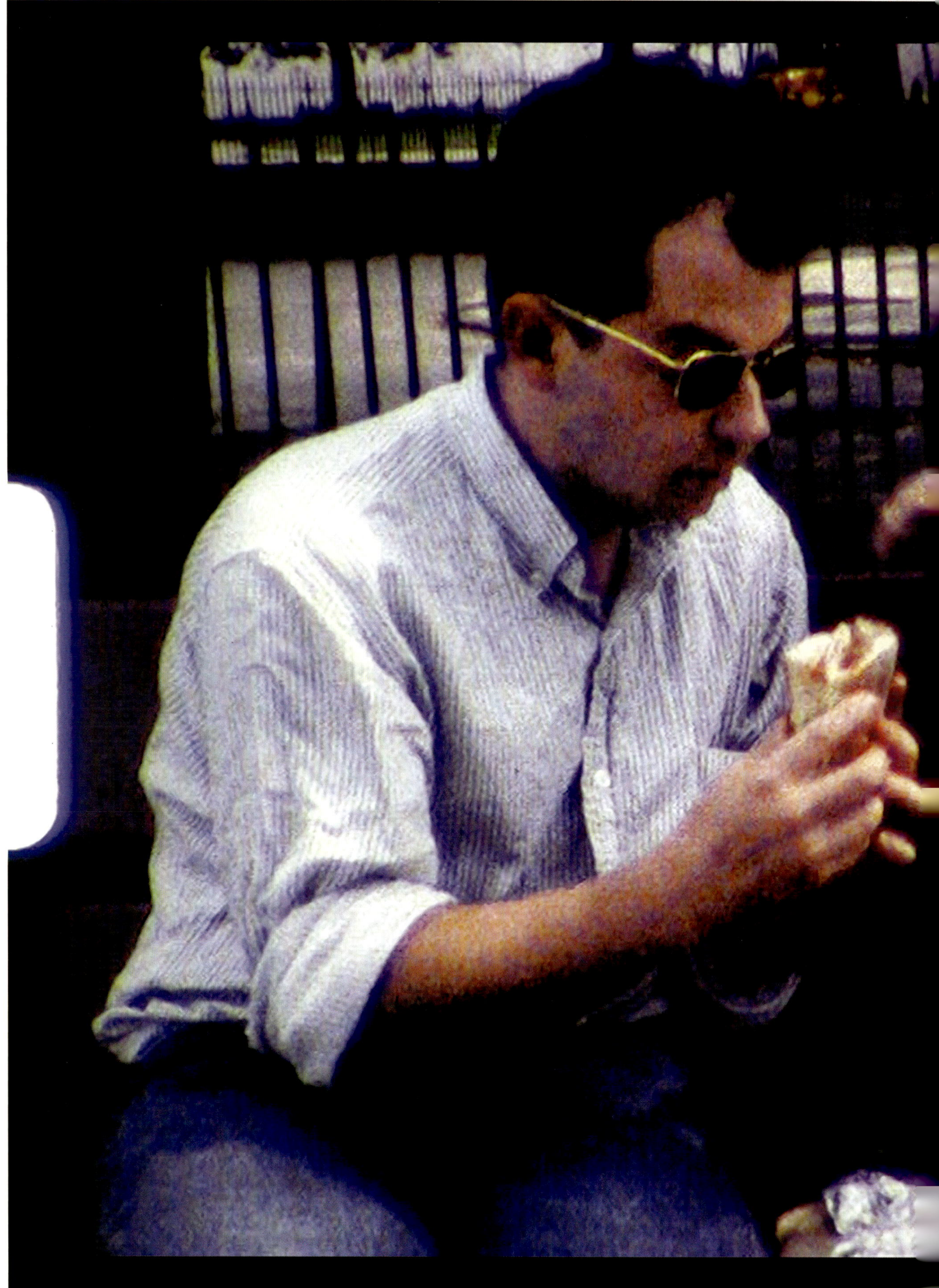

Fig. 37

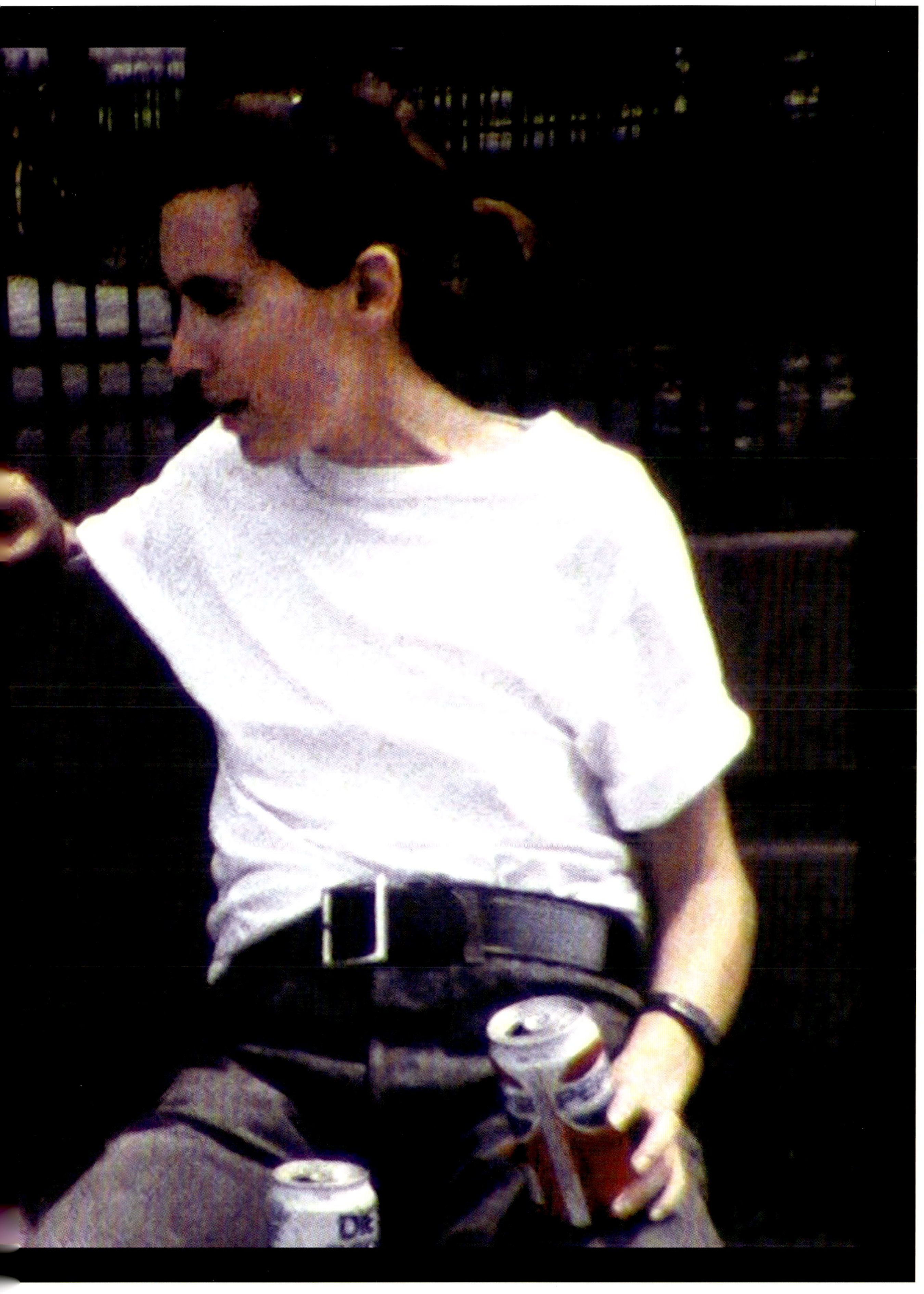

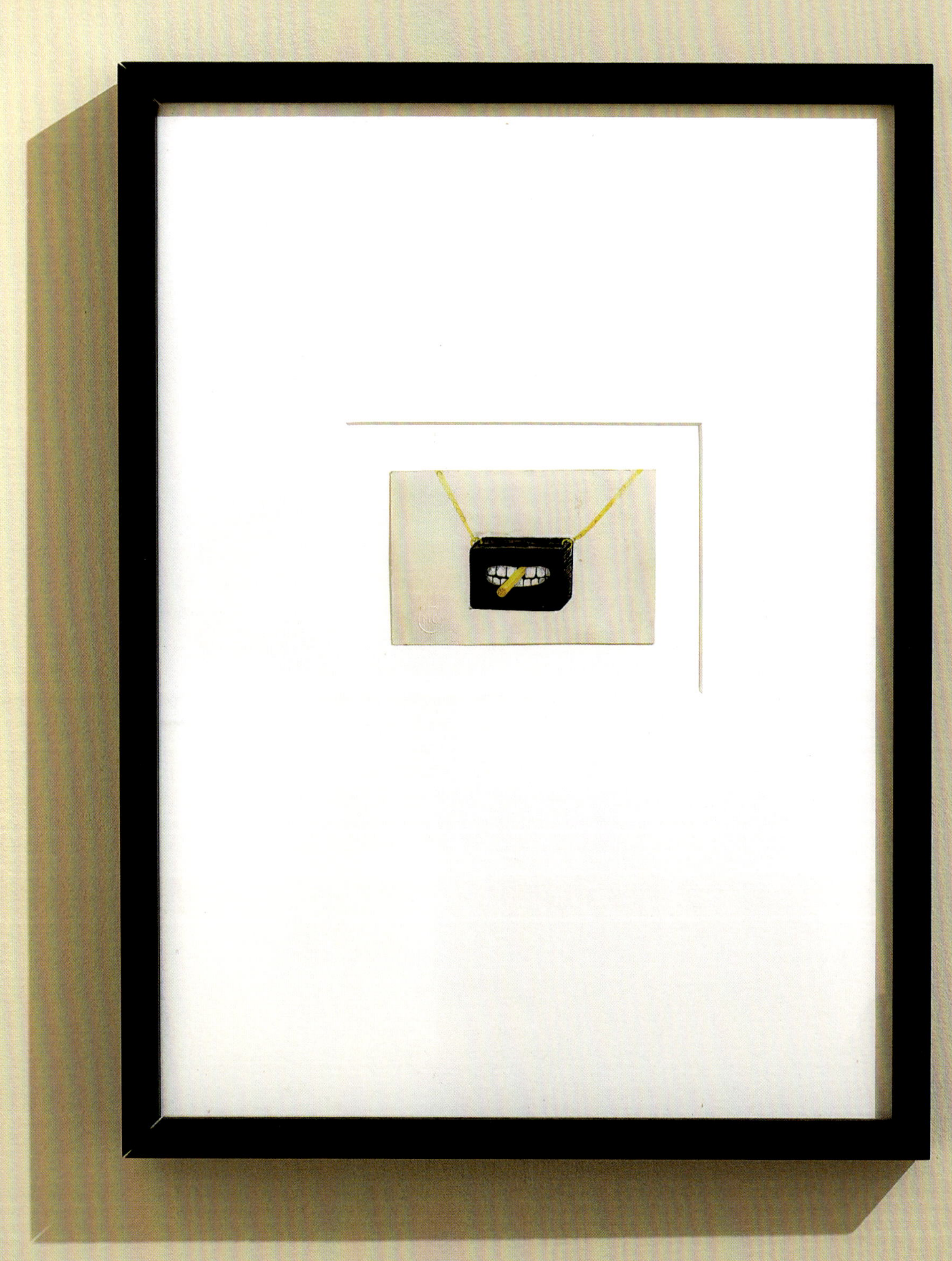

III.

In the audio clip, Tobias Madison admits to his girlfriend that yes, he had strangled her, and yes, he had thrown her head against a brick wall. But she had to understand. She caused this by turning the light on while he was sleeping. He is calm, pragmatic. He understands that she is taping him, and he is sorry that something inside him has caused him to behave so terribly. But she has to understand; she turned on the light.[5]

IV.

The grotesque aesthetic emerged in the fifteenth century, when fantastical designs of satyrs and chimeras, hybrids of flora and fauna, were discovered in ancient Roman ruins and reimagined by Renaissance artists, who were drawn to the hedonistic, liberated expression these images suggested. But with the ascendance of the Vitruvian ideal, and the determination that the classical phantasms were products of the decadent phase of Nero's Golden House, thereby signaling the decline of Rome, such forms which did not occur naturally were recast as foul and crude.

"How can the stem of a flower support a roof, or a candelabrum pedimental sculpture? How can a tender shoot carry a human figure, and how can bastard forms composed of flowers and human bodies grow out of roots and tendrils?"[6] Vitruvius had asked. The answer is: not without help. Not without prosthetics or cosmology or pharmacology or surgery. Not without design and intervention. Not without care, and not without a collective investment in magical thinking. Bodies are only determined if we are unwilling to see them otherwise. The grotesque, as Mikhail Bakhtin in his study of Rabelais mused, resides in the point where bodies enter into each other, where forms are mutually constructed.[7] Where they touch. There is no moral assignation for the grotesque, only the color of risk that accompanies welcoming the other in; life and limb.

The thing with group shows is that they highlight the transitivity of artworks, and Berger's dentate design only emphasized this effect. Group shows are always propositions wherein artworks participate in an encompassing field of signification. The assumption is that a work consents to be acted upon in this context.[8] The Vitruvian question for this grotesque body, the body of Berger's exhibition, became over the course of the show a nonconsensual one: How can someone familiar to me do something so gruesome? How can I trust myself when I didn't anticipate this horror? And what is to be done with the objects that remain?

life and limbs was organized around the theme of artworks that "trouble the limits of what a body can consume, process, reach, and become," and it was taken to task. For the artists involved, the curator, the institution, the transitive nature of objects and exhibitions alike became untenably clear. The limits of what a body, what a social body, what an exhibition, can process were materially troubled. One object spoke over the rest.

The presentation of bad objects requires a fraught calculation of risk and reward. For example, the space of the exhibition can usher actual violence into theoretical abstraction—ideally, this would allow for new ways to perceive and consider the conditions and contexts of that violence with an eye toward its eradication; however, it might simply aestheticize and neuter the violence, or worse, fetishize it. Moreover, offering up the work of a malignant artist could be construed as validating his worldview and would certainly contribute to his cultural and likely financial capital. However, when the details of Tobias Madison's abuse came to light, his work had already been selected for the exhibition, complicating the terms of such appraisals. Amid calls to deplatform the artist, Berger wrestled with the proposition of adjudicating an event she was on no grounds to assess. Ultimately, she kept his work in the exhibition; she wore a stained garment.

I wonder, when an artist who is embedded in a social and ideological fabric is revealed to be deeply corrupt, is it even possible to excise him or scrub him out? What is the shape of his blemish, are its edges defined? Or, like mold, has it already compromised the integrity of the whole? Like art, abuse doesn't happen in vacuums. It cannot be reckoned with if it isn't brought to light. When a bad object persists, it affirms that our previous understanding of the world was not stable. To remove the bad object from view is to return to the space of euphoria; to remove the stain is to return to fashion. To confuse

Fig. 38

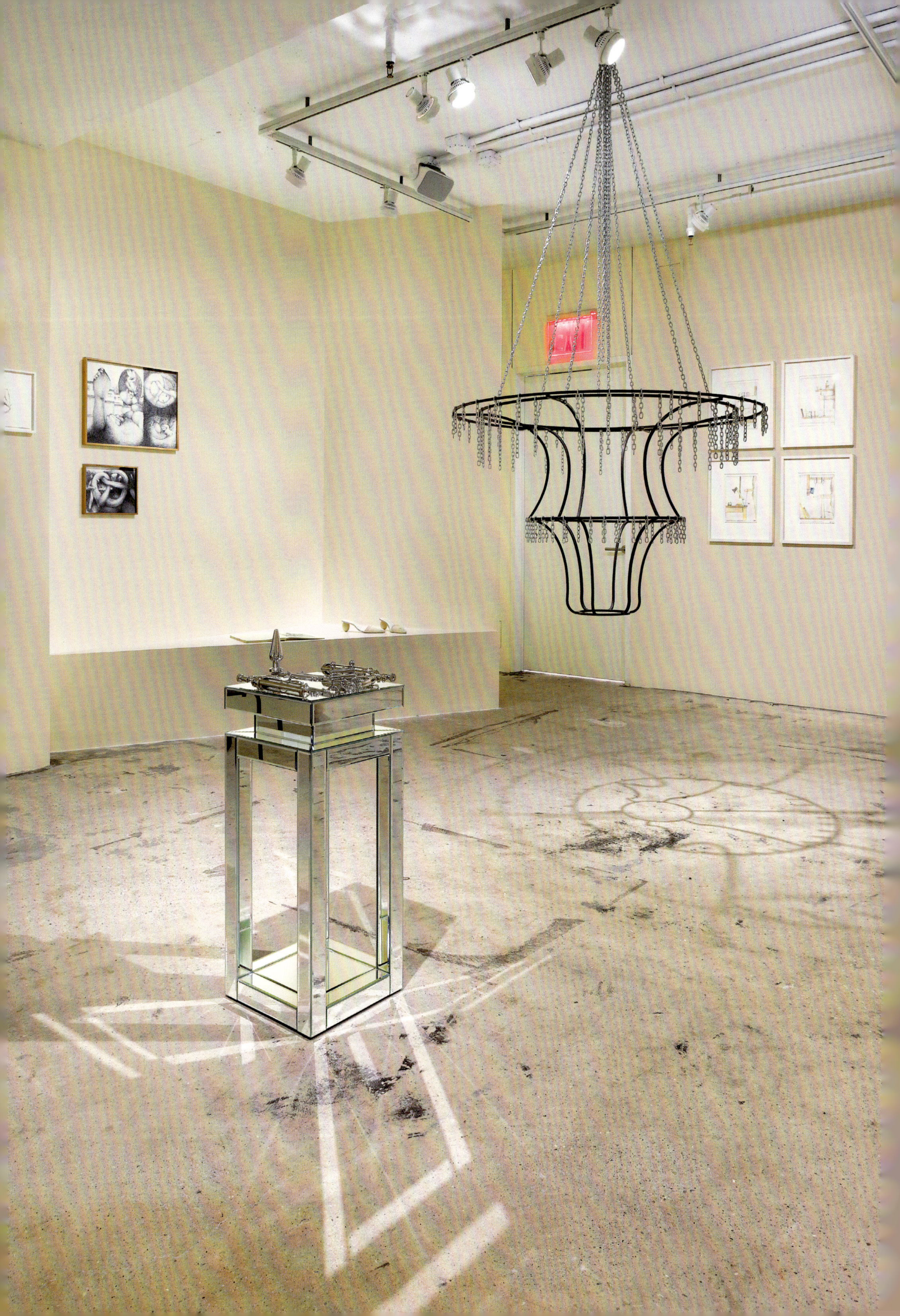

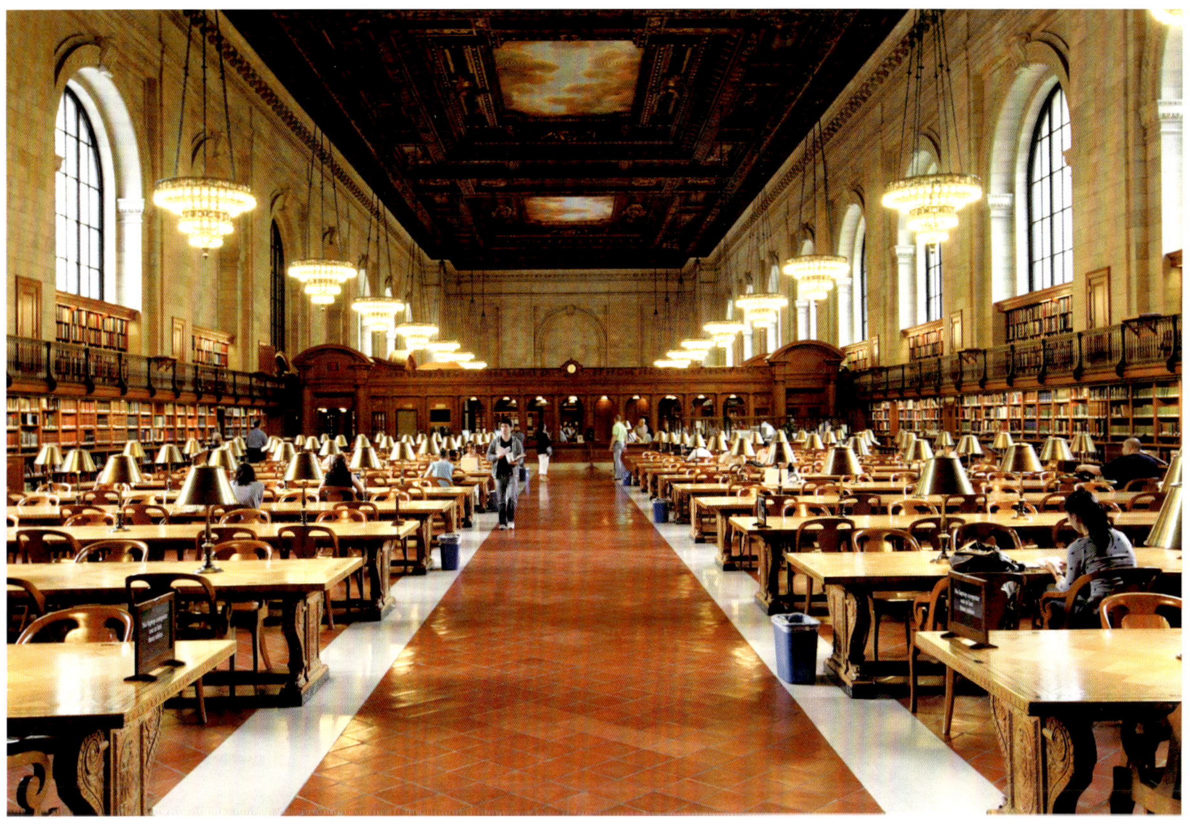

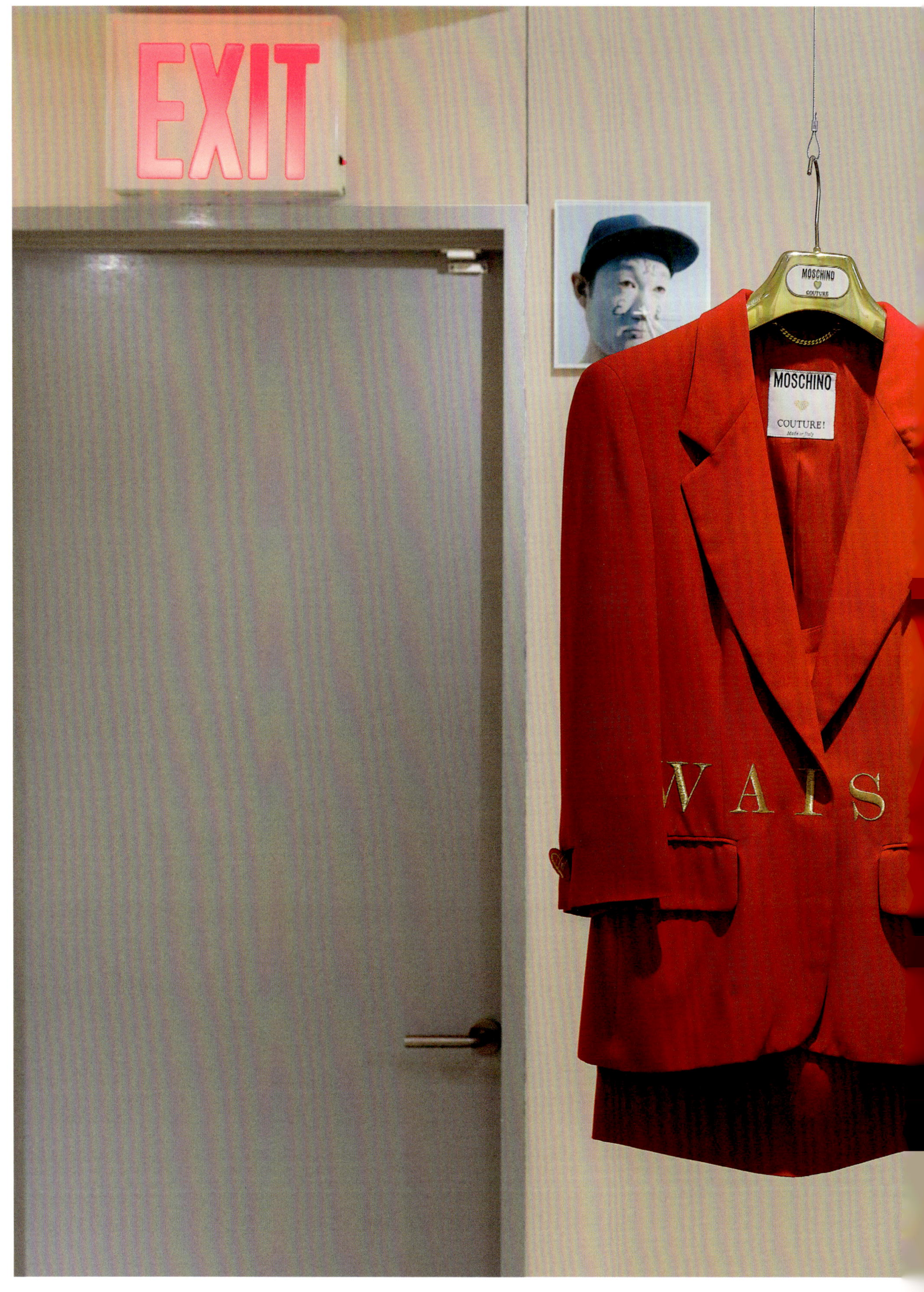

Fig. 41

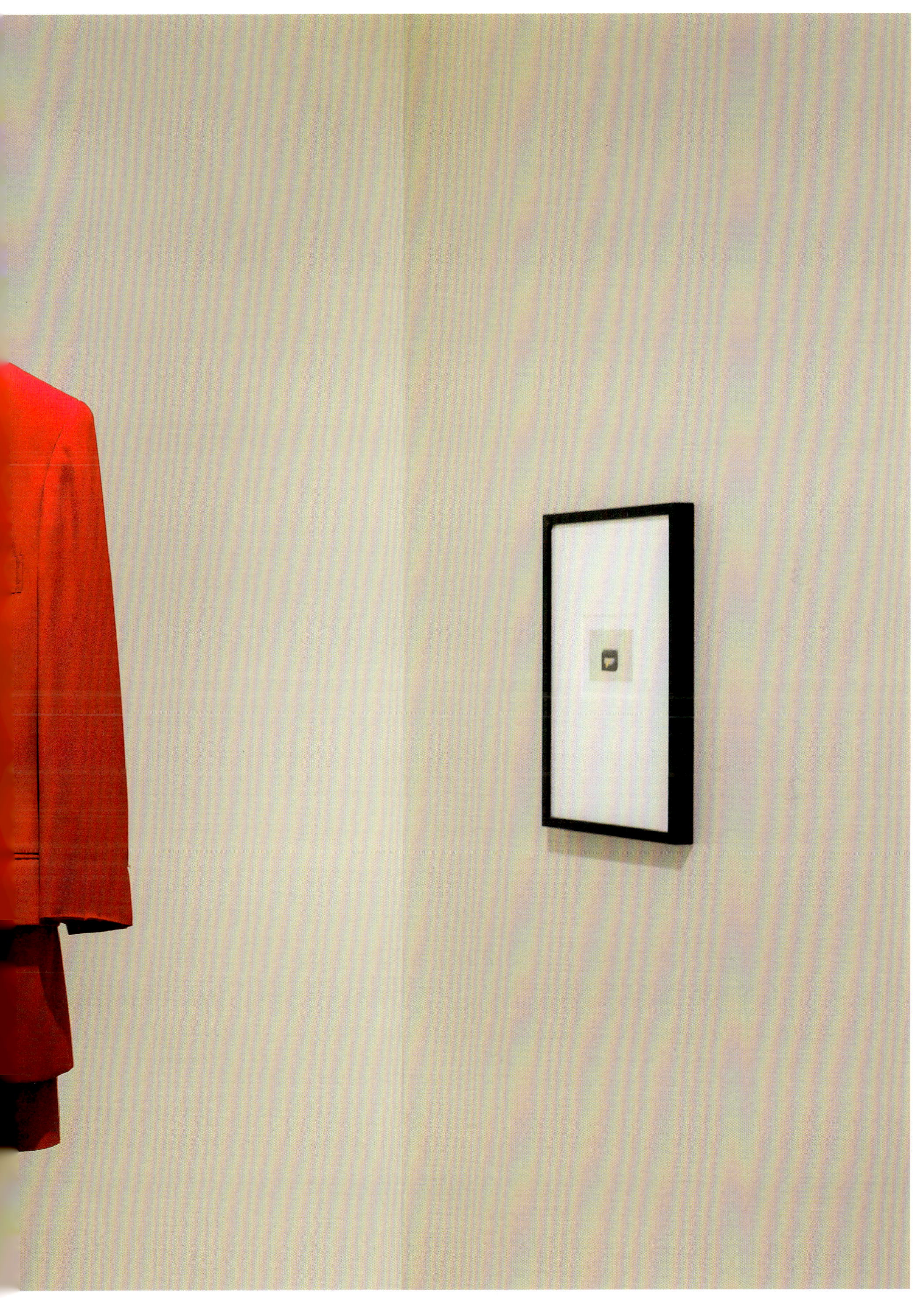

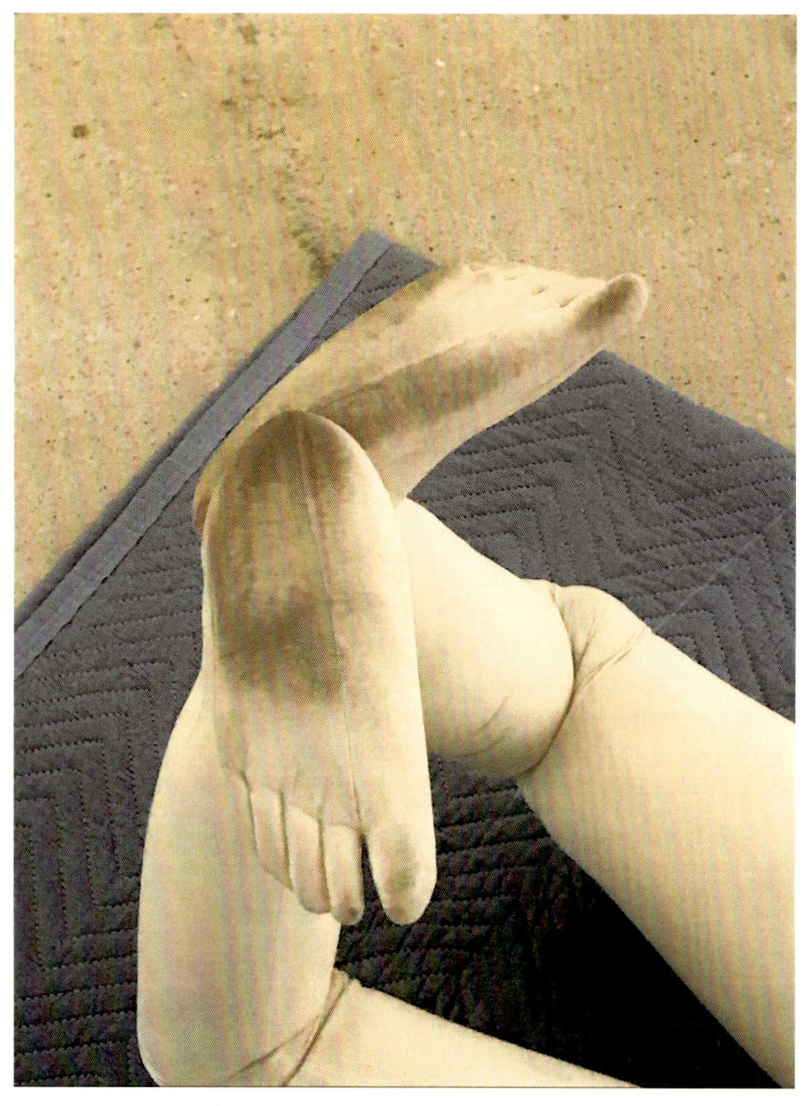

Fig. 42

presentation with affirmation is to void the possibility of criticality, recalibration, and change. Is this a reckoning?

At the center of *life and limbs* was Lutz Bacher's *Pregnant* (2009), a stuffed, white fabric doll of a supine, pregnant woman whose legs are inverted at the knee and held in the air. Dirt is on her heels. Her arms are held in *bras bas*, awaiting choreography or embrace, and her neck is craned just so. She is a picture of dependence. Mike Kelley described the grotesque body as "an accumulation of pieces at odds with each other—a group of parts that refuse to become whole."[9] As for me, I started this essay before Tobias Madison pled guilty to criminal counts of assault and harassment and finished it one month after the coronavirus sank its teeth into New York City. I can tell you, in mourning, I want to retreat into metaphor for its magical properties. I can tell you, in anger, that there is no whole. I can tell you, alone, that the network is the only frame, and it is unknowable. In midair, I can tell you the ground has never looked more appealing. Defund Tobias Madison. Believe women. Let his objects be stains, let them be shit.

V

It wasn't this exhibition's task to offer up prescriptions for the social lives of bad objects or the punishment of bad actors. And with this essay, I hope to do quite the opposite of conscript the works in *life and limbs* to the role of some Oedipal chorus or bind them to another artist's name. But it's true that there are guides here, and testaments, to the most intimate and vexing project of reorienting ourselves to our own bodies and to the bodies of others as they tell us more about their needs and flaws, as they betray us. In *blood in blood out* (2017), a sculpture by Lucia Elena Průša (with whom Berger exhibited at Galerie Kunstbuero in 2015), a framed garment-assemblage features a gaping *Death-Becomes-Her* aperture where the wearer's stomach would be. The object allows for the ambiguity of whether the proposed garment would fail the expectations of a typical body or the proposed body would fail the expectations of a typical garment. The point is to draw attention to the material and semantic interdependence of coverage and exposure.

Notes

1 Anna-Sophie Berger, *MANUAL*, Museum moderner Kunst Stiftung Ludwig, 2016.

2 Roland Barthes, *The Fashion System,* tr. Matthew Ward and Richard Howard (New York: Hill & Wang, 1983), 237.

3 Suhail Malik has articulated these conditions in his argument for "art's exit from contemporary art," observing that contemporary art's constitution is based on a logic of escape that inherently reifies the power structures it often aims to critique. See the roundtable on free speech with Malik, Hannah Black, Howie Chen, Jamillah James, and Ajay Kurian, "Freedom at the Expense of Others," in *Frieze*, no. 202, April 2019, 132–38.

4 David Joselit, "Painting Beside Itself," *October*, no. 130, Fall 2009, 125–34.

5 https://www.instagram.com/p/CNiV-twni2A/, last accessed on May 18, 2022.

6 Jodi Hauptman, *Beyond the Visible: The Art of Odilon Redon* (New York: Museum of Modern Art, 2005), 21.

7 Mikhail Bakhtin, *Rabelais and His World* (Bloomington: Indiana University Press, 1984).

8 This formulation of consent was expressed by artists, such as Tiona Nekkia McClodden and Sahra Motalebi, participating in the 2019 Whitney Biennial, when protests against Warren B. Kanders, chairman and CEO of the defense manufacturing company Safariland, shifted the framework of and politicized participation in the exhibition.

9 Mike Kelley, "Foul Perfection: Thoughts on Caricature," *Artforum* 27, no. 5 (January 1989).

Fig. 43 →

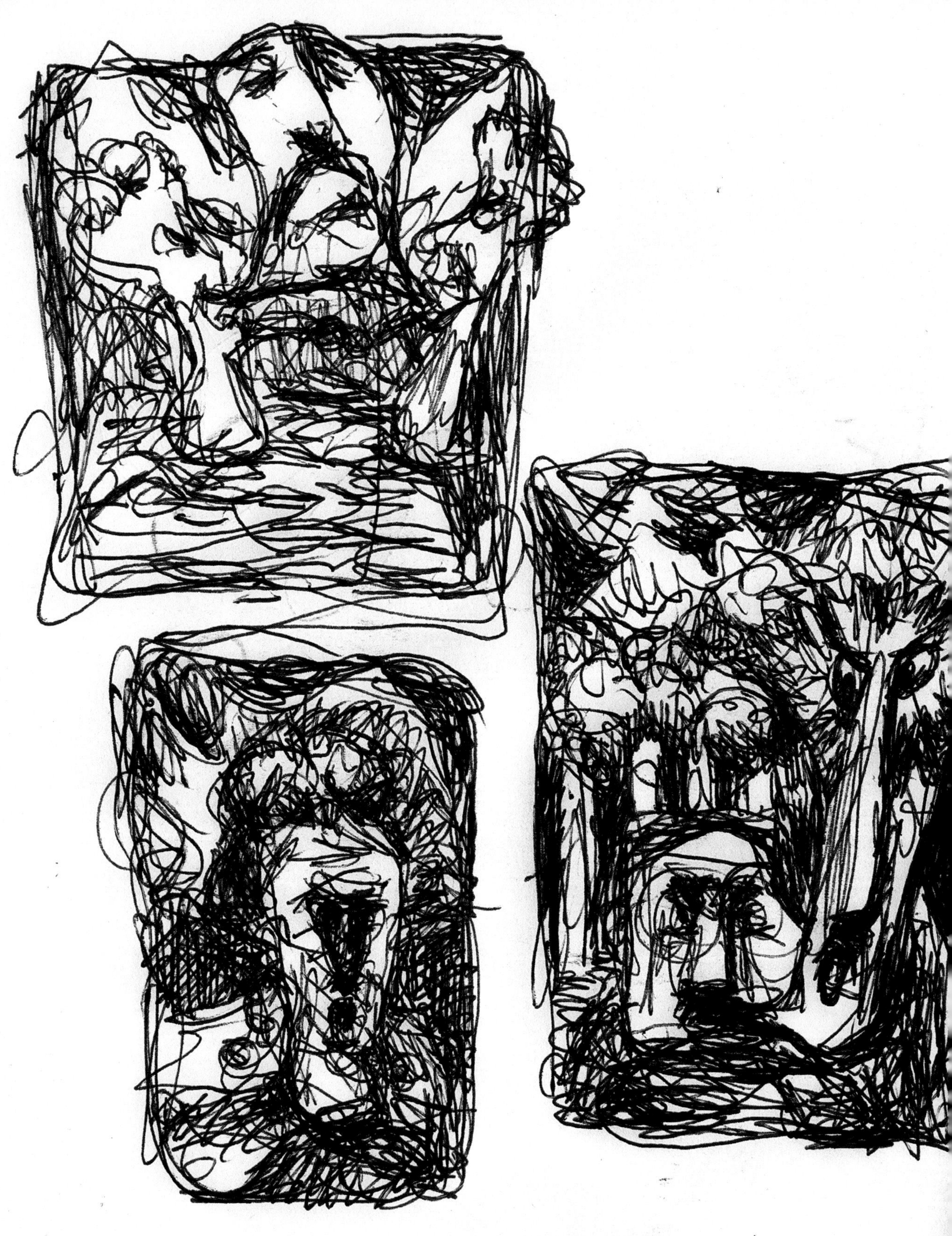

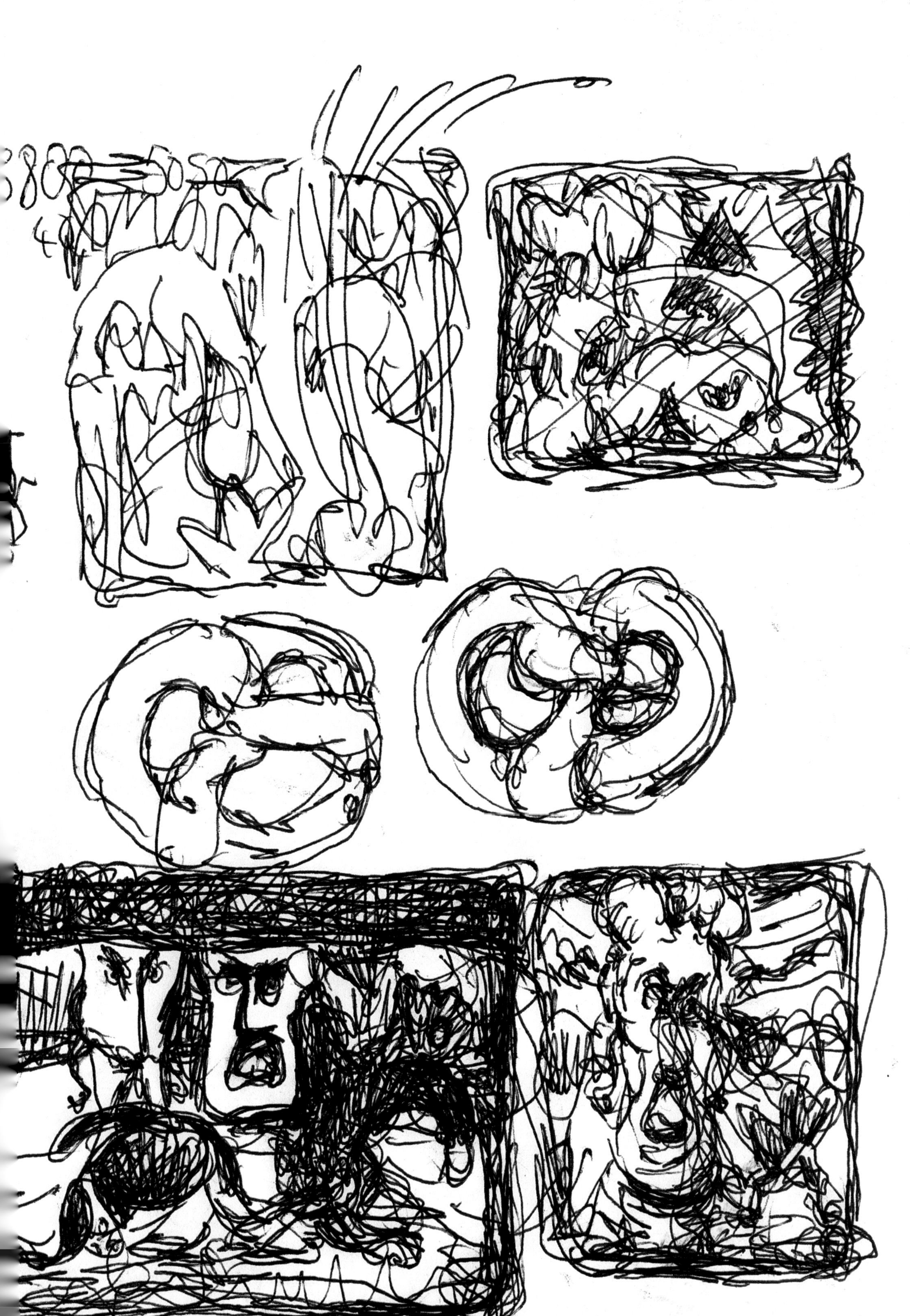

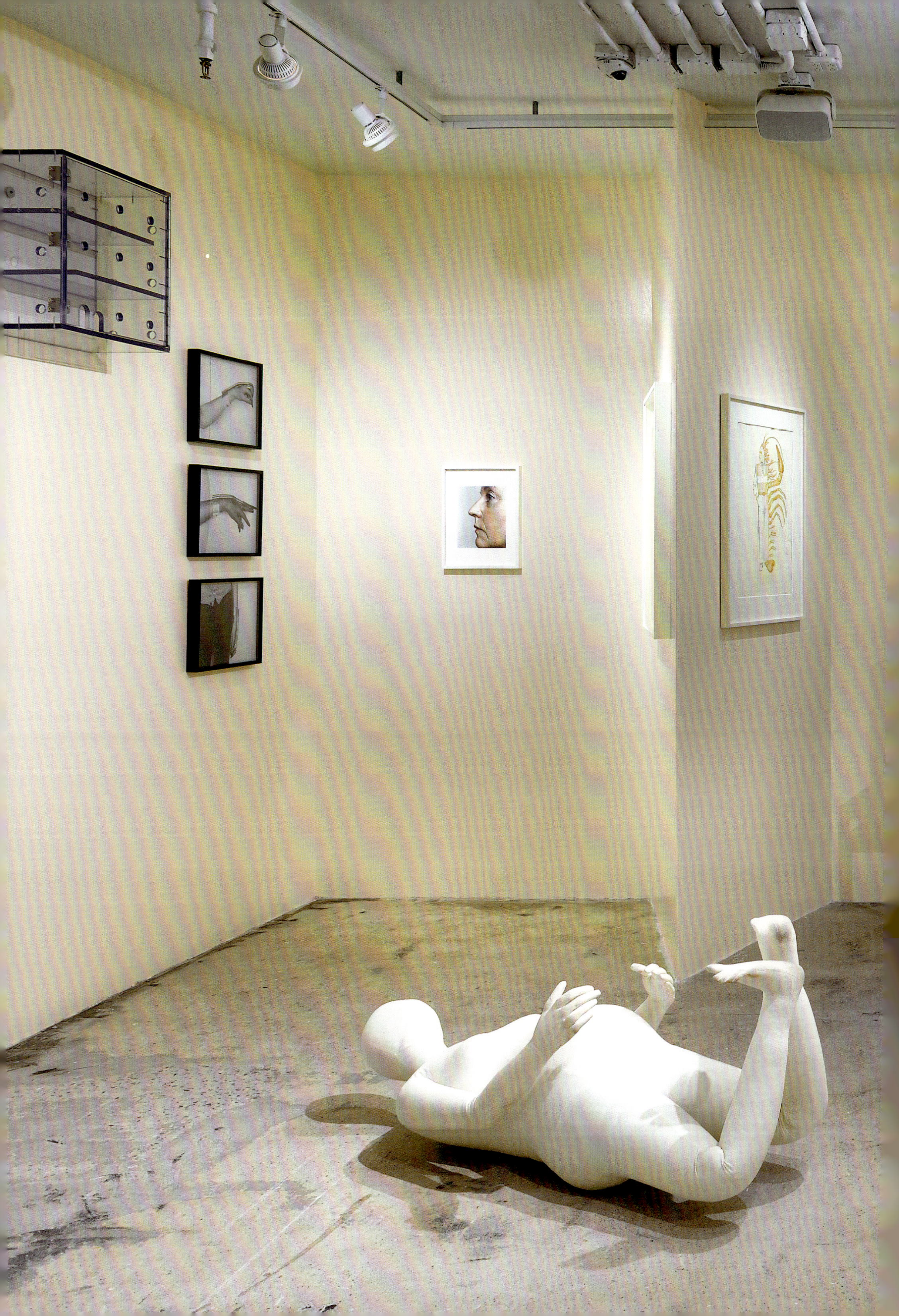

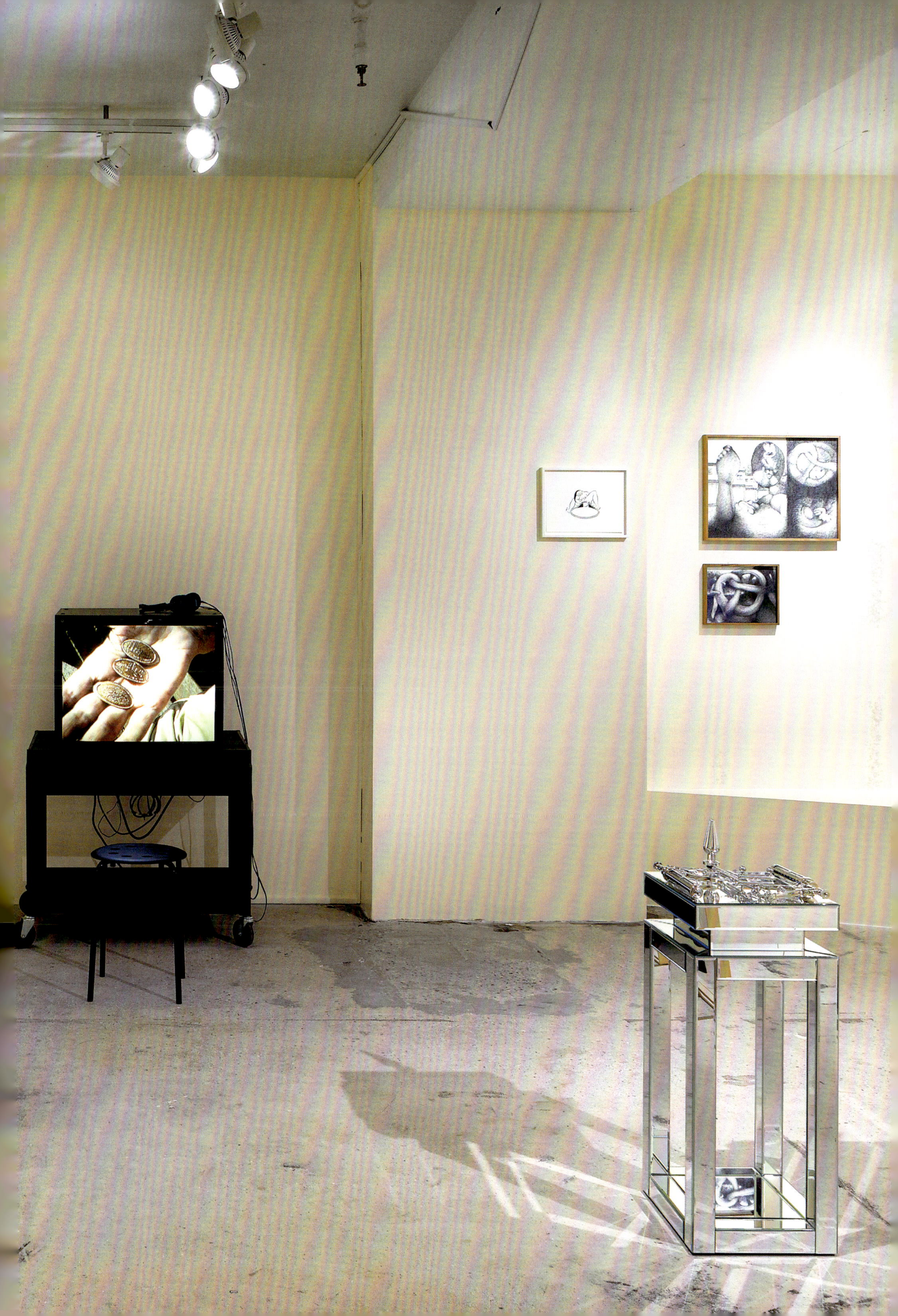

← Fig. 44

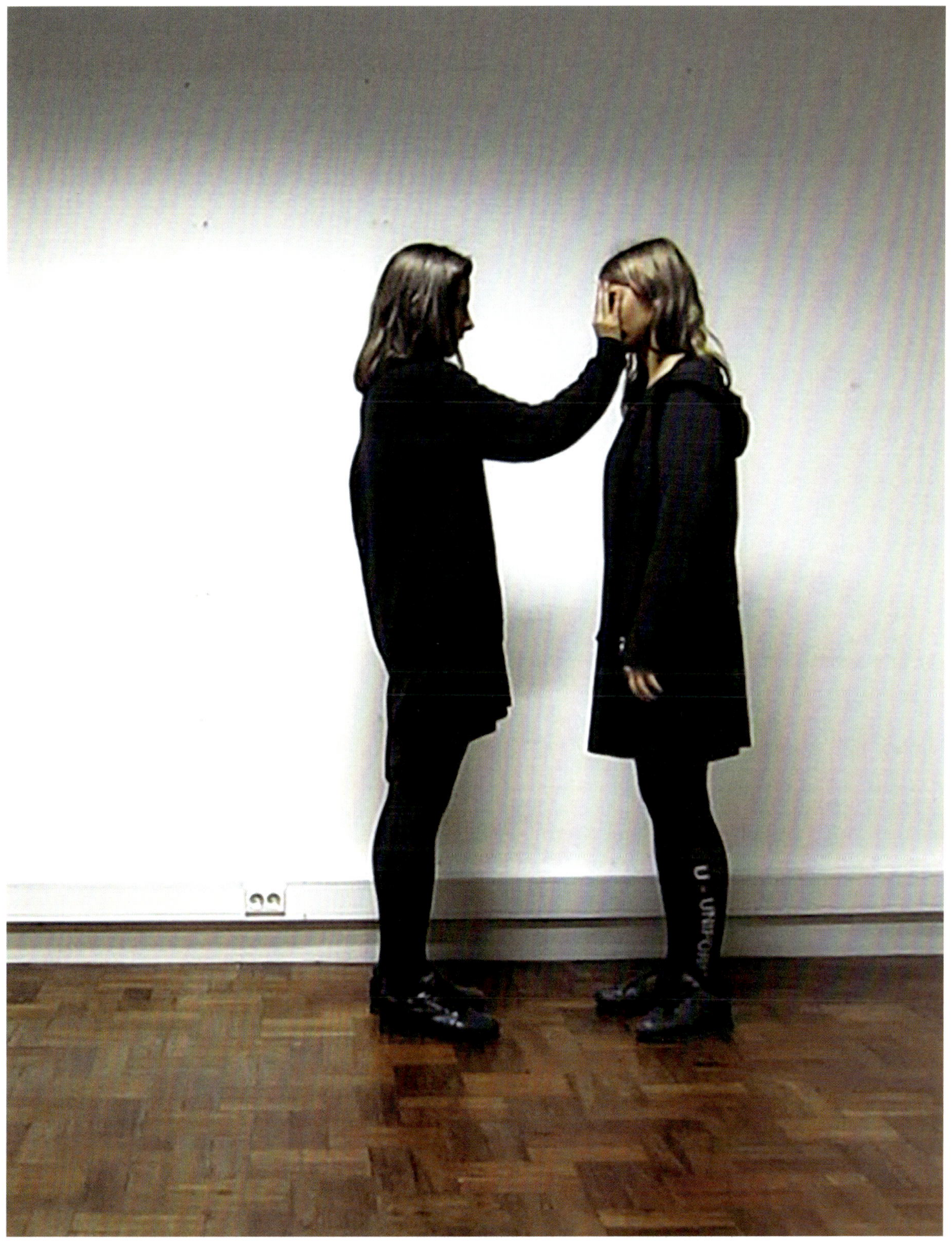

Fig. 45

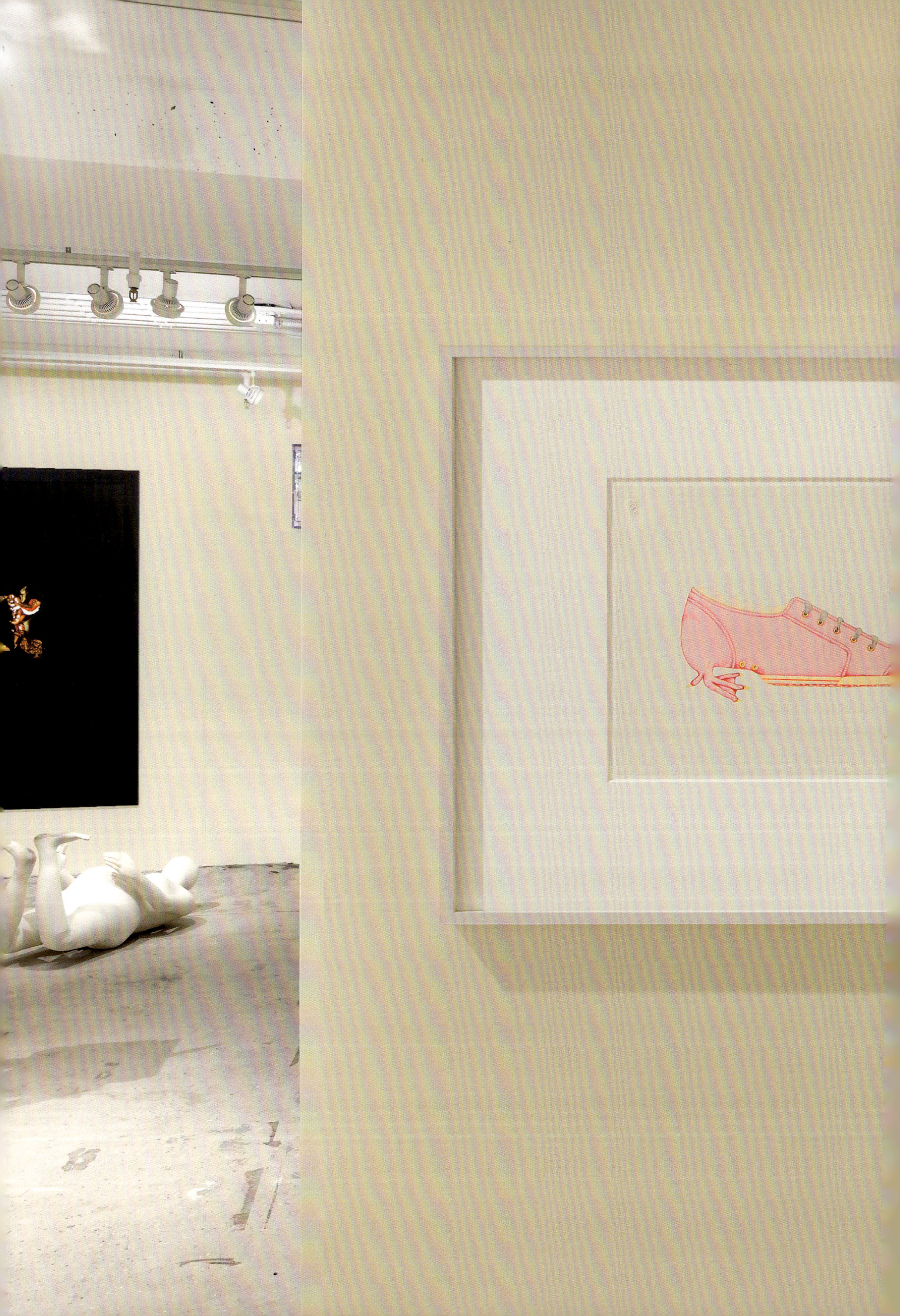

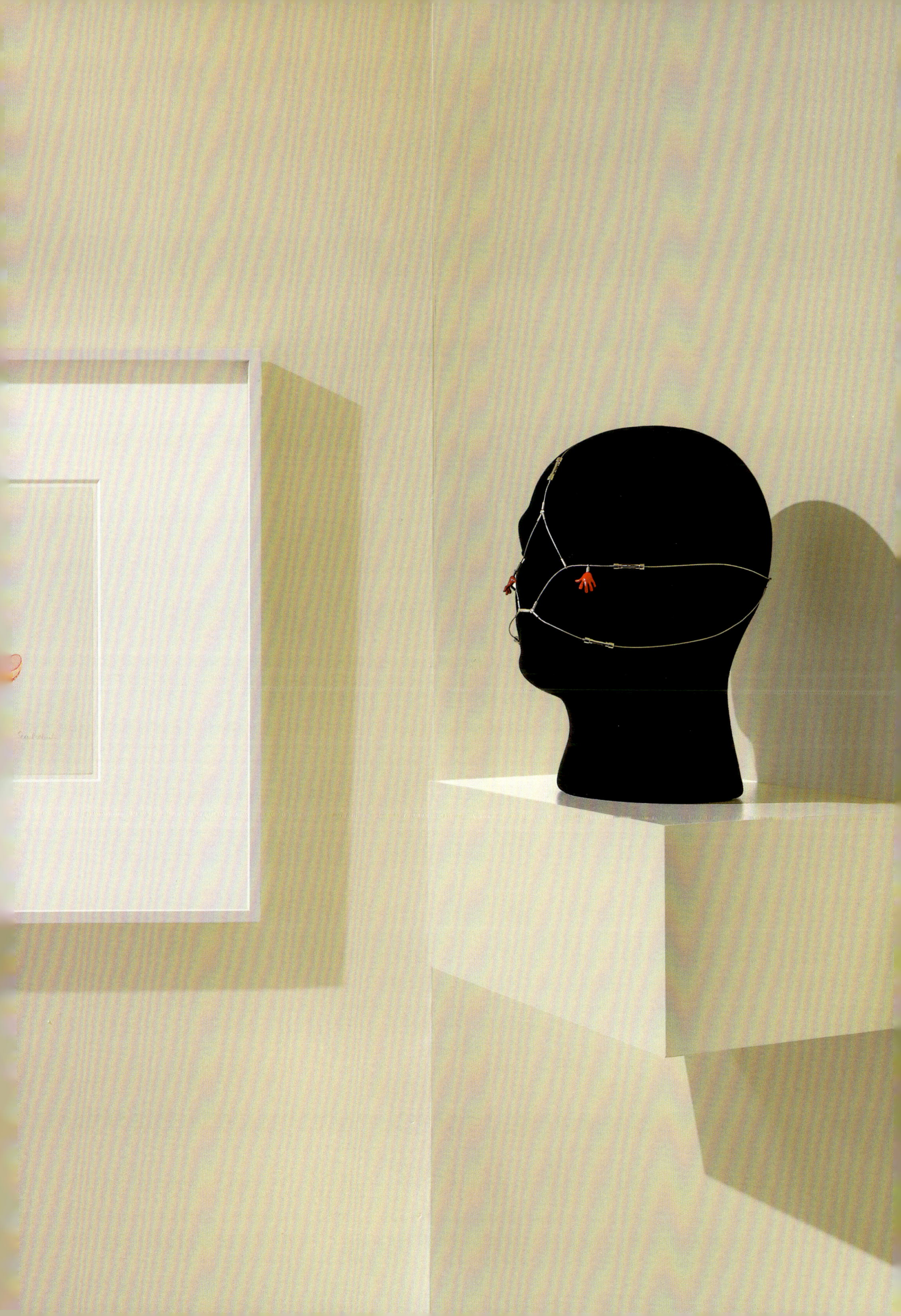

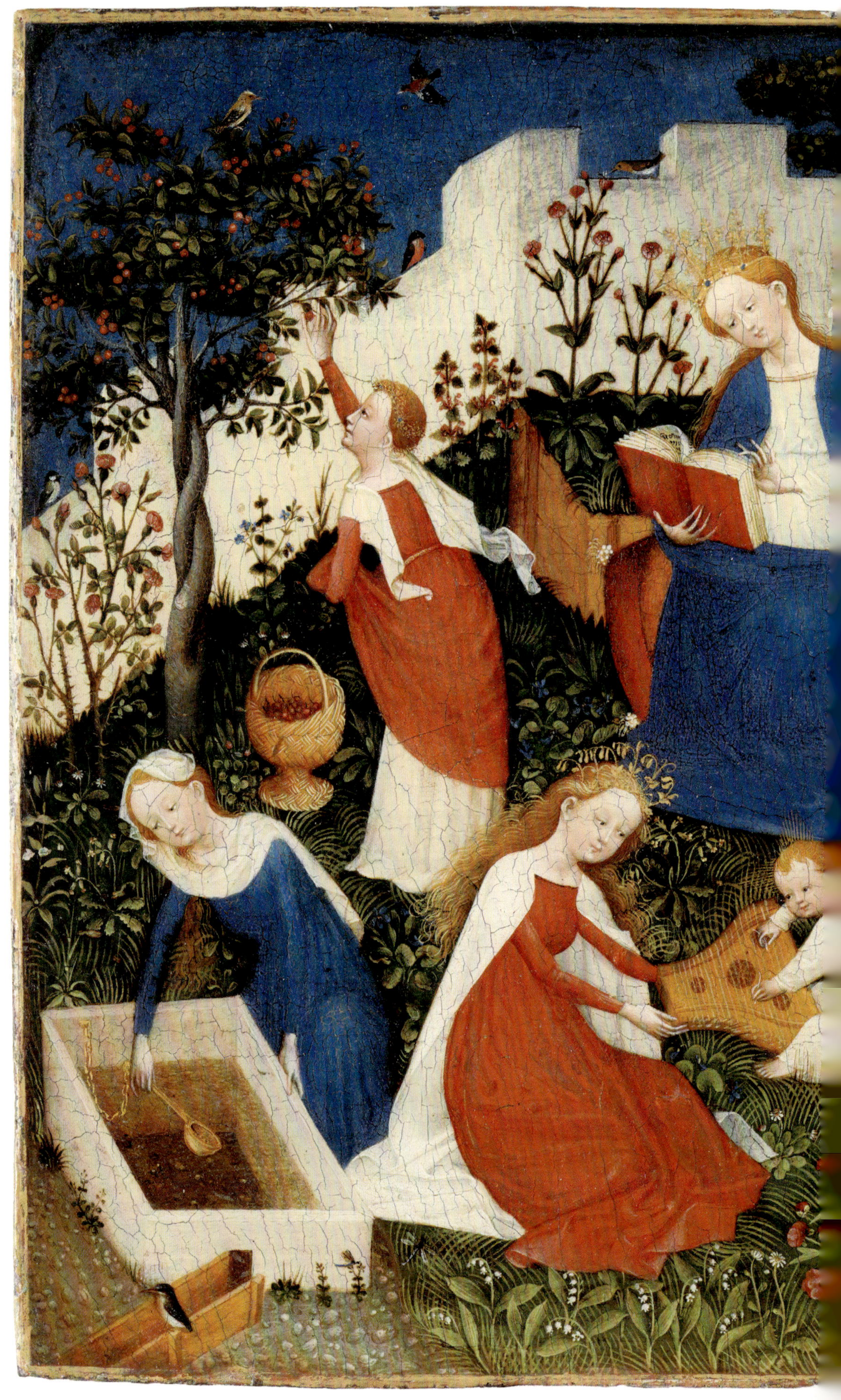

← Fig. 46

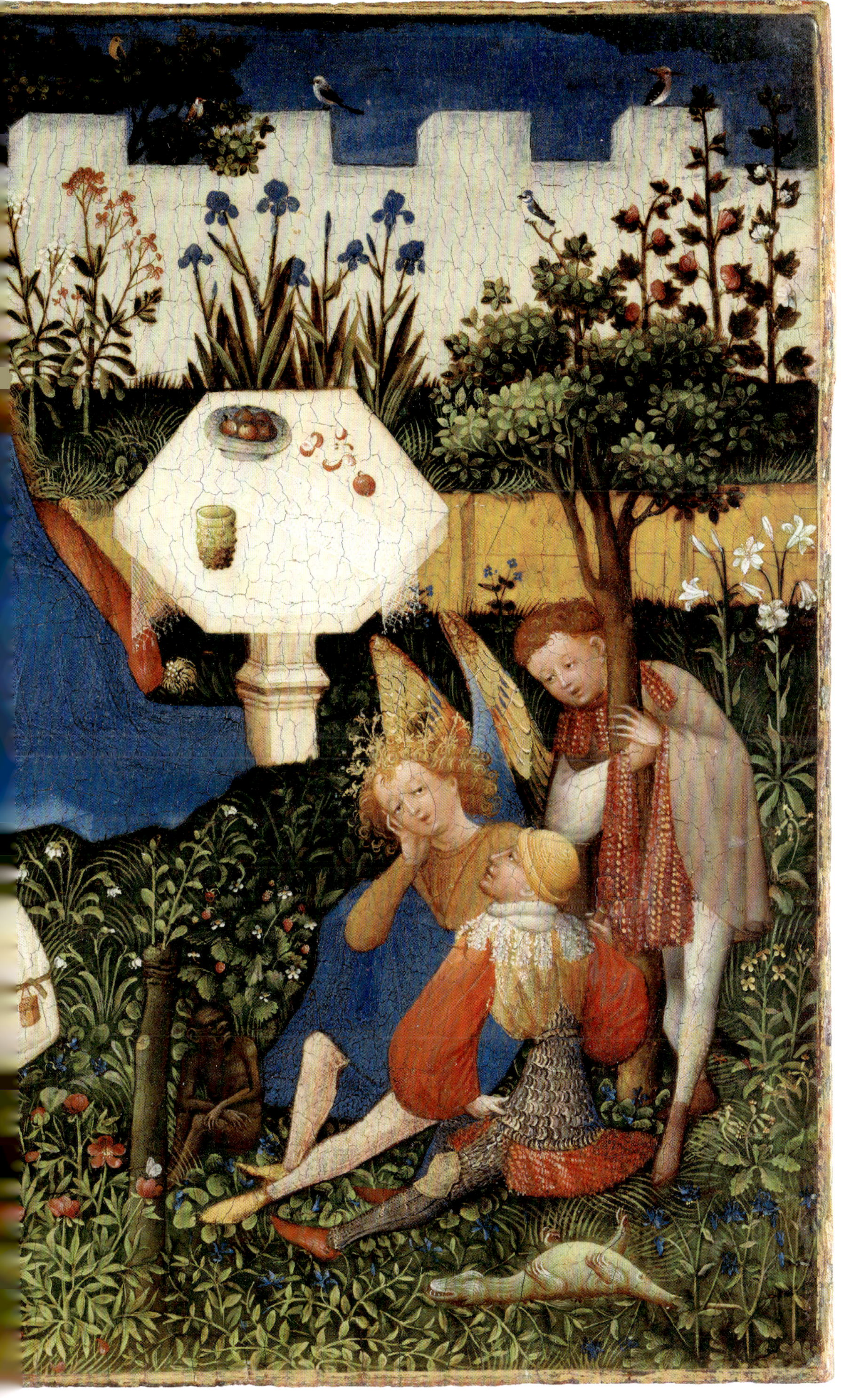

Fig. 47

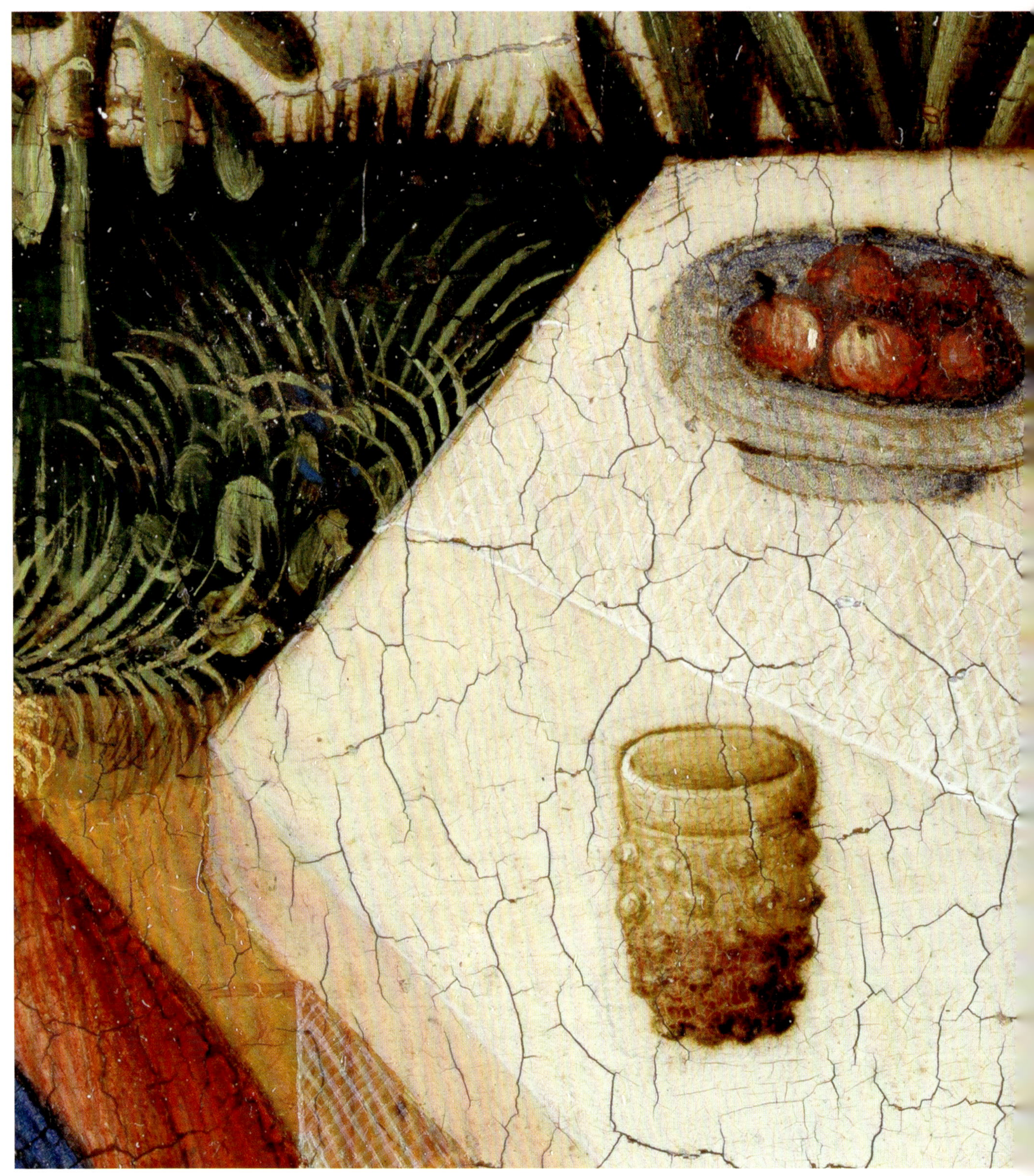

Fig. 48

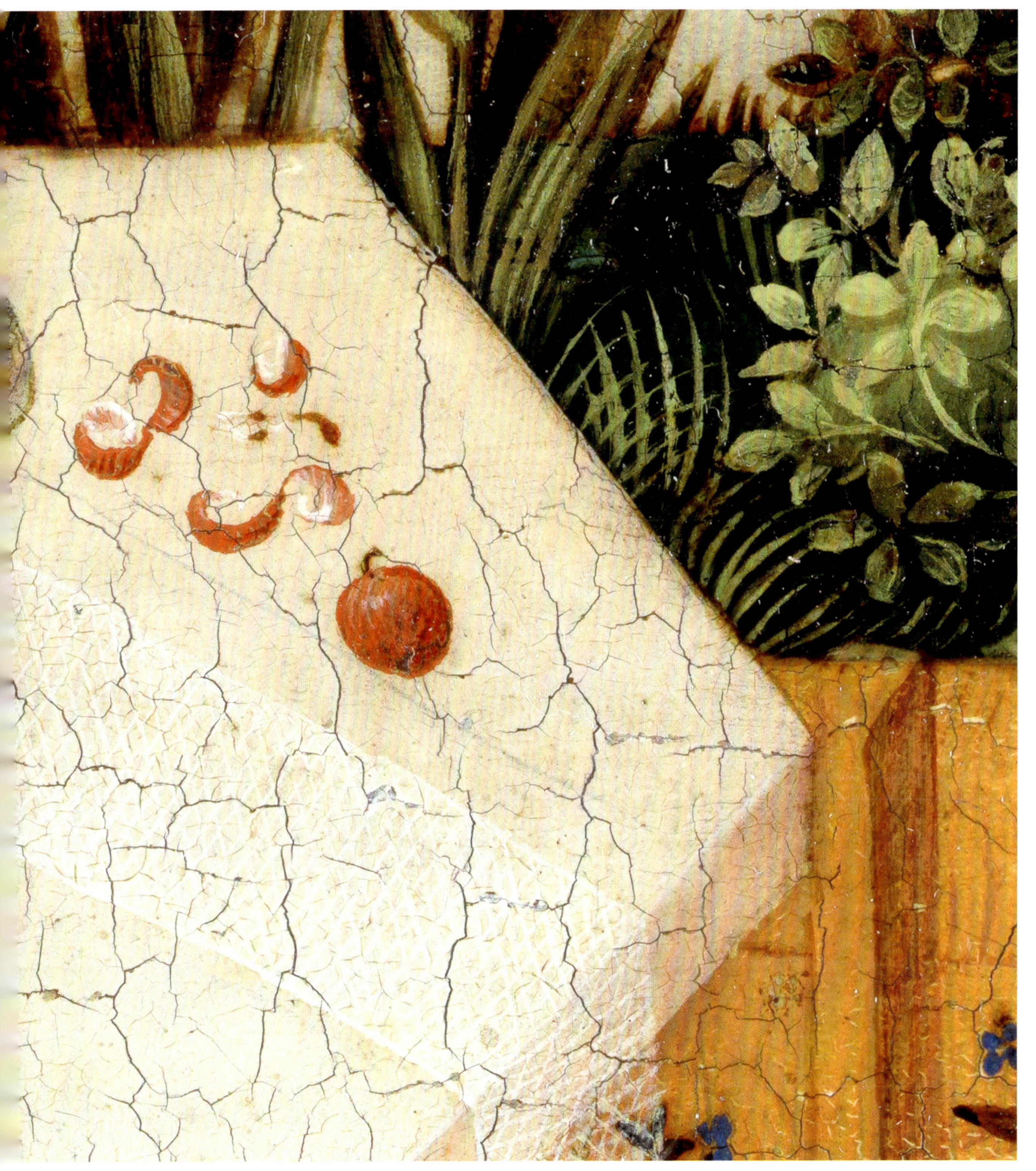

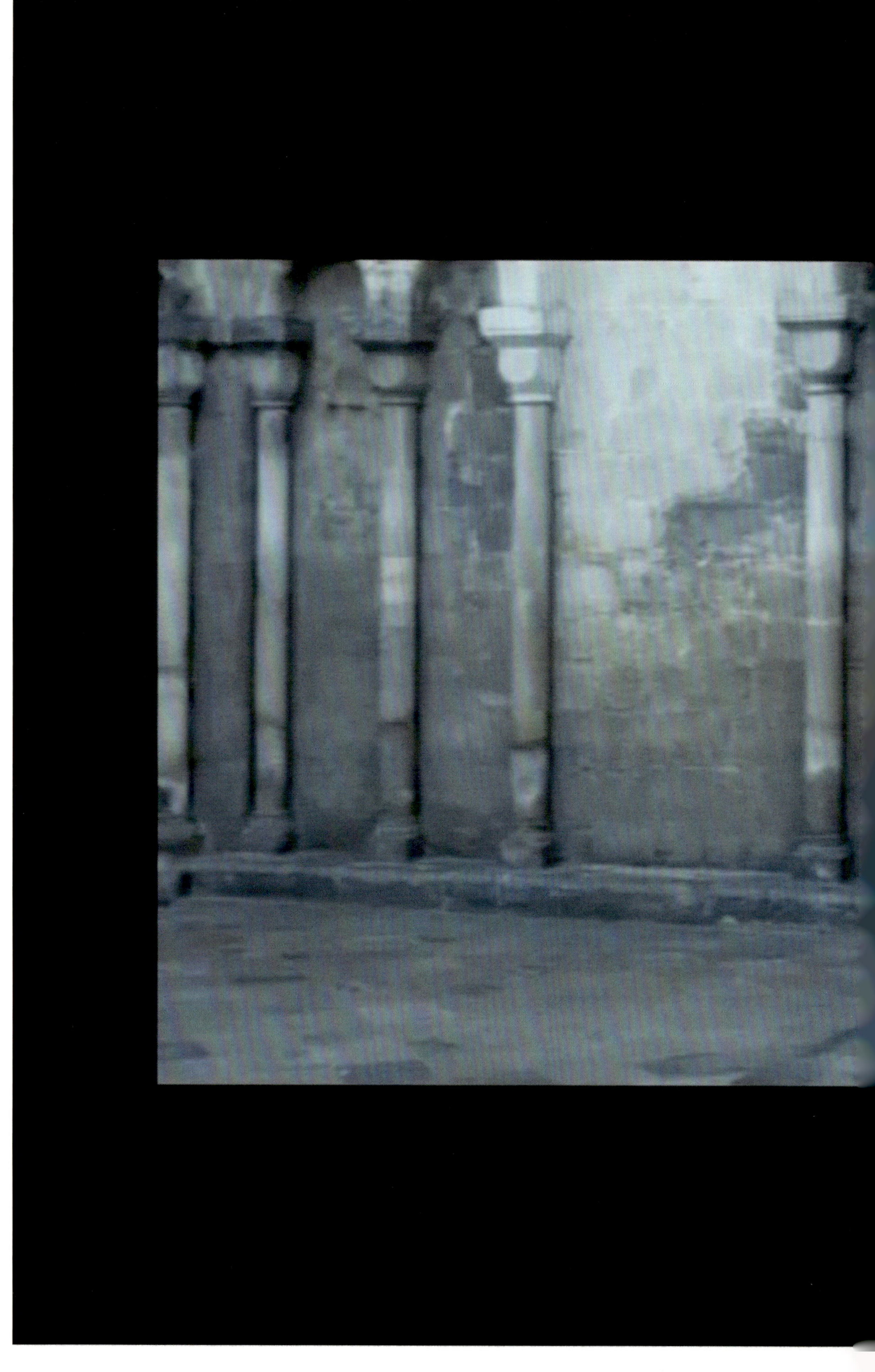

Fig. 49

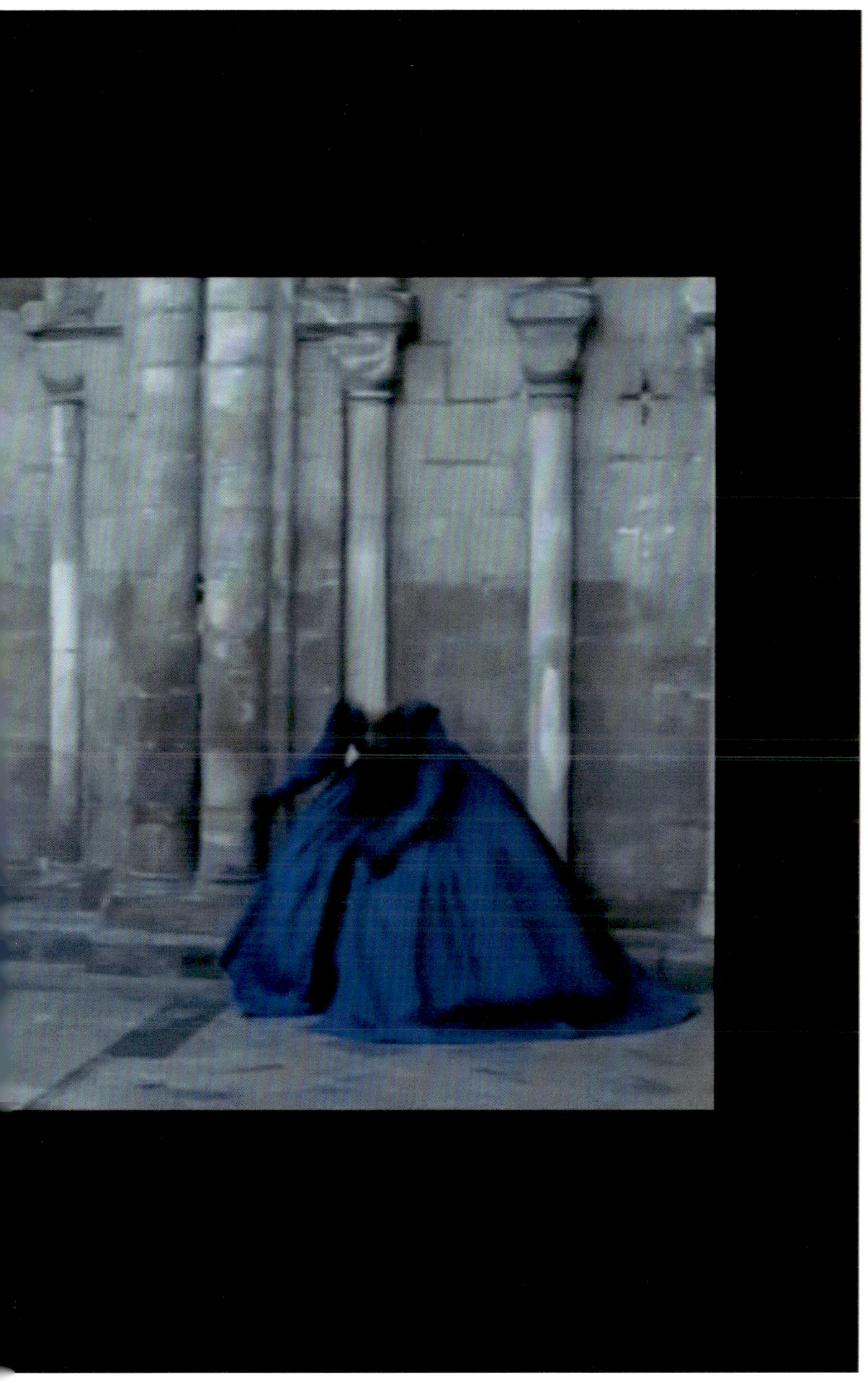

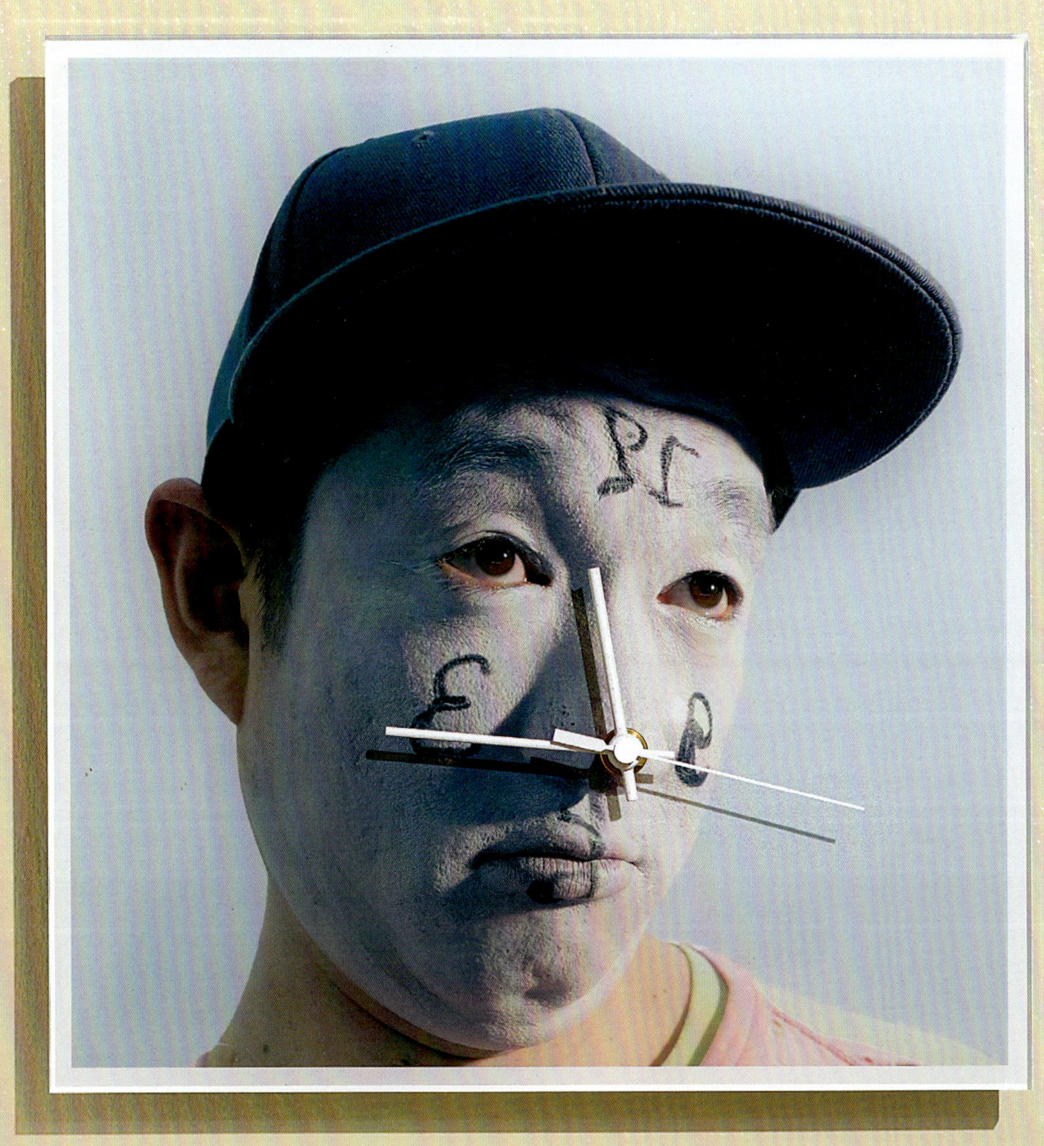

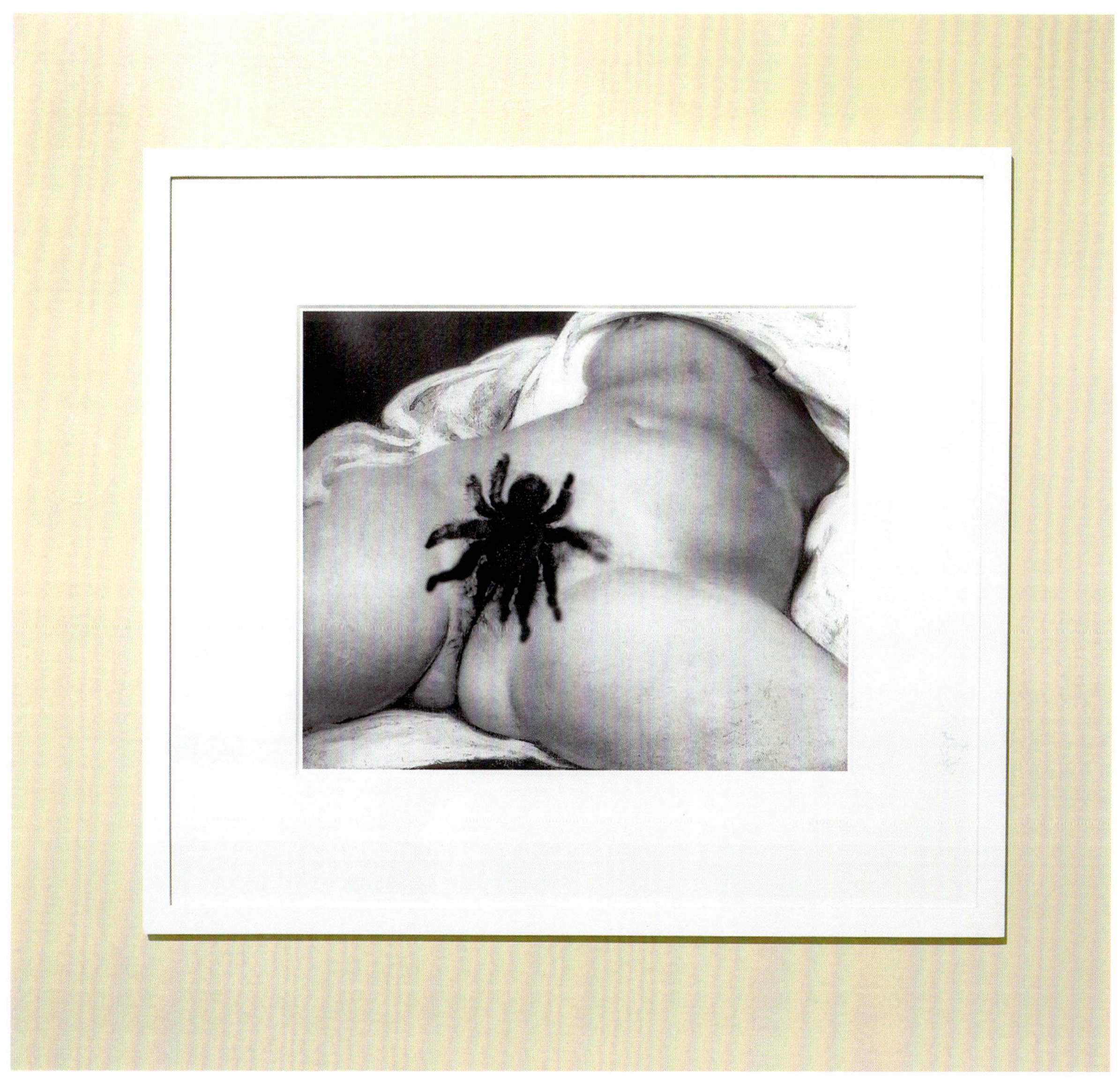

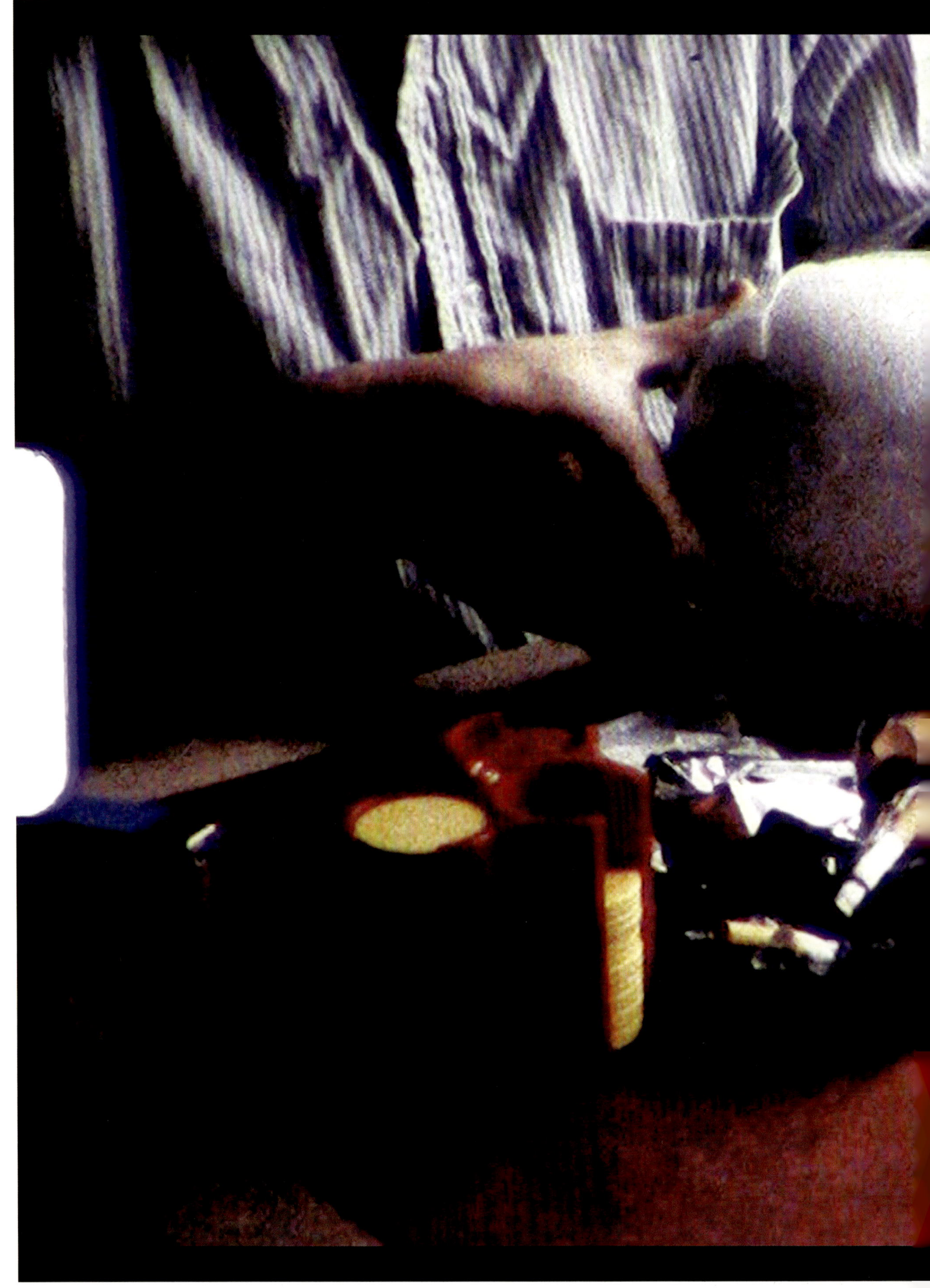

Fig. 52

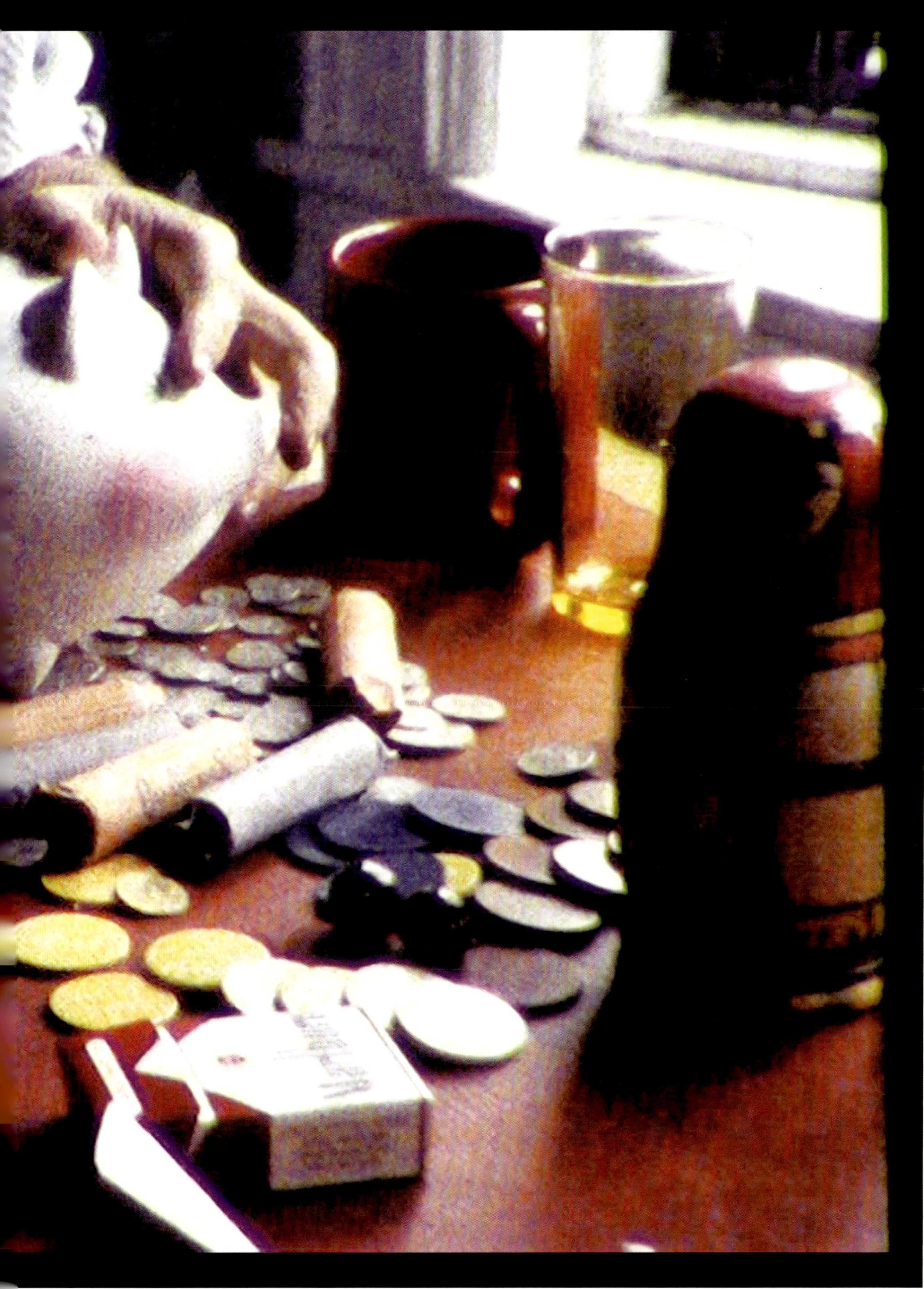

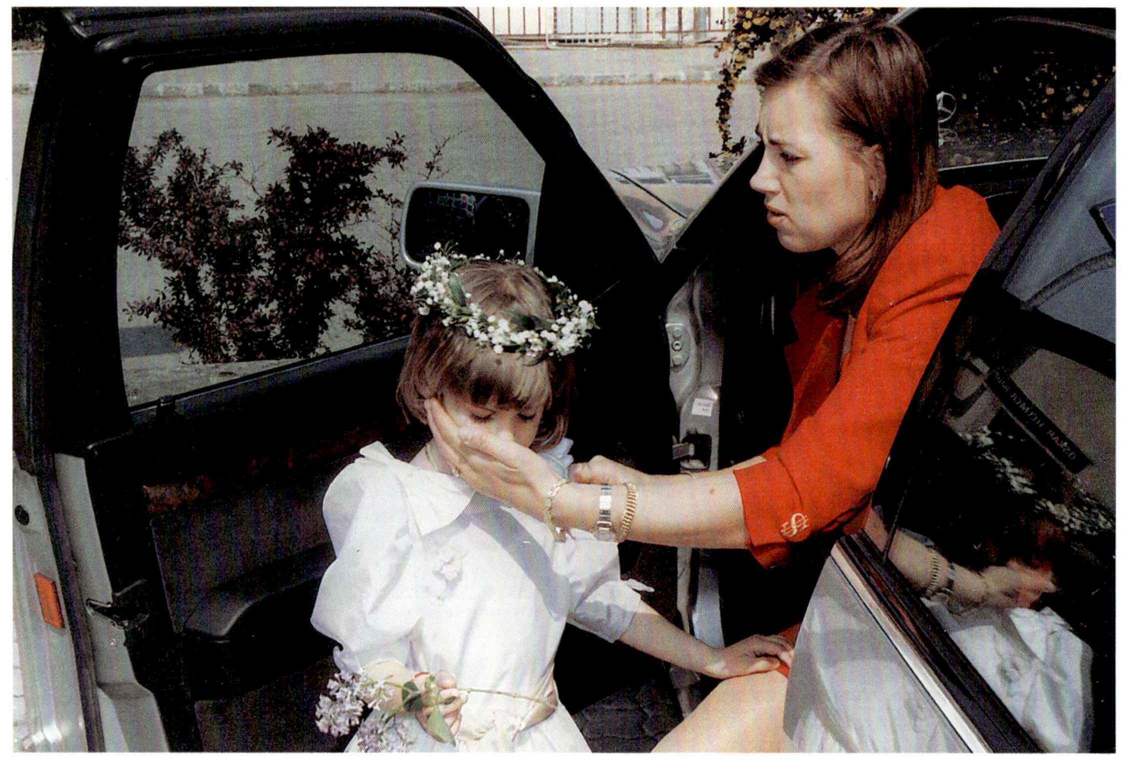

Fig. 53

Family Photographs

In the photograph, my mother is sitting on the driver's seat of a silver Mercedes, with both her legs placed outside on the sidewalk. Her auburn hair is loose and she is wearing the red Moschino suit jacket and a matching skirt, sheer tights, a watch, and two golden bracelets. On her left cuff we see a small golden dollar sign on a button. She is looking at me at six years old in a white festive satin gown. Reaching out with both hands, she touches my cheek lightly. My hand is placed on her thigh. It is the day of my first communion. I am wearing a wreath of small white flowers and green leaves and I am holding on to a lilac twig. The suit my mother is wearing is a design by the late Franco Moschino for his 1991 collection. Fashioned from red rayon, the jacket features gold embroidered lettering spelling out the words "Waist of Money" around the waistline.

When I first started taking my own photographs, I had a very brief documentary phase. Long before I reached any sort of conceptual undergirding for my photographic proclivities, such as Martha Rosler's argument against the *victim photography* of meliorism (*Documentary, as we know it, carries (old) information about a group of powerless people to another group*[1])—and long before I grew weary of taking pictures—I gave up snapping photos *of* strangers. I remember my father's self-developed photographs hung in clip frames around the house, taken before he, too, gave up: stark black-and-white compositions of street scenes, still lifes of half-burnt candles, and Tina Turner concerts—these pictures were difficult to map onto my full-color reality. The compositional rigor of my father's first technical investigations into depth of field, light, shadow, exposure is where I started off, his old Canon camera preciously clasped, soon to be left behind. Like I said, back then I had no moral or conceptual reasoning to feel dubious about the invasion and secrecy of the documentary photograph.

What I did know, intuitively, was that the image I was trying to take required a quasi-authentic nonchalance, a conscious non-awareness. To catch an old woman frown as she made her way across an even older square, felt like cheating.

Perhaps what I knew was simply that these photographs had been taken and used in museums and in magazines and repetition would not recover the fraught relationship between the subject and the camera. The photographs I proceeded to make for the next years predominantly involved my close family, mostly my younger sister—prepubescent at that time—and my mother. Obviously, these endeavors were neither always planned or sketched, nor did I conceive of them as works of art. But I felt I was collecting material, rehearsing, and therefore they predate the work I would go on to exhibit later. I took pictures of my mother in the nude and wearing clothes. I photographed her when she didn't want me to (under feeble protest). I was always convinced that in truth she liked it. Sometimes I styled and directed her and I never asked permission to share my compilations of pictures on whatever digital media platform we were then using. My objectification of my mother's body was the terrain that felt most authentic to me. Still unbothered by weighty considerations of the libidinal connotations of family relations, I self-organized an exhibition titled "my mother's closet." In it, one photograph features the red Moschino suit hung outside on a garden fence amid other elements of my mother's wardrobe: dresses, skirts, tops, a pair of lederhosen. She herself, crucially, is in that same photograph, naked, on the left side of the frame, pulling out weeds. She is wearing a straw hat and is not looking at the camera.

I staged the scene, insofar as I involved my family in my projects and ideas. I wanted to show that these clothes belonged so intimately to my imagination of my mother, as her present self and as a younger woman with a past I could not access. These clothes constituted the eerie residue of her past body. Far from simply functional, they were attached to the memories of the situations in which they were worn. My mother herself, naked by default in our large garden, came to the scene naturally, or I should say, my photographic appraisal of her body existed alongside her performativity, nourished it, without either of us having to communicate about it.

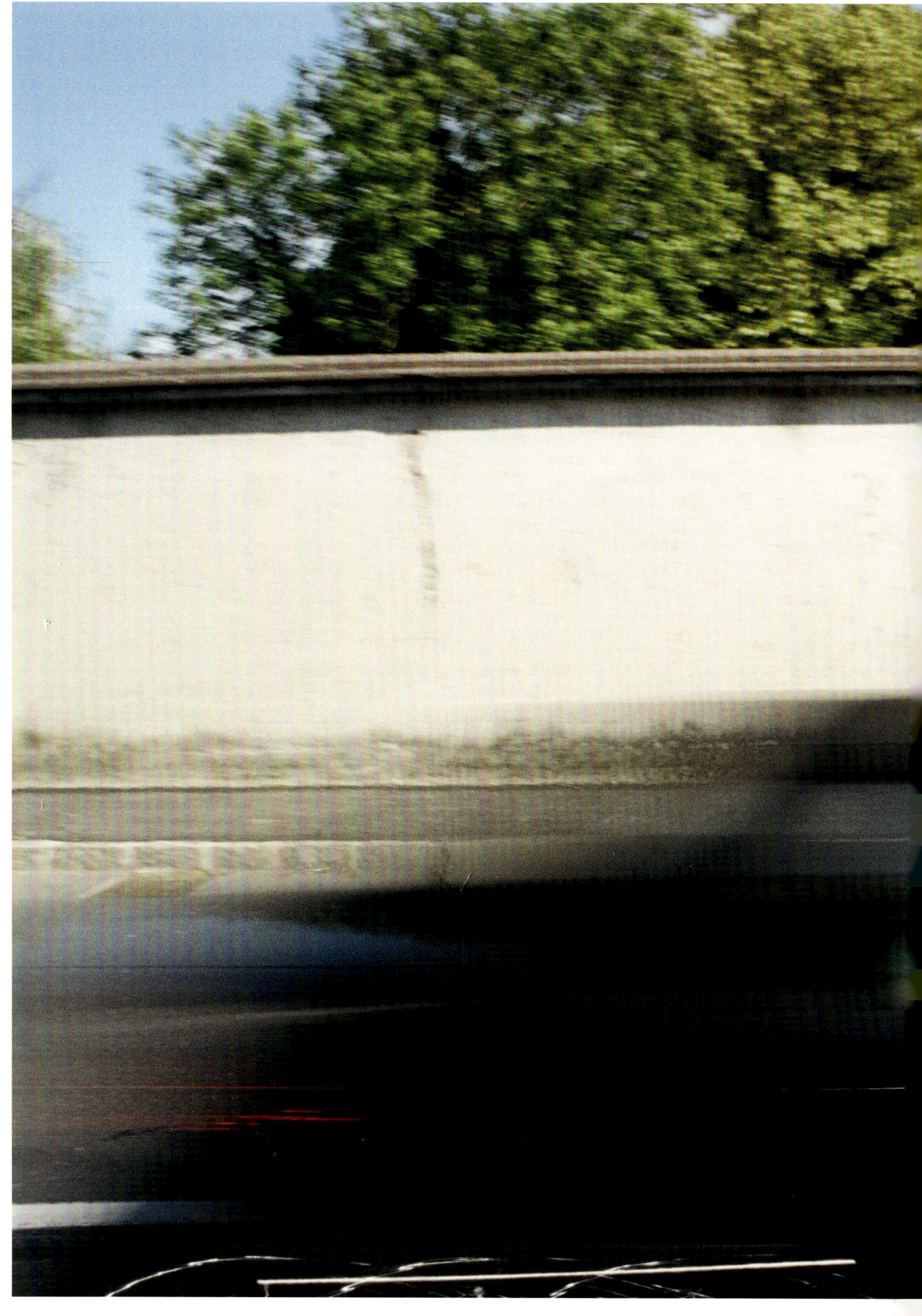

Fig. 54

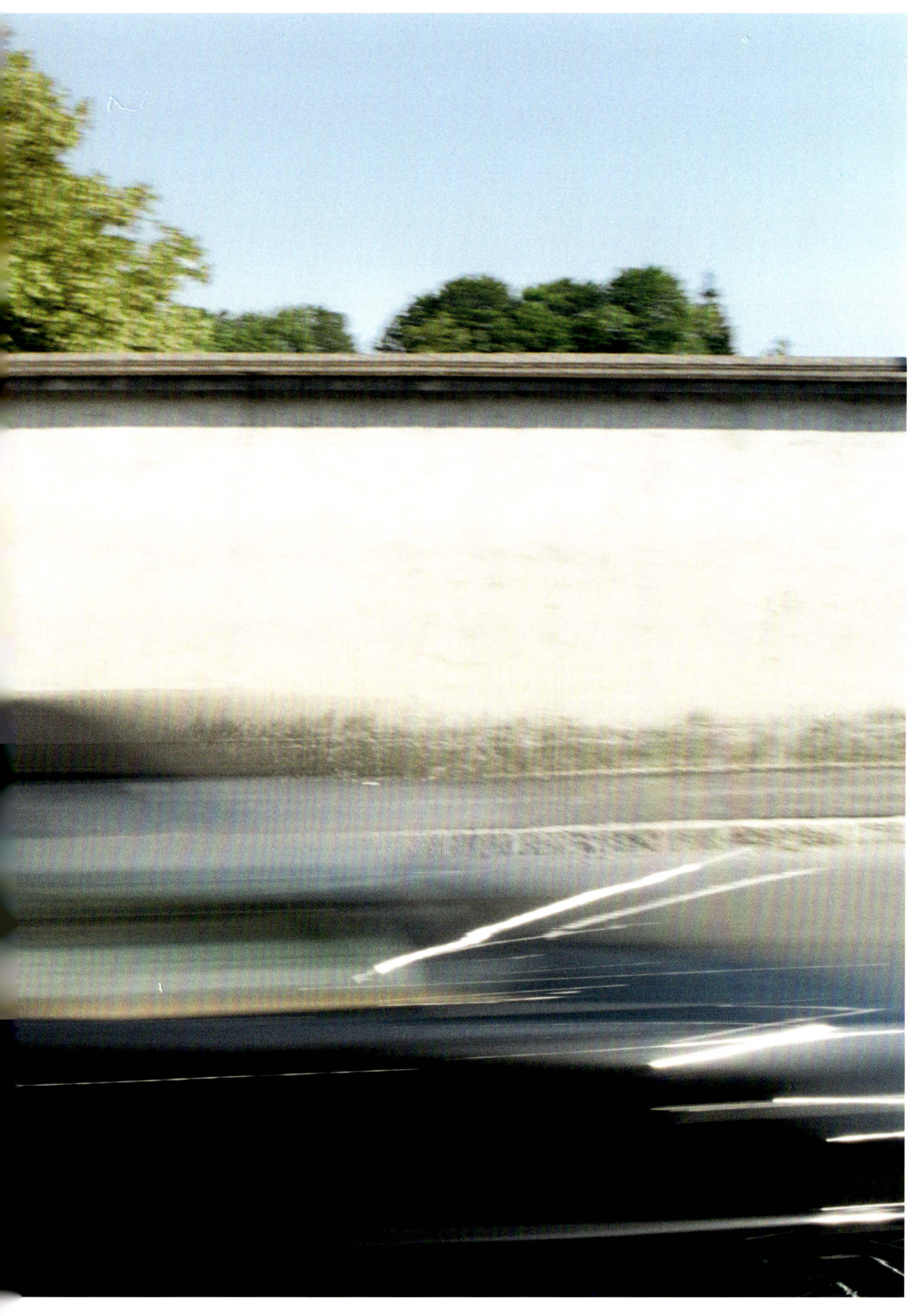

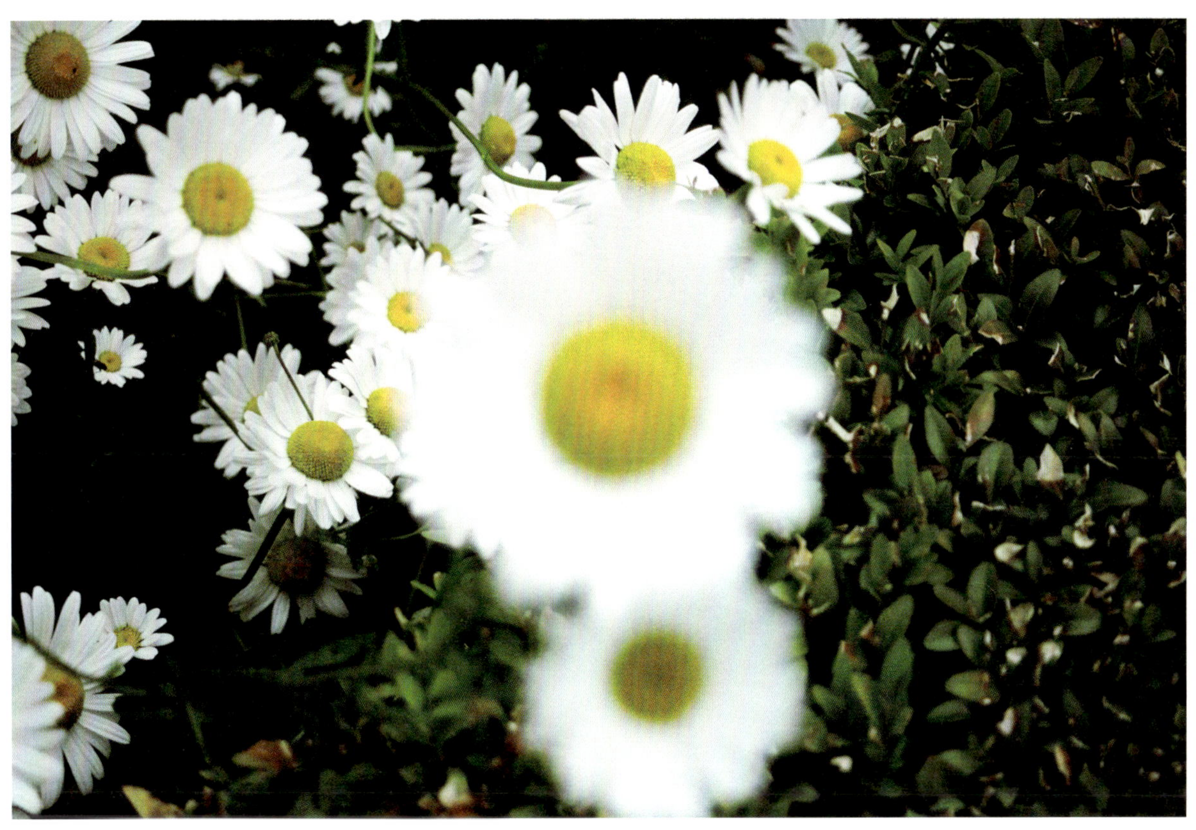

Fig. 55

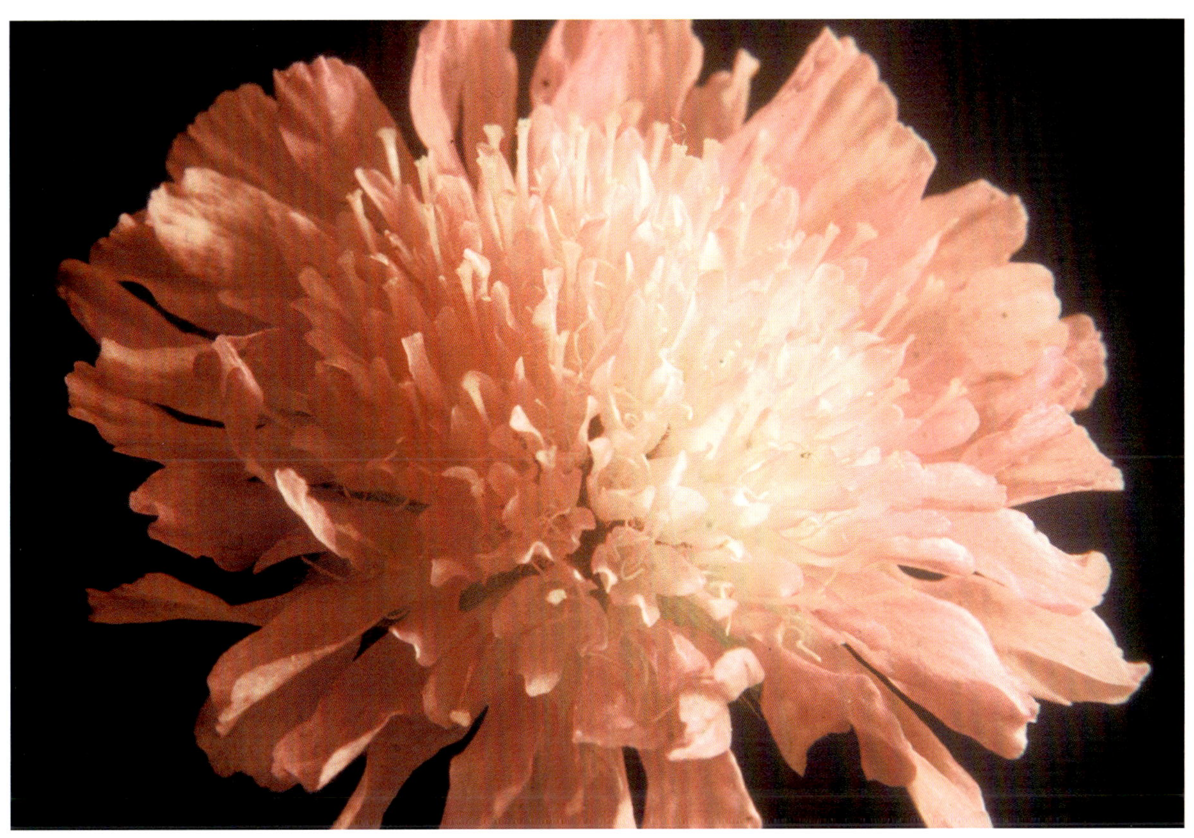

Fig. 56

Waist of Money

Though I uprooted my mother's suit from the subjective context of my family—exhibiting it as an object in *life and limbs*—the photograph of my mother wearing it for a significant religious event offers other perspectives on the joke told "on a waist" about a "waste." I would like to sum up some of the symbolic and perhaps literal potential in this object as a garment to be worn. Despite the fact that I do not think a literal, stable interpretation of clothing signs is possible, I think this potential is where my own artistic attraction to the suit starts.

A first interpretation can be subsumed under the phrase "the joke's on her." A woman—not necessarily for lack of intellect, but disinvested in the concrete meaning attached to garment signs, even if they are as literal as a semantic message—wears a suit that she chooses naively based on availability within contemporary fashion and aesthetic proclivity. The designer, if we cast him as knowing or accepting the textual message as literal "waist of money," treats her body like a vehicle for surplus capital. The woman wastes money and wears her own fashion victimhood.[2]

A more dandyish interpretation would see the wearer as understanding the concrete textual meaning and choosing it as a self-irony of sorts, potentially as both pertaining to her status as woman and her class status as owner of a luxurious item. This Oscar Wildean woman could be cast as both self-deprecating and emancipated: inhabiting a history of (mis)interpretations and therefore owning them. This approach pertains to a proto-queering of gendered stereotypes.

Then there is the question of status and class as it relates to a statement about money and its waste: perhaps the woman does not reflect her class status, but understands the suit as broadly transgressive and flamboyant in contrast to the sociodemographic climate she inhabits. The understanding of the suit is less literal than formal: blunt gold embroidery, red rayon, short skirt. She is content to provoke a feeling of, if not tastelessness, then inappropriateness, spectacularism. Within the setting of practiced Catholicism and despite the sentence being spelled out perhaps in a foreign language (English), the meaning of such formalism can easily be categorized as provocative if not indeed intolerable. Although church communities have undergone rapid transformations in the ongoing secularization of Western Catholicism with congregations steadily shrinking even in the rural parts of Europe, the rituals that structure liturgy still extend to comportment and wardrobe. A *waist of money*, although the living hallmark of Catholic clergy, is most definitely not considered proper for a first communion. So, even without a lexical understanding of the suit's message, the garment could be perceived as formally un-suitable and hence offend. If understood literally, we would assume the outrage to be a given, although judging from the omnipresence of textual slogans printed on garments—anything along the line of kids' T-shirts featuring "Life Is Fruity" or "Sorry I'm Bad"—in all areas of civic life, we cannot be too sure of this.

Hence, we come full circle: perhaps the suit is formally canonized within the fashion of its time and therefore intuitively not perceived as radical at all. Symbols such as dollar signs, skulls, or crosses used on clothing tend to hardly evoke outrage but rather are conventionally seen as abstracted aspects of a fashionable look. The suit then signals blandly to those uninitiated to or uninterested in its self-referential pun, exactly what the sentence references: a luxurious, elegant suit on a woman who can afford it and who is therefore either distinguished from the lesser affluent—a chic lady—or simply dressed her best for church.

Franco Moschino—La classe non è ACQUA

The initial pages of Franco Moschino's publication *X Anni di Kaos!*[3] remind me of the domestic intimacy in the photographs I took of my family: Franco himself appears constantly, candidly shot clowning through his own "Imaginary Inventory." An early campaign poster features a portrait of his team, his mother, and close collaborators.

His particular design can be approached through many lenses of fashion history. But what jumps out at me as I look through this collection of Moschino's work is Catholicism: ornate exuberance despite or because of the reality of man (woman) as inherently guilty and specifically as a result of the Counter-Reformation; a 1980s genre of womenswear designed predominantly

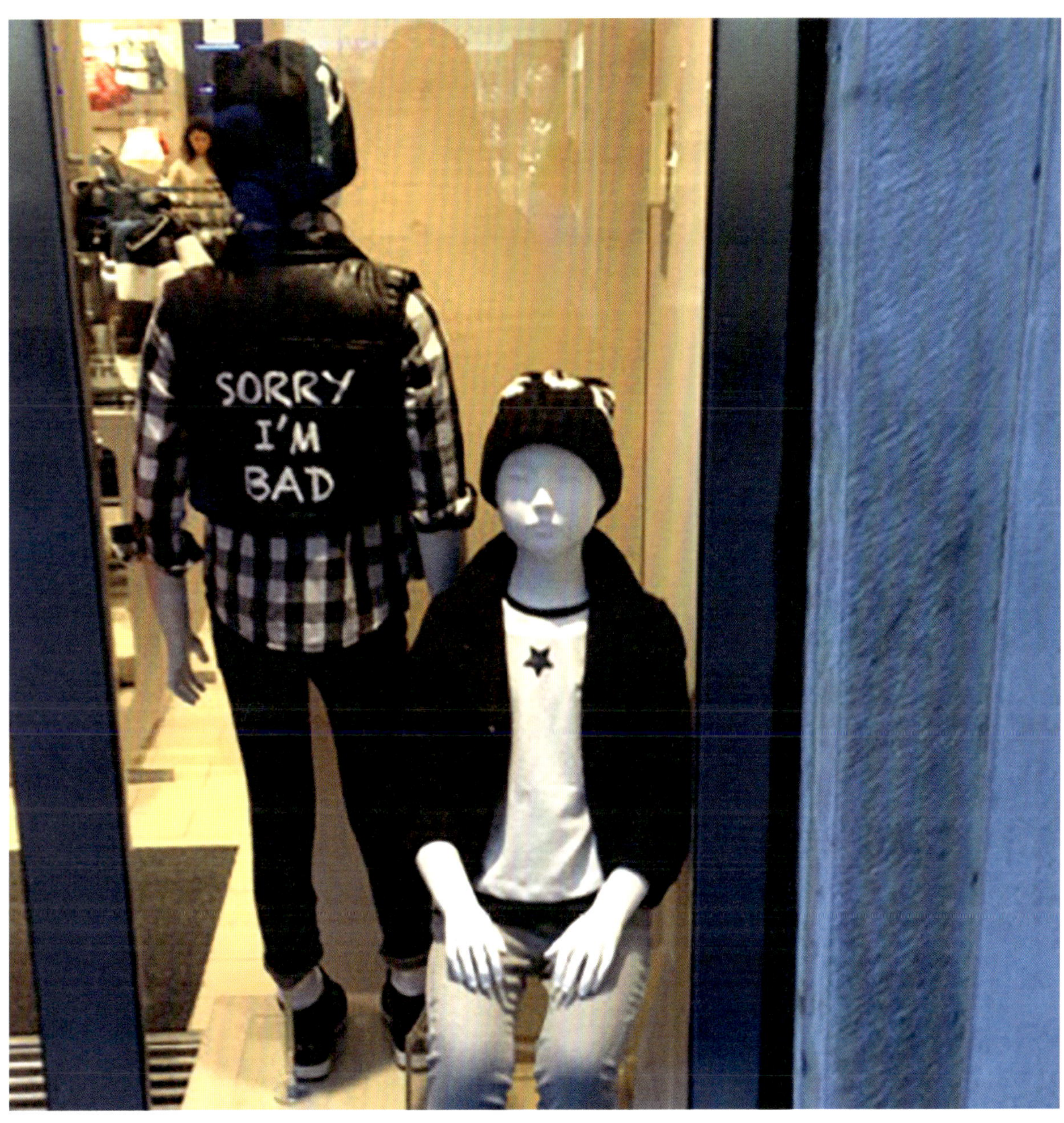

Fig. 57

BIJOUX
SHOES
LEATHER
BAGS
COUTURE !
JEANS
SWIMWEAR
HOSIERY
SCARVES
MOSCHINO

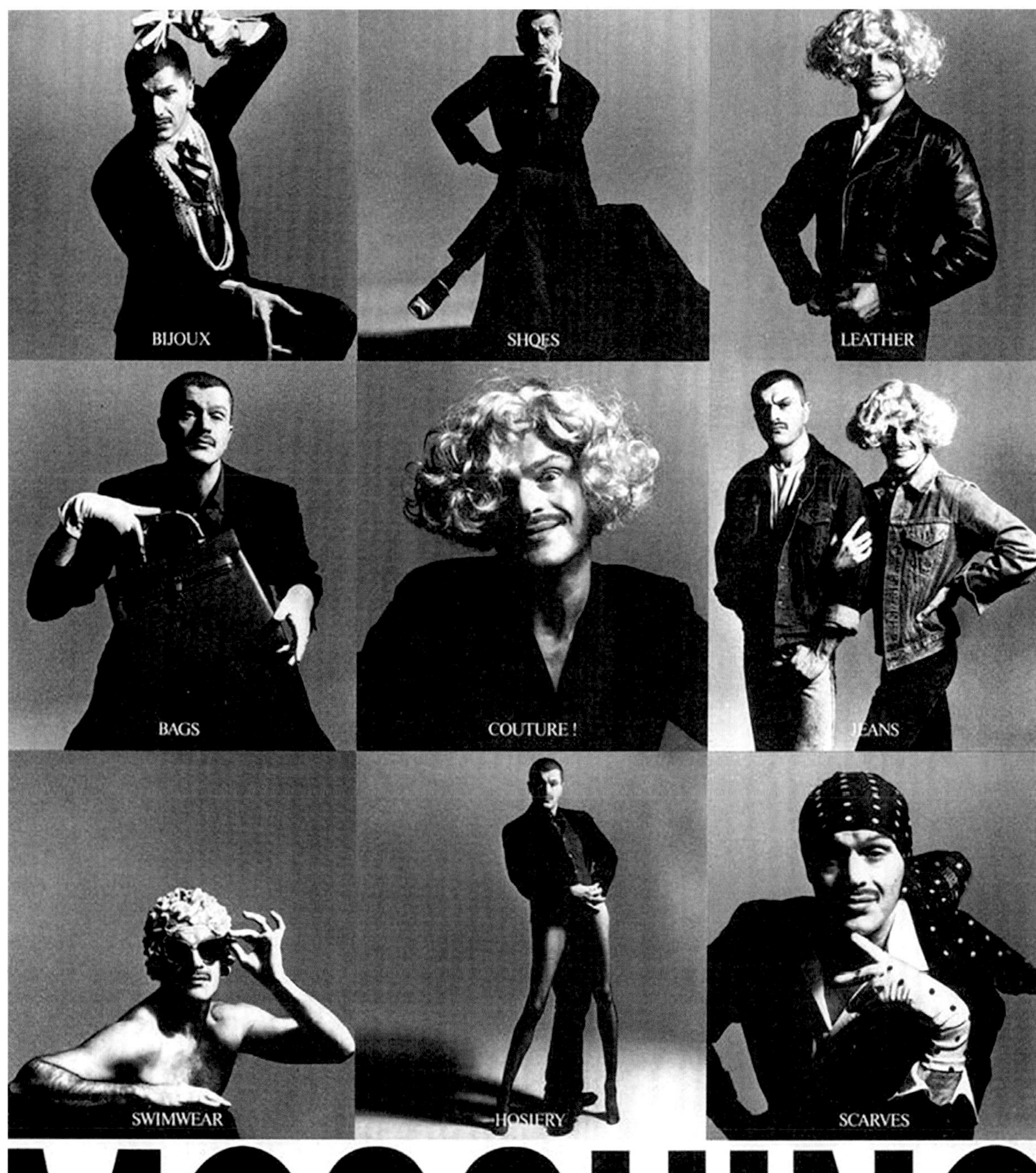

Fig. 58

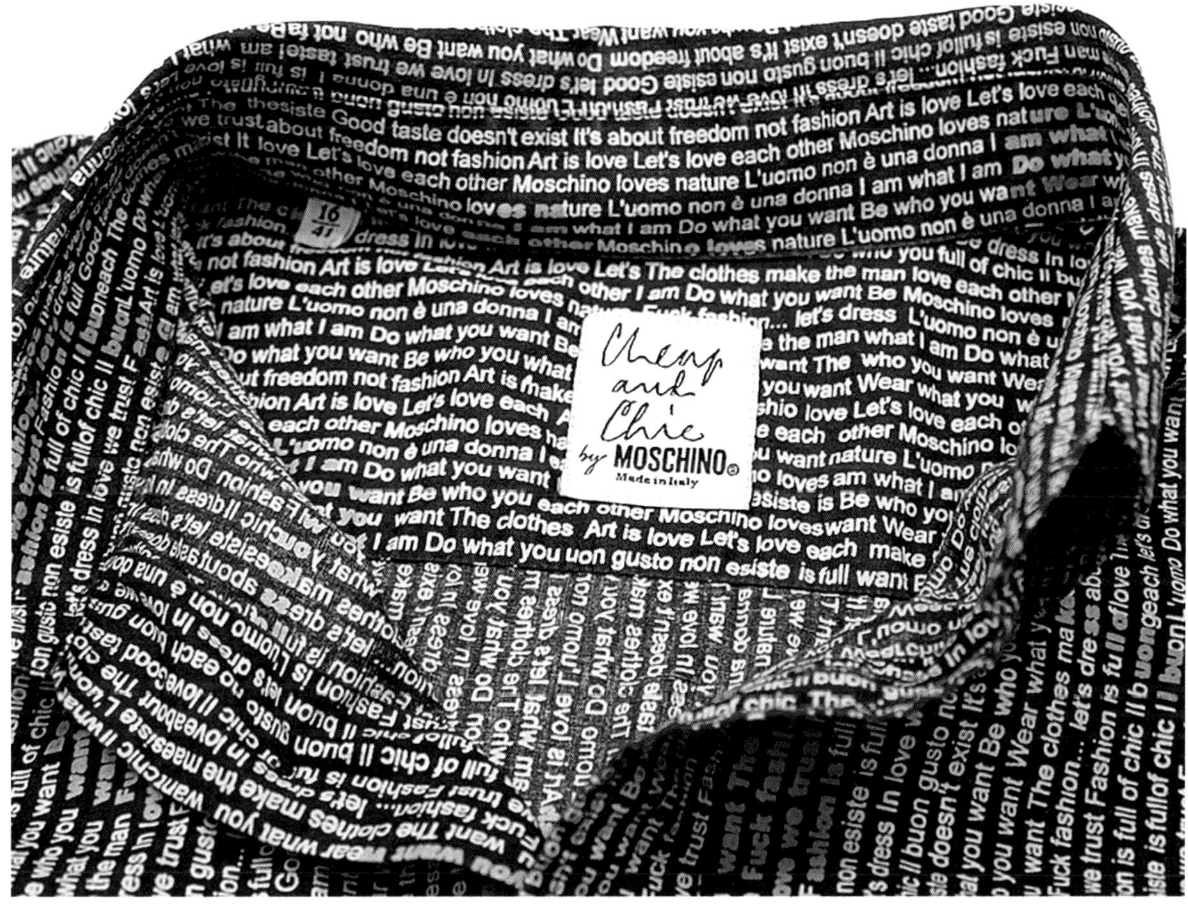
Cheap and Chic
by MOSCHINO
Made in Italy
Good taste doesn't exist It's about freedom not fashion Art is love Let's love each other Moschino loves nature
L'uomo non è una donna I am what I am Do what you want Be who you want

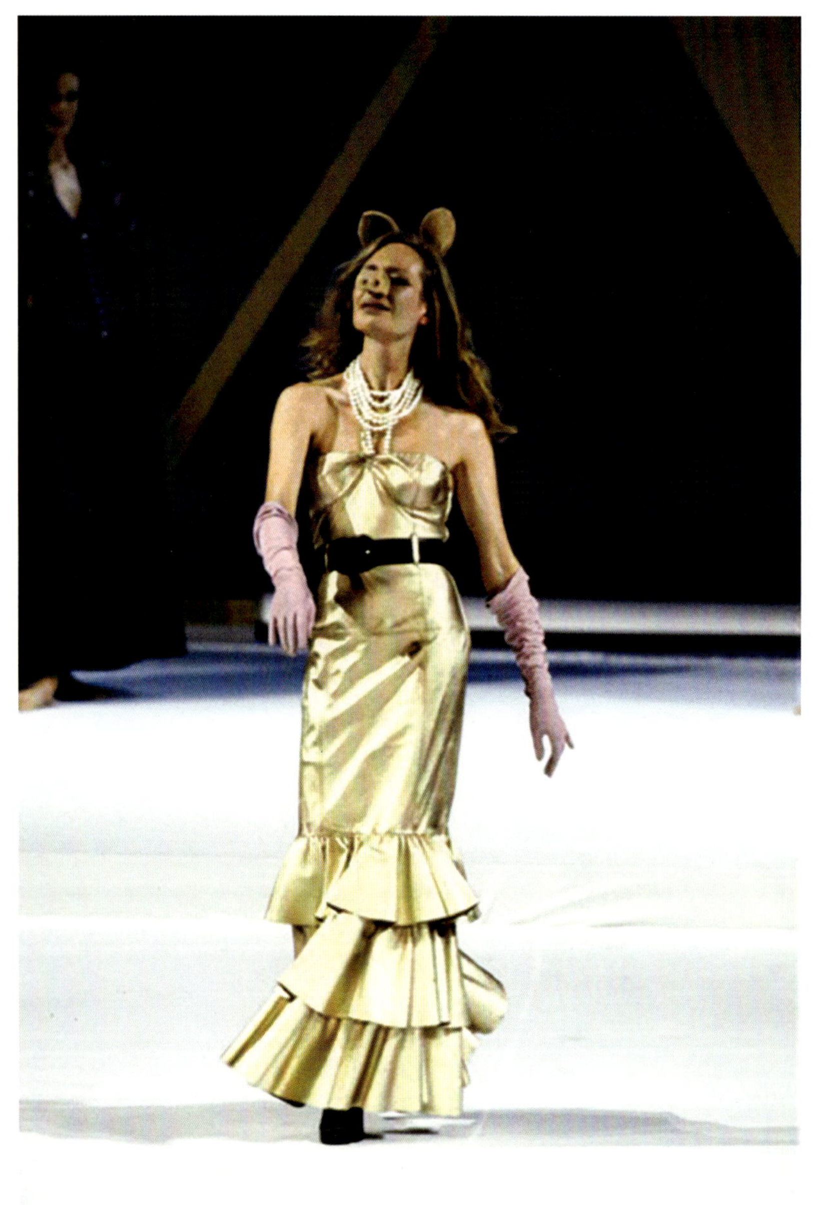

Fig. 60

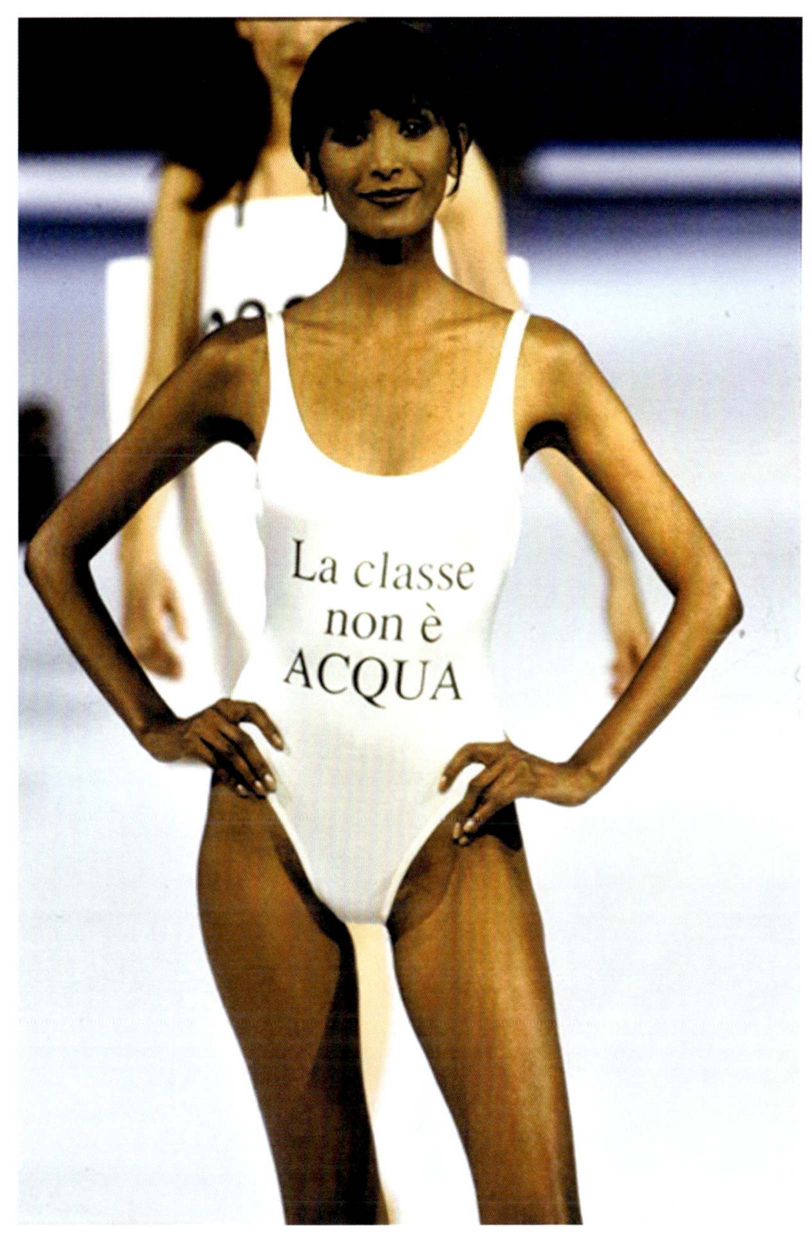

Fig. 61

by gay men looking at their mothers suspended between postwar economic boom and a still traditionally gendered civil life; and the self-referential punch lines that connect garment to corpse, indebted to Surrealism, *commedia dell'arte*, and postmodern discourse.

The aim of Moschino is to give the consumer total freedom. The impositions are removed, if you still like what you wore last year, wear it again this year and even the next year. If you feel better in an uncomfortable dress or pretty shoes, that are too tight, that's fine, if you are a fashion victim and are reassured by a label that's fine too, if you think you have good taste and don't, carry on! Basically, Moschino means that you can choose your clothes with the same ease that you would choose something to eat![4]

The disarming naïveté of this very fashion-kind-of statement holds an important clue to the conceptual framework of his production: a negation of taste-based exclusion and a renouncement of high and low. Everything can be included and nothing *does not fit*. With this and the comparison to food, it highlights an approach that can be easily denounced as superficial or anti-intellectual, but that is more closely indebted to the particular sensuality of clothing, not what is commodified in advertising, but what is, in reality, beyond apprehension of theory and taste. It is the rejection of the trope of art as concrete intellectual meaning making. To quote Fran Lebowitz, "I have news for you, Mr. Baker. If you can eat it, it's not art. Okay? If you can say, 'I'll have that, and a cup of coffee, that's not art! That's a snack!"[5] While Lebowitz's disavowal of food as "art" here of course pertains to a much mediatized lawsuit in the US in which a baker claimed to be in their right to religious freedom when refusing to bake a wedding cake for a gay couple, it is significant that Moschino would call upon the specific orality of food intake as a counter to what I would presume to be his environment of rigid, class-based fashion habits—unspoken but definitive—and it suitably mirrors Adorno's denunciation of what he calls the "culinary" use of art as a critique of the expansion of art to and the inclusion of popular culture.[6] The ideal of a gut-based style is understood as a popular counterapproach, akin to the child that gets to pick its school outfit for once. Whether this aspiration is at all practically applicable in daily styles is of course questionable.

Franco Moschino's particular humor permeated not just the designs he created during his short span of production before his untimely AIDS-related death, but also the printed matter and media campaigns that accompanied his collections. In interviews, he appears fiercely doubtful of fashion as an industry, referring to himself as a decorator, rather than a designer. His marked emphasis on ethics in production and fabric choice seem curiously out of place in the early '90s. The Moschino woman that came into existence on the threshold of the '80s and '90s is both conventionally feminine and goofy. It is a curious convergence that a dislike for unnecessary spending, *wasting*, defines both nascent consumer criticism and the traditional ideas of modesty as taught in Christian catechism and ethics. Finally, the mind–body schism as upheld by Christian scholastic teachings influences the modern image of fashion as flimsy and flippant. It is therefore not possible to analytically separate some of Moschino's *leibfeindliche* (body hostile) phrases from this older, broader argument against fashion in general as expendable, and, with the development of the uniform male suit parallel to republicanism, female garments as nonintellectual.

While many of the seminal Moschino pieces did not attempt to deconstruct patterns, they rather used fashion's symbolic repertoire—the suit, the dress, the skirt, the blouse—as surface to be clowned and as pinboard for jokes that aim at deriding both fashion's status as luxury good as well as its consumers as members of a class able to afford them. Between moralism and critical materialism, pieces such as a white swimsuit from the 1994 collection printed with the slogan "La classe non è ACQUA" (You can't BUY class) can never be fully classified as either. Whether the proverb in its original Italian reading is meant to refer to the impossibility of money (oh dirty money) to buy *noblesse* (nobleness) or whether it hints indeed at the material reality of the static class relations that still structure the societies we live in, we cannot decide through the garment qua object sign.

One more remarkable look from that same runway show, which was conceived as a best of the outfits from former seasons, features a model in a golden, ruffled lamé bustier gown with a patent leather belt around her waist. She wears lilac evening gloves and an opulent multi-stringed pearl necklace. The both conservative and cheap conventionality of this assembly is rendered comical by her headdress and face mask: she dons pig ears and a small pig snout. The logic of carnival weaves together animal and human features to deconstruct the worldly order. Here, the comparatively small gesture alters the outfit from formally banal to sociologically complex. We think of Miss Piggy here less because of an actual animal likeness but because of the puppet's apt caricature of American small-town struggle: once again Moschino here operates more as a theater director than as a designer. What is staged is aspiration to style without class-based knowledge of elegance or a sense for dos and don'ts.

Franco Moschino's Dada stance included campaign slogans such as "Fashion is full of chic" (read: fashion is full of shit) alongside ads that featured endangered species. Naturally, he received not only canonic cult status but also performed well within the confines of commerce, creating several labels: Moschino (women's and men's main line), Moschino Cheap and Chic (women's secondary line, created in 1988, consolidated in 2014 into Boutique Moschino), and Love Moschino (women's and men's diffusion line, known as Moschino Jeans from 1986 to 2008), in order of exclusivity.

Almost thirty years later, with self-referential symbolism and social awareness endorsements now sturdily inscribed in fast fashion, to make a simplistic criticism of such seemingly self-ironic although complicit fashion statements risks making the classic mistake that theory makes when evaluating fashion. To put it this way: yes, to sell expensive couture that self-consciously stages its own wrought relationship to wealth, class, and the social realities of the world, might appear in a post-ironic discourse as innate, indeed as vulgar. However, to understand fashion at all, attention must be paid to the social, both semantic and non-semantic. To speak of fashion and its meaning, to try and attribute it at all, is where theory tends to become stuck, unable to locate the aesthetic as well as its sociopolitical radicality. It is perhaps here, where the relationship gets tricky, when we attempt to locate the role of the woman wearer—mannequin on the runway, conspicuous consumer, rich lady, victim, vamp, subject, object; my mother. As Elizabeth Wilson points out, "The triviality of dress is the fetishized idea that makes it possible for us to continue—even as we denigrate it (in fact because we denigrate it)—simultaneously to indulge our fascination with it, and further, constitute it as the vehicle for deeply significant ideas, aspirations, and feelings."[7]

Lady Wealth: Waste & Waist

One of the chapters of Moyra Davey's 1990 video *Hell Notes* is titled "Meatball Hero." In this scene, the artist herself recapitulates the psychoanalytical relationship between money and excrement while talking to a friend eating a meatball sandwich: *In the unconscious, money and property are the symbolic equivalents of excrement and that's because things—property and money and things in general—are all equated with that which is cast off from the body, that which is alien to the body. That doesn't mean that money has no worth, has no value; actually, it means the opposite: we value money because we value our shit. And the paradox of this—this is the paradox of the money complex—and there is a reason why money cannot make us happy. Actually, Freud said that wealth cannot bring happiness because money is not an infantile wish. The whole concept of money would need to be fully invested with the idea that it was shit which then became food. You see if it became food it would sustain the infantile wish for a completely omnipotent, self-replenishing, self-sustaining, immortal body and then it would bring happiness. Then money would bring happiness. If money were shit which then become food it would fully satisfy the infantile desire.*[8]

There is hardly a more apt staging of the context of Davey's investigation than the capitalized *Waist of Money* gold embroidered across a woman's stomach, if you will. *Waist* here has become a homonymous synecdoche for a *waste* that is both guttural, in that it denotes the intestinal apparatus of a human body, and synonymous with the aforementioned (if playful) accusation of expendable consumption. In the logic of the grotesque, the body made up of organs, constituted by nature, is here the very location of the transaction transcribed psychoanalytically above: ingestion turning food into excrement. In Bakhtin's (arguably revisionist) reading of Rabelais's writing, the emphasis is not on the symbolic, psychoanalytical aspects of the intestinal, but on the comedic debasement of the world through the physical as he locates it in the Renaissance traditions of the folk and carnival:

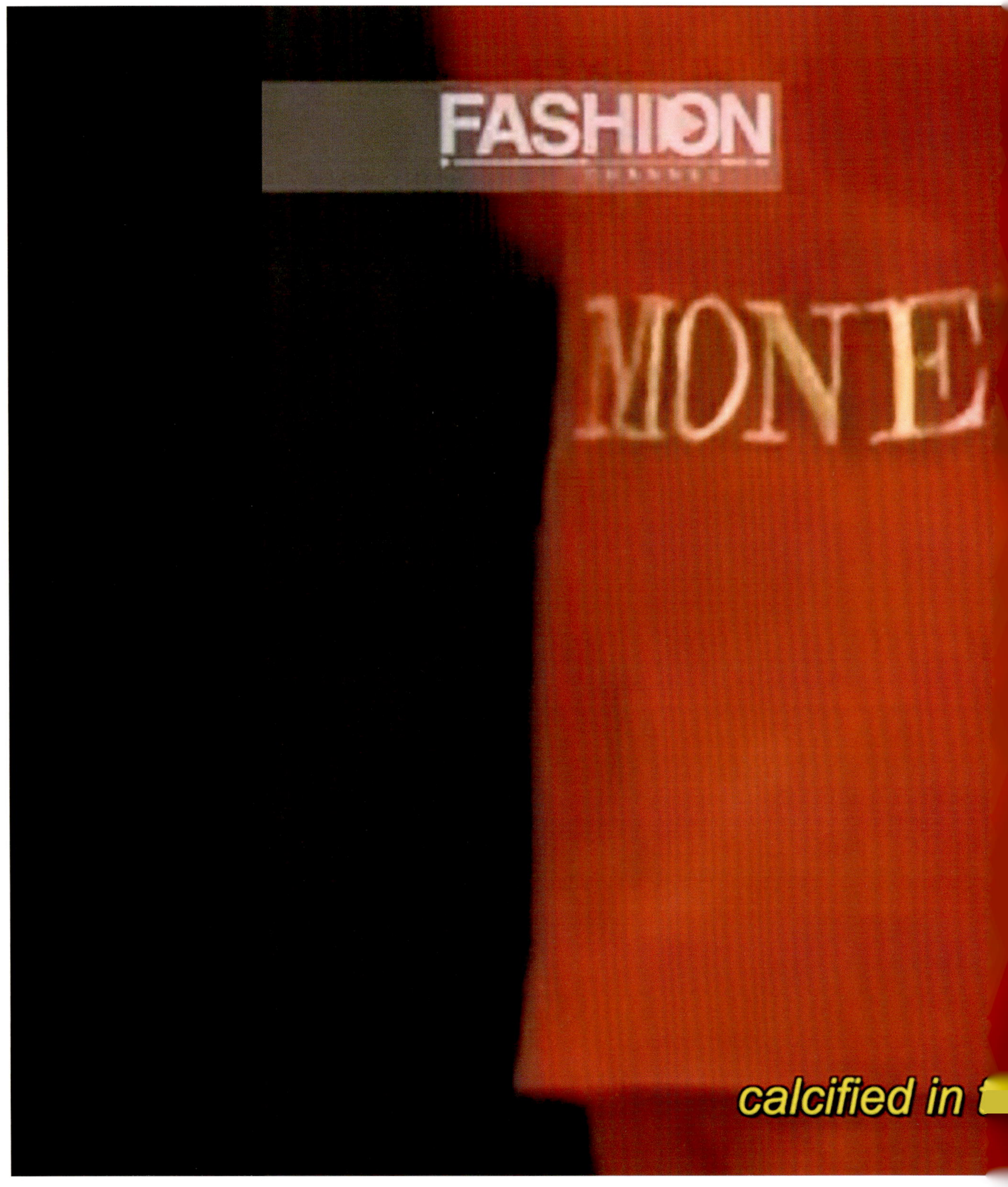

Fig. 62

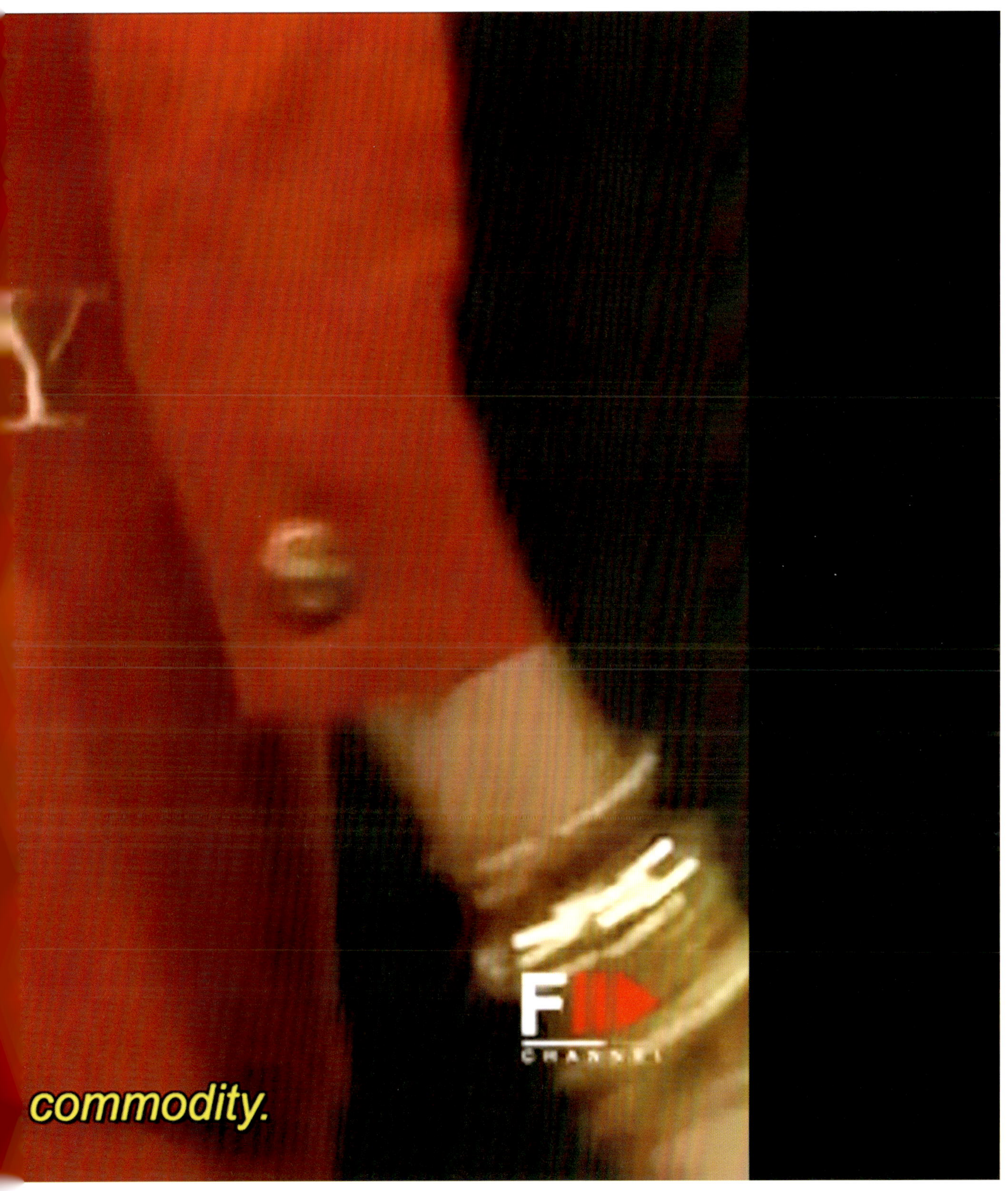
commodity.

Tripe, stomach, intestines are the bowels, the belly, the very life of man. But at the same time they represent the swallowing, devouring belly. Grotesque realism played with this double image, we might say with the top and the bottom of the word.... This is why the main events in the life of the grotesque body, the acts of the bodily drama, take place in this sphere. Eating, drinking, defecation and other elimination (sweating, blowing of the nose, sneezing), as well as copulation, pregnancy, dismemberment, swallowing up by another body—all these acts are performed on the confines of the body and the outer world, or on the confines of the old and new body.[9]

However, in the Moschino suit, this physical body is indissolubly tied back in with its symbolic death as location for the commodity that is fashion.[10] Philipp Ekardt refers to this aspect in his study of Walter Benjamin's writing on fashion as "a woman's body is the place where labor goes to die":[11]

The vocabulary of death, secondly, forms part of a theory of commodification, understood as a process by which labor, initially imagined as "alive" (cf. the Marxian notion of "living labor"), mortifies into "dead labor," ready for the exchange process (the *Umschlag*, the circulation of commodities) to ensue. Fashion, as the site for these processes, is thus defined as the frame in which the mortification of woman into allegory and woman into commodity take place.[12]

Benjamin's specific and unrealistic denegation of woman's body as that of an active agent—as a worker—potentially both exploited and industrious, has to be linked to the history of female repression and the contested aspects of female self-determination since the onset of the woman question as political subject matter. If we were to ask with this in mind who is doing the wasting of money here, we can take recourse to Virginia Woolf's seminal essay *Three Guineas* from 1938, in which she expounds the limits of female agency in a society based on money still predominantly earned by men and in spite of having earned the right to vote. In her fictional response to a letter asking "How are we to prevent war?" she reasserts her focus on the material circumstances of women already introduced in *A Room of One's Own*: "So magically does it [Arthur's education fund] change the landscape that the noble courts and quadrangles of Oxford and Cambridge often appear to educated men's daughters like petticoats with holes in them, cold legs of mutton, and the boat train starting for abroad while the guard slams the door in their faces."[13] More simply put: the historical casting of woman as both economically passive and frivolously wasteful functions as a self-perpetuating contradictory fable which permeates fashion's tropes throughout the twentieth century and arguably up until today. Waist of Money personified remains an ambiguous entity, with the most fascinating tension located precisely in agency: the chimera of a passively gold-adorned corpse and that of lady wealth, shrewd and defiant.

If we were to leave aside for a moment Benjamin's gendered notion, then the image of *fashion as the place where labor goes to die* denotes an important, almost vulgar intimacy of human and ware. The shroud of dead labor, the enstrangement of man from his work under industrialized capitalism, here is stuck or glued skin tight to the body—and if indeed fashion and its clothes are taken as literal derivates of a production process seen as corrupt, the image that is created is completely apt in its moribundity. In this reading though, fashion and its garments are forever detached from animation through the wearer, from the shirt that dresses the naked body as a need for protection and from the citizen garb of individuals: "The body . . . symbolizes our defenseless object-ness. Getting dressed means to camouflage its object-ness, it is to claim the right to see without being seen, or in other words to be pure subject."[14]

From the standpoint of fashion history, the waist is itself an important marker not only physically and therefore pertaining to pattern technology but also ideologically: many of the radical shifts in historical as well as contemporary fashion have corresponded to a proverbial loosening and tightening of the waist as the narrowest location of an average female body. The waist is hidden and exposed in more or less clear convergence with the respective religious, moral, and even more so the socioeconomic ideologies of any one system of power.

One famous technological waist-revolution is brought about by the invention of the set-in sleeve in the Middle Ages, whereby pattern-making is revolutionized from rectangular cuts following

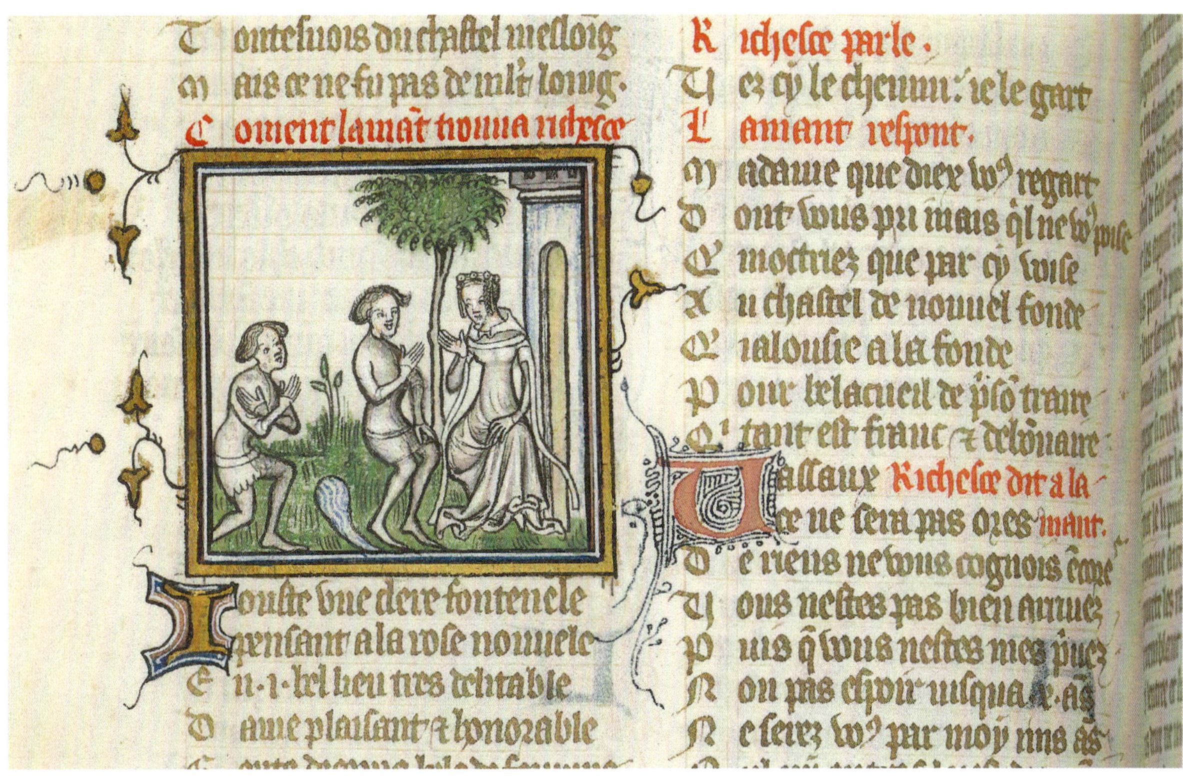

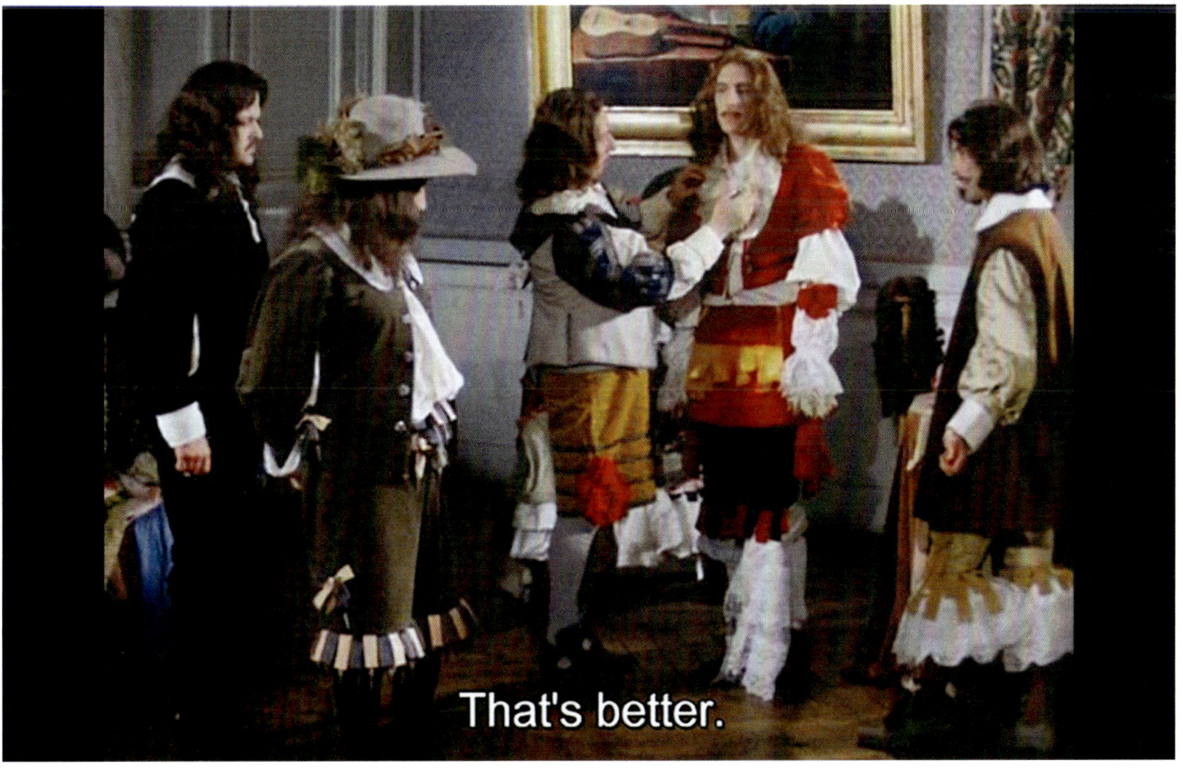

Figs. 63, 64

THE BIG STICK
LAW OFFICE
LADIES WAIST
&
D ESSMAKERS
U NION
OCAL 25
W MOURN
OU LOSS
WE MOURN OUR
LOSS
UNITED HEBREW
TRADES
OF
NEW YORK.

FILM
GORILLAS

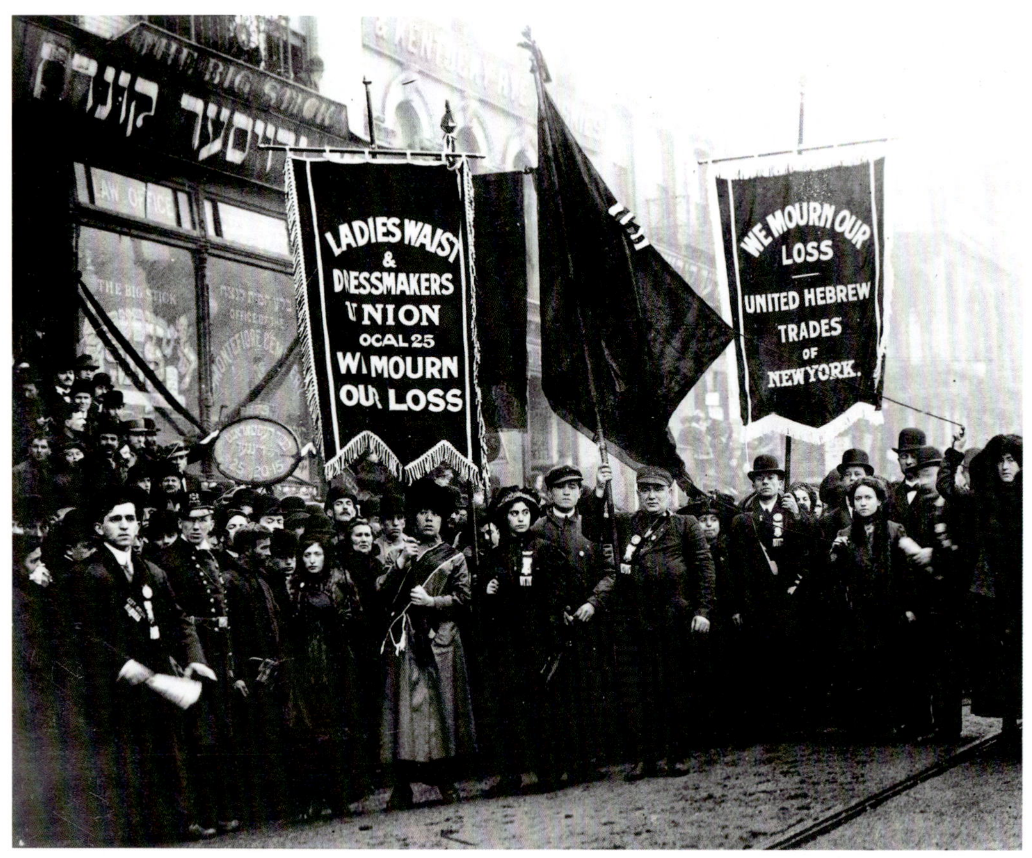

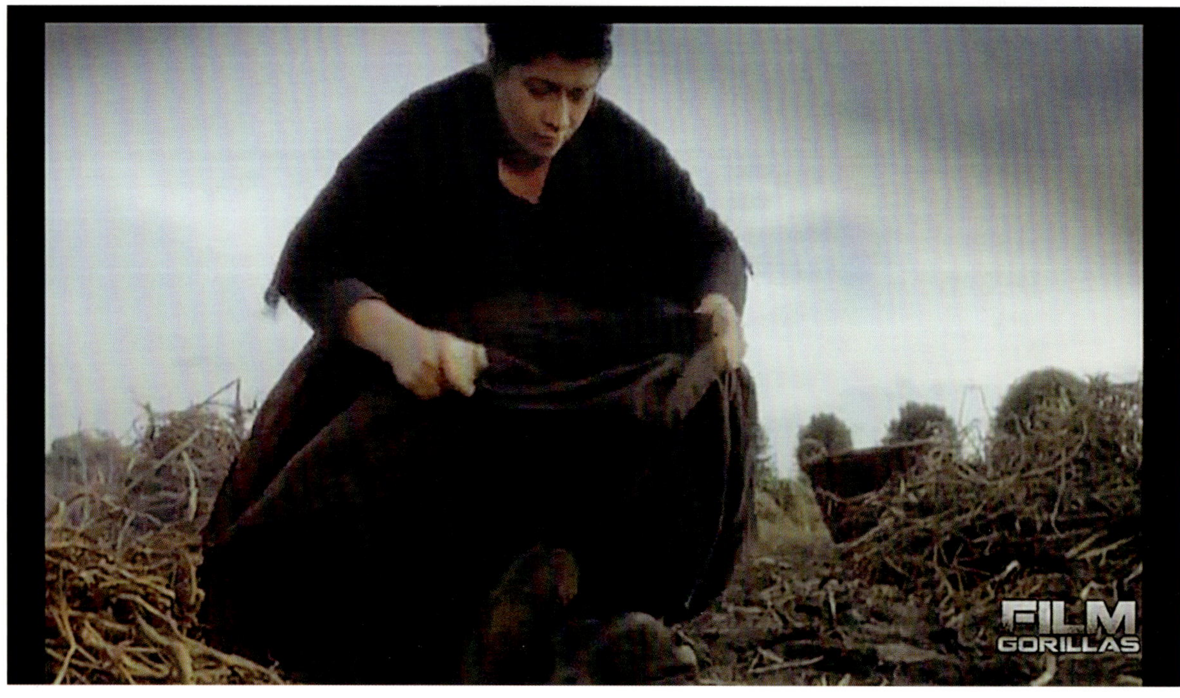

Figs. 65, 66

warp and weft, to round shaped tailoring—allowing for garments to follow the curved form of the body, thereby enabling more freedom of movement. While the wasp waist that follows this invention is at this moment in time even more pronounced in male clothing, clothing items such as the coat-hardy are worn by both sexes and they are categorized by tailored sleeves and tight bodices widening into long dresses at the hip. Below is a description of a miniature illustrating a scene in the famous medieval poem "The Romance of the Rose." The poem is intended to teach about the art of romance in a medieval court setting. Throughout the narrative the Lover encounters various characters as metonyms for virtues. The word *rose* here is used both as the poem's main female protagonist and as a symbol for female sexuality writ large.

He [the Lover] is depicted first approaching, then addressing the female personification of Wealth. He wears the hourglass-shaped doublet, with a low, narrow belt, and chaussembles (hose equipped with leather soles). His loose hair, parted in the middle, is that of a youth. Lady Wealth wears a cote hardy with tippets: slender strips of cloth attached to her upper arms (instead of the elbows, as was more customary). Her shoulders are draped with a chaperon, with its hood thrown back, and braids frame her face.[15]

And in quoting from "The Romance of the Rose": *Wealth had a purple robe. Now don't take it as a trick when I tell you truly and assure you that nowhere in the world was there a robe so beautiful, so costly, or so gay. The purple was covered with gold embroidery which portrayed the stories of dukes and kings. The collar was very richly edged with a band of gold decorated with black enamel. And you may know for certain that there was a great plenty of precious stones which emitted flashes of brilliant light. Wealth had a very costly belt which encircled her outside the purple robe. The buckle was made of a stone that had great power and virtue, for he who wore it on himself feared nothing from any poison; no one could poison him.*[16]

There is well-founded doubt in contemporary costume history as to the actual literalness of the effects of state-sponsored or religious sanctioning of any one time's fashion. The history of sumptuary laws is a telltale of failed attempts at regulating sartorial consumption—of the proverbial *wasting of money*. Throughout history from the antiques on almost every culture has at varying degrees instituted rules regulating the consumption of the materials for its citizens' daily fashions, usually on religious or moral grounds and naturally corresponding to strict class lines. For example, hemlines were mandated to be shorter for the lower classes, first as a practical result from suitability for hard labor and an insistence on recognizable class division; later, to prevent spending among the impecunious; and even later, as a quasi-protectionist measure at the onset of international trade:

> *The excess of apparel and the superfluity of unnecessary foreign wares thereto belonging now of late years is grown by sufferance to such an extremity that the manifest decay of the whole realm generally is like to follow (by bringing into the realm such superfluities of silks, cloths of gold, silver, and other most vain devices of so great cost for the quantity thereof as of necessity the moneys and treasure of the realm is and must be yearly conveyed out of the same to answer the said excess) but also particularly the wasting and undoing of a great number of young gentlemen, otherwise serviceable, and others seeking by show of apparel to be esteemed as gentlemen, who, allured by the vain show of those things, do not only consume themselves, their goods, and lands which their parents left unto them, but also run into such debts and shifts as they cannot live out of danger of laws without attempting unlawful acts, whereby they are not any ways serviceable to their country as otherwise they might be.*[17]

In Roberto Rossellini's *La Prise de pouvoir par Louis XIV* we find a fantastic cinematic rendering of the literalness that fashion theory dreams of: a Louis XIV newly awakened to the potential of his individual power—his mentor and spin doctor of absolutism Cardinal Richelieu just having died—confides his plans to change court fashion in order to bind the apostate aristocracy more closely to his court:

LOUIS XIV: Mr. Fouquet had adopted those German fashions. We'll take the most luxurious part from it. Mr. Fouquet saw in it no more than an instrument of glory. We'll make political use of it so that the nobles won't be able to think of anything but their doublet. A suit like this one, Mr. Colbert,

Jezeichnet v. L. Brand Prof.
Gestochen v. J. E. Mansfe
Eyerweib.
Vendeuse d'oeufs.

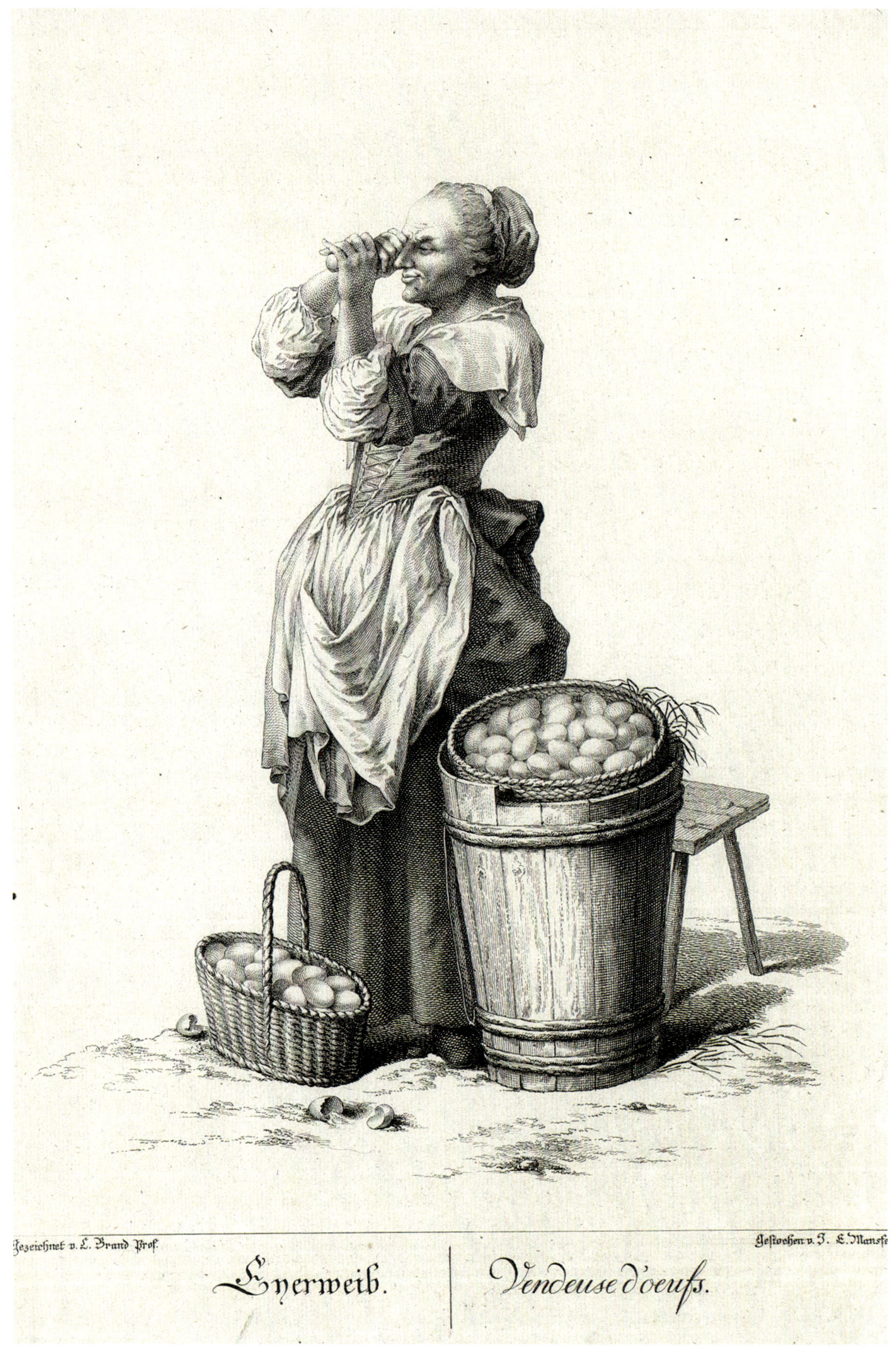

Fig. 67

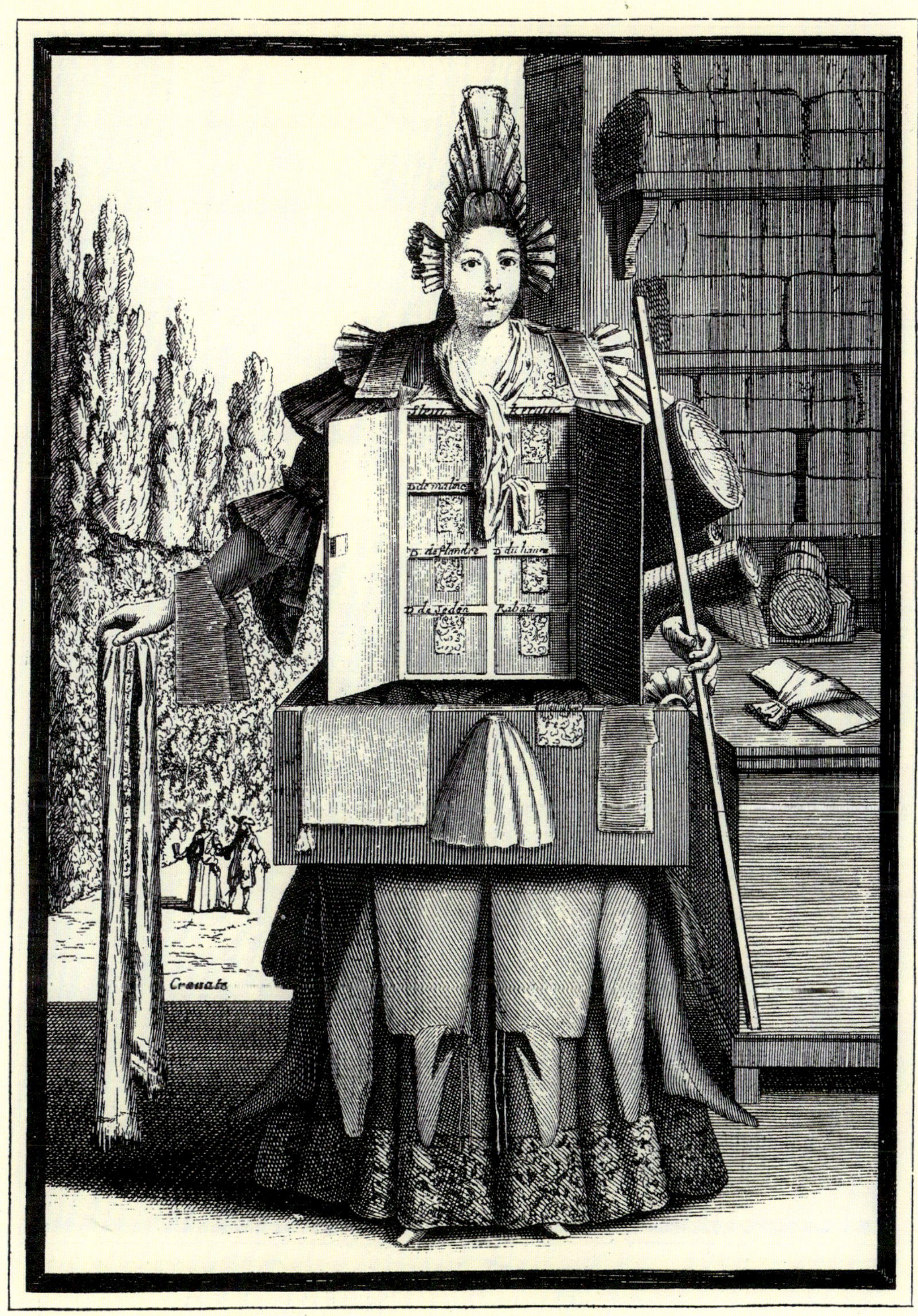

Habit de la Lingere

Aparis Chez la Vefue N. de Larmessin Rue S.t jacques à la pomme d'Or — *Auec priuil. du Roy*

Fig. 68

should represent a year's income for a gentleman of the court. . . . Mr. Fouquet understood that minds are governed more by appearances than by the true nature of things . . .[18]

In the film, the richness of style characterized above corresponds with a literal excess in material: ruffles are added to trousers, fabric is doubled. The religious moralism of historic clothing ordinances here is suspended in favor of an invitation to deficit spending as political strategy for power and dependency. Another notable example of the desire to phenomenologically link fashion to economics is the hemline index first introduced by American economist George Taylor in 1926. He suggests that hemlines rise and fall in accordance with the American stock exchange—thereby drawing a connection between affluence and audacity in style as in shorter skirts.

Ladies Waist

As a counterpoint to these monarchic strategies it is important to mention the history and legacy of both pre-industrial and industrial Weavers' Uprisings. In contrast to the personification of the wasting waist above called upon, female labor historically and traditionally linked with the textile arts and technologies—such as weaving, spinning, sewing—had been the location of many seminal uprisings. The Silesian Weavers' Uprising from 1844 is just one example, famous for its literary treatment by German poet and author Heinrich Heine. As a demographic, women (and later, women migrants in particular) ranked for reasons already mentioned among the most exploited in the textile industries that relocated from Western Europe and the US to Asia and the global South, and still do to this day. The Triangle Shirtwaist Factory fire in New York City in 1911 is seen as the deadliest industrial disaster in the history of the city. The fire caused the deaths of 146 garment workers—123 women and girls and 23 men—who died from the fire, smoke inhalation, or falling/jumping to their deaths. Most of the victims were recent Italian and Jewish immigrant women and girls aged fourteen to twenty-three.[19] They had been locked into the premises to prevent idling and smoke breaks. The disaster did not lead to immediate change in labor law but the strikes that had started prior to the catastrophe were continued and helped spill into progressive changes to labor safety regulations during the Roosevelt era. Countless disasters of similar scope continue to unwind in the global production sites of cheap textile goods.

A selection of prints from engravings in the collection of the MAK in Vienna from 1775 by Johann Christian Brand features professions of the marketplace subsumed under the term *Kaufruf* or the specific beckoning call of salespeople in the marketplace. These prints include saleswomen such as the *Eyerweib* (egg woman) in the process of performing a quality test on one of her eggs whereby she lifts the egg to her eye and holds it against the light. The emphasis here is evidently on a scientific and naturalistic depiction of the professions in the Habsburgian empire.

In his essay "Language and Clothing," Roland Barthes mentions a different kind of attempt: Nicholas de Larmessin's costume grotesques from around 1700. We find here, at a moment in time when traditional trades would soon be subject to grave changes under the all-encompassing influence of industrialization and mechanization, an almost nostalgic casting of the professions as "clothed" in the objects that make up their trade. The depictions extrapolate an understanding of a craft as literally defining the features of a craftsman's appearance. The *Habit de l'Architect* displays different types of columns and architectural ornaments as body parts, the *Habit de la Lingère* presents a female vendor of underwear with her display table fitted around her waist like an immense angular skirt, on which her goods are affixed for display, while her torso is made up by a triangular drawer: "in this fantasy, clothing ends up absorbing Man completely, the worker is anatomically assimilated to the respective instruments and in the end it is an alienation which here is described poetically; Larmessin's workers are robots avant la lettre."[20] In contrast to the alleged passivity of the not-working but consuming woman discussed above, the immobility of the worker turning incrementally into a robot includes a tradition of progressively alienated labor.

What strikes me is the symbolism of those women's skirts. The trope of this female garment at the onset of the industrial revolution is different when looked at from the location of the marketplace rather than under the auspices of fashion. These skirts, arguably dirty at the hem from trailing, constitute the animatedly layered cosmos of the female proto-entrepreneur. While there is no doubt about the impracticality of skirts vis-à-vis pants, the symbolic ontology of this garment which spans a space from its fixed position at the waist over genitalia and legs formally evokes a sort of on-body tent, a carried space. It relates intimately to the picture of the first scene in the movie adaptation of Günter Grass's *Tin Drum*. The chapter in the book is aptly titled "Der weite Rock" (The Wide Skirt) and in it the protagonist's great-grandmother Anna Bronski, harvesting potatoes in a field in 1899, saves a criminal from capture by the local police by hiding him underneath her *four potato-colored skirts*. Yet, as we learn in the next scene, underneath these skirts she is impregnated by the very criminal she saves and bears his child. While this scene can be naturally interpreted as rape with all the resulting societal consequences for a pregnant non-married woman, I have always understood it visually within the realm of the uncanny in relation to the female mothering body. Skirts here are what constitute this realm. In regard to the historical materialism of Marxist critique, we have to include the image of the body of the mangled woman proletarian—exposed, violated, and exploited—both as worker and as object of unwanted sexual attention.

"Through all ages—when the pavement was grass, when it was swamp, through the age of tusk and mammoth, through the age of silent sunrise, the battered woman—for she wore a skirt—with her right hand exposed, her left clutching at her side, stood singing of love—love which has lasted a million years, she sang, love which prevails, and millions of years ago, her lover, who had been dead these centuries, had walked, she crooned, with her in May."[21]

Habitus and milieu
Painted on my skin[22]

A discussion of habitus and milieu is unavoidable when trying to locate agency in the way we dress. If we tend to commonly accept the impossibility of complete independence from social class, religion, nationality, ethnicity, education, and profession, fashion is still popularly conceptualized as a field of extravagance or experimentation. The makeover testifies to this in the bluntest and most popular sense. Personally, I tend to locate fashion's relative potency in inciting awareness and emotions in people not particularly schooled or alerted to its ontology through both the basic fact of its location on the human body and the non-verbal societal understanding of materials—here, fabrics. Both of these statements are in keeping with French sociologist Pierre Bourdieu's understanding of social processes as generally un-self-aware of the structural rules that underlie them. Habitus, with Bourdieu, is composed both of the particularities of physical comportment—the way one walks, stands, gesticulates—as well as the way one thinks, feels, and takes action: "The schemes of thought and expression he [each agent] has acquired are the basis for the intentionless invention of regulated improvisation."[23] It casts our agency as at all times dependent on the structure of the society we are socialized in while we reciprocally reproduce the social setting through our actions.

Andrea Fraser's performance *May I Help You?*, first performed in 1991 at American Fine Arts Co. in New York City, features female characters sometimes impersonated by the artist herself. The script for the performed monologue is composed of text fragments culled from Bourdieu's sociology, literature, and various interviews, papers, and articles investigating what broadly amounts to the lifestyle and self-representation of the white Anglo-Saxon middle class in America. The actor plays the role of a gallery salesperson or director addressing an audience of unspecified visitors to a museum or gallery. In the original performance, the gallery walls were hung with one hundred *Plaster Surrogates*—wall works by artist Allan McCollum—that served as the exhibition-cum-backdrop for the performance.

"Loving something means having it with you. Your collection expresses the texture and quality and even the smell of your life. It reflects everything about you, from the condition of your teeth to the way that you love. You're branded by the objects you love. They mark you as the property of your culture, the property of your class. (She turns to an art object.) Now, imagine this picture tattooed on my shoulder. It's like that. Imagine the clothes that I'm wearing and the rest of my environment have been painted on my skin, and then the whole thing is turned inside out so that it's the stuff inside the shoes, the sofa, the dining room.

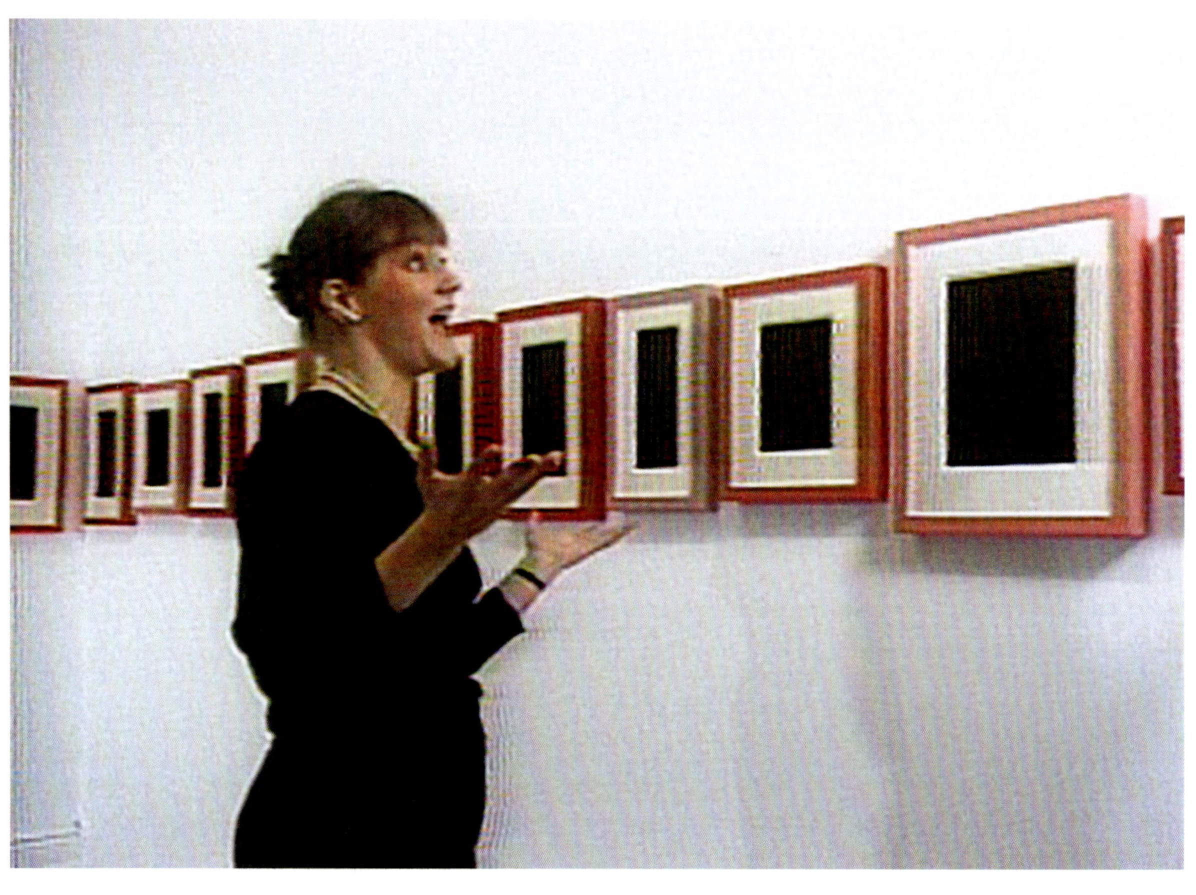

Fig. 69

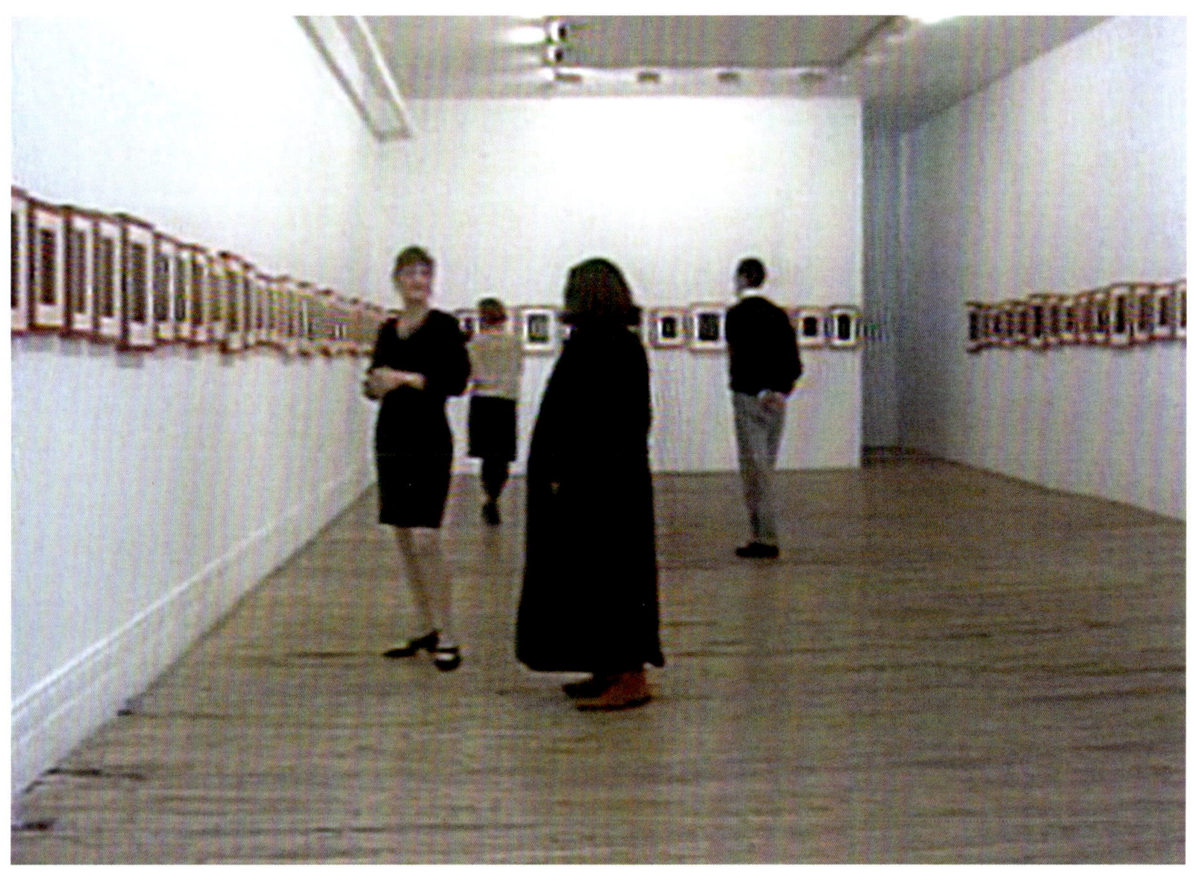

Fig. 70

You know, these are the things for which you'll be remembered. These are the things for which you'll be loved. It's always with you. It's inside. And it's outside, at the same time, for everyone to see. It's a prison."[24]

Fraser viscerally evokes an intimacy of inside and outside: the image of a tattoo as a radicalized version of what clothing qua clothing really already is: the visible extension and projection of the body in the world, as conditioned by habitus and milieu. The exaggerated invocation of the dangerously conspicuous aspects of our use of objects recalls Simone de Beauvoir's assertion that by projecting oneself into things we turn ourselves into objects.

Although the character and tone of the performer switches between various degrees of candid self-confidence and class awareness, the typology of the chosen outfits allows for a location of the character as broadly middle class, business style. Ledlie Borgerhoff, performer in the original staging, wears a black ensemble of top and skirt, kitten-heeled Mary Janes, a wristwatch, and a classic pearl necklace.

Fraser's suited characters aided by the theoretical context of their monologues perform a headier version of the Franco Moschino mannequins. But there is a general likeness in the exaggeratedly and consciously deconstructed manner and comportment of these characters, that share in an understanding of the complexity of the socially conditioned self as investigated by Bourdieu. The similarity in antics is particularly palpable in a moment during the Moschino S/S 1991 runway show that also featured the Waist of Money suit. Archived via YouTube by the Fashion Channel, we see Pat Cleveland in a red outfit consisting of a frilly, ruffled top over red chinos. On top of the outfit, she wears a jacket fashioned precisely in detail and color after an airplane life vest. As Cleveland turns, we can indeed read the letters LIFE JACKET embroidered on the back of the vest. With an earnest and professional expression, she goes on to demonstrate the safety features of the vest—just as we know them from airplane cabin safety demonstrations—before eventually taking off the jacket and casting it aside on the edge of the runway.

While Fraser's female characters transcend the confines of the woman as exploited housewife, her entanglements with the commodities she affords do not free her, as much as her male consumer counterpart, from dependency. While Bourdieu has been criticized for the determinism of his thesis, we can wrench from his theory the relative and conditional field of action available to a human being. Within our quasi-statistical memories of what is socially possible and what is unspokenly forbidden, we constitute our existence as agents, and we do so despite this knowledge. It is ultimately not useful to disavow the capacity for conditional choice if we are to constitute an ethics for a functional society. From a psychological, behavioral standpoint fashion signs, always *a kind of sign in decline*,[25] allow for a nuanced field of obscure significations that are made use of in a communicative sense, often nonverbally, whether we can call them emancipatory or not. The tension of fashion arises precisely at the intersection of the negative connotations of objects as corruptive simulacra indebted both to Christian anti-material ethics and the critique of commodification in Marxism and their psycho-material relevance to humans as meaningful objects of desire: libidinal, fetishistic, and transitional.[26]

Post Scriptum
Domestic Mending
How We Waste

I was raised with a culturally Catholic, middle-class understanding that I was *not to waste* but more as a behavioral etiquette than as a rule that extended from an ethical or moral position. My sister and I were spoiled, but money was used as a means to exert power and to discourage flocking from the family home. To brag or to throw around food was considered in bad taste. But, to mend a ripped garment, to repair an object of use (unless it was excessively exquisite) was, as far as I remember, not the norm. I remember my mother as extremely smart in understanding the management of both her business and our household and I am not suggesting she would throw away clothes barely used. But as I find myself stitching funny bespoke patches on a bathrobe that has ripped at two different locations, I think about what the difference between my mother's relationship to money and objects and my own really is, besides a basic understanding of our respective professions' class status—as a former factory owner and a self-employed artist.

Having grown up in a large family of eight siblings with a mother who was a housewife and extremely industrious in manufacturing almost everything that could be made by hand without a workshop, my mother, in her own words, craved to leave the chaos of the perpetually disorderly household. As my grandfather was a veterinarian, the family was perceived as upper middle class in the countryside, his profession one of high importance in a rural community where industry was only slowly replacing agriculture. All eight siblings, five of them women, spanning thirty years between the youngest and the eldest, went on to study or to get degrees. The financial burden of raising and sustaining the family was substantial and my mother, in moving out of her parents' home and later in marrying, craved economic independence: it had been impressed on her that there could be no more financial support from her parents after she graduated. What I am considering these days, when I compare myself with my mother and try to describe my socialization and class status, is whether it is sufficient to view my mother's reluctance to mend (as I and my partner now like to do) as a sign of her aspiration toward an economic class with an ability to spend money on new things. The more I think about it, the more I think that what might be closer to the truth is that she was attempting to transcend the symbolic dominance of her mother, who, as the perfect *Angel of the House*,[27] embodied the image of woman and wife as the fixer of domestic problems, a possessor of a readily available maternal handiness that supplied solutions and attended to things in nonindustrial fashion.

My mother worked full time and she suffered under the small-town suspicion that she was neglecting her children. Not braiding your child's hair and buying a school lunch rather than making sandwiches from slices of bread are now almost comical ciphers in stories of Western motherhood after the war. It leads us full circle to the communion photograph with my child-self wearing a handmade box-tree wreath. My mother's own memory of the event itself is one of defiant pride connected to this object. Despite her self-affirmed clumsiness in binding it, after skipping out on the weekly training sessions with the other mothers, she still has it in her possession: a token of her resilience.

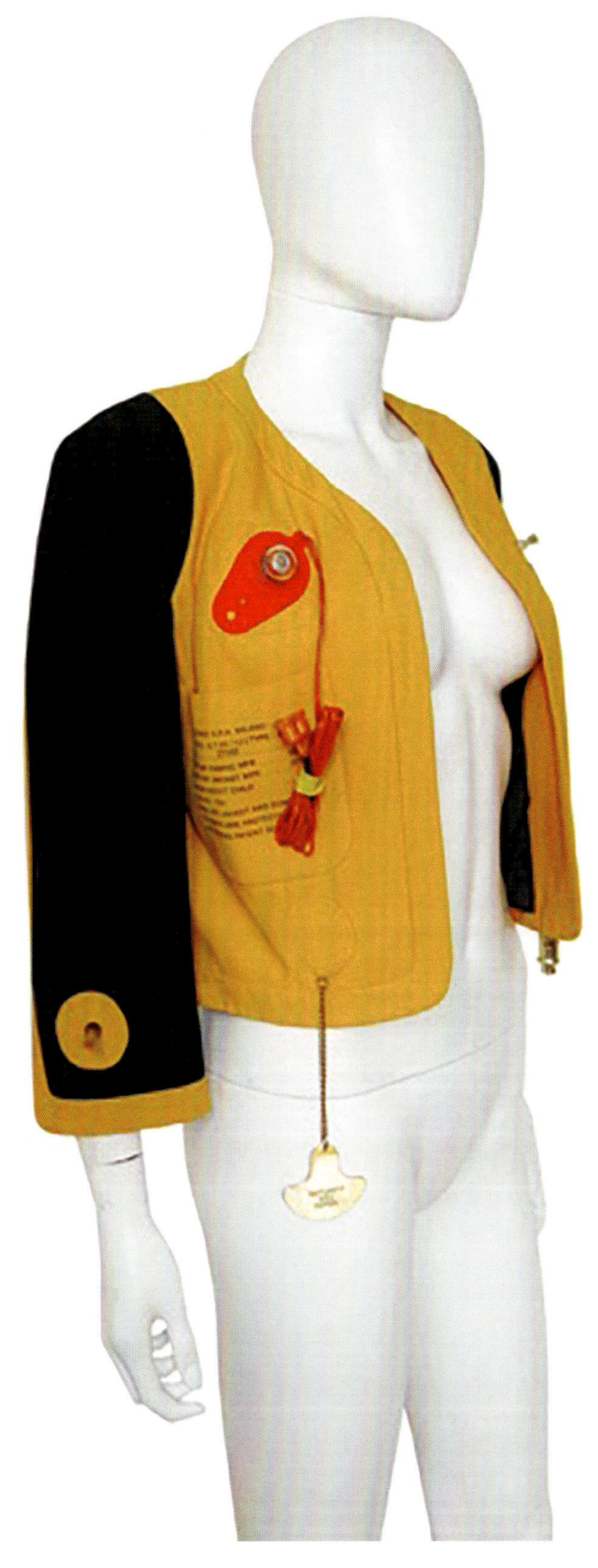

Fig. 71

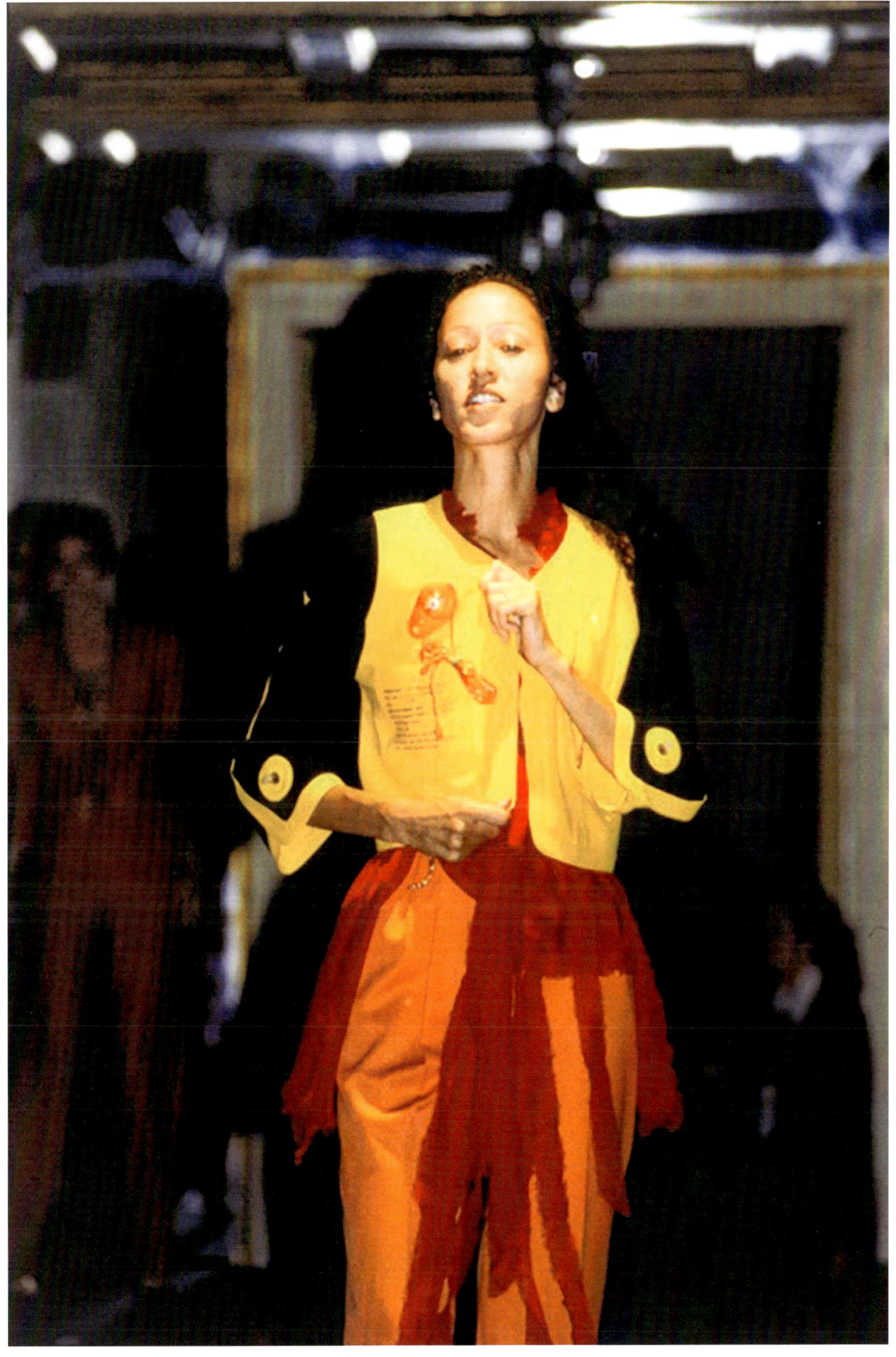

Fig. 72

Notes

1 Martha Rosler, "In, around, and afterthoughts (on documentary photography)," in *Decoys and Disruptions: Selected Writings, 1975–2001* (Cambridge, MA: MIT Press), 179.

2 What is left untouched here is whether or not she afforded the suit through her own financial means, although this does not directly alter the meaning of her appearance or her choice of the garment. It does however pertain to the question of woman's class status as complicated by Virginia Woolf's term "daughters of educated men" and by any other of her oblique dependencies be they to man or different sponsors. It is important to stress that economic dependency does not, in my opinion, make self-scrutiny impossible. But in an investigation of milieu this should be mentioned.

3 Franco Moschino and Lida Castelli, eds., *X Anni di Kaos! Moschino 1983–1993* (Milan: Lybra Immagine, 1993).

4 Ibid., 15.

5 *Pretend It's a City*, episode 1, "Pretend It's a City," directed by Martin Scorsese, featuring Fran Lebowitz and Martin Scorsese, released January 8, 2021, on Netflix.

6 See Theodor Adorno, "Art and the Arts," in Juliane Rebentisch, *Aesthetics of Installation Art* (Berlin: Sternberg Press, 2012), 100.

7 Elizabeth Wilson, "Magic Fashion," *Fashion Theory* 8, no. 4 (2004): 383.

8 Moyra Davey, *Hell Notes*, 1990, Super 8 film with sound, transferred to HD video, 28:44, courtesy of Galerie Buchholz, Berlin/Cologne/New York.

9 Mikhail Bakhtin, *Rabelais and His World*, tr. Helene Iswolsky (Bloomington: Indiana University Press, 1984), 162.

10 See Philipp Ekardt, *Benjamin on Fashion* (London: Bloomsbury, 2020).

11 Ibid., 203.

12 Ibid., 200–201.

13 Virginia Woolf, *Three Guineas* (Harmondsworth: Penguin, 1977), 8.

14 Jean-Paul Sartre, quoted in Ariella Azoulay, *The Civil Contract of Photography* (New York: Zone Books, 2012), 211.

15 Description of "The Lover Encounters Wealth," illuminated by the Master of the Bible of Jean de Sy, ca. 1380, in Guillaume de Lorris and Jean de Meun, *Romance of the Rose*, The Morgan Library & Museum, accessed August 1, 2020, https://www.themorgan.org/collection/Illuminating-Fashion/9#overlay-context=collection/Illuminating-Fashion/9.

16 Guillaume de Lorris and Jean de Meun, *The Romance of the Rose*, tr. Charles Dahlberg (Princeton: Princeton University Press, 1995).

17 “Enforcing Statutes of Apparel, issued at Greenwich, 15 June 1574,” Elizabethan Sumptuary Statutes, accessed August, 2021, http://elizabethan.org/sumptuary/who-wears-what.html.

18 *La Prise de pouvoir par Louis XIV*, directed by Roberto Rossellini (1966; New York: Criterion Collection, 2009 [*as The Taking of Power by Louis XIV*]), DVD.

19 Wikipedia, s.v. “Triangle Shirtwaist Factory fire,” last modified March 28, 2022, 16:28, https://en.wikipedia.org/wiki/Triangle_Shirtwaist_Factory_fire.

20 Roland Barthes, *The Language of Fashion*, tr. Andy Stafford (London: Bloomsbury, 2013), 50.

21 Virginia Woolf, *Mrs Dalloway* (Harmondsworth: Penguin, 1996), 90.

22 Andrea Fraser, “May I Help You?,” in *Texts, Scripts, Transcripts*, ed. Carla Cugini (Cologne: Walther König, 2013), 22.

23 Pierre Bourdieu, *Outline of a Theory of Practice*, tr. Richard Nice (Cambridge: Cambridge University Press, 1977), 79.

24 Fraser, “May I Help You?,” 22.

25 See Barthes, *The Language of Fashion,* 81.

26 The term *transitional* is used in reference to the work of D. W. Winnicott. See Winnicott, *Playing and Reality* (London: Tavistock, 1971).

27 Virginia Woolf, “Professions for Women,” in *The Death of the Moth and Other Essays* (Harmondsworth: Penguin, 1961).

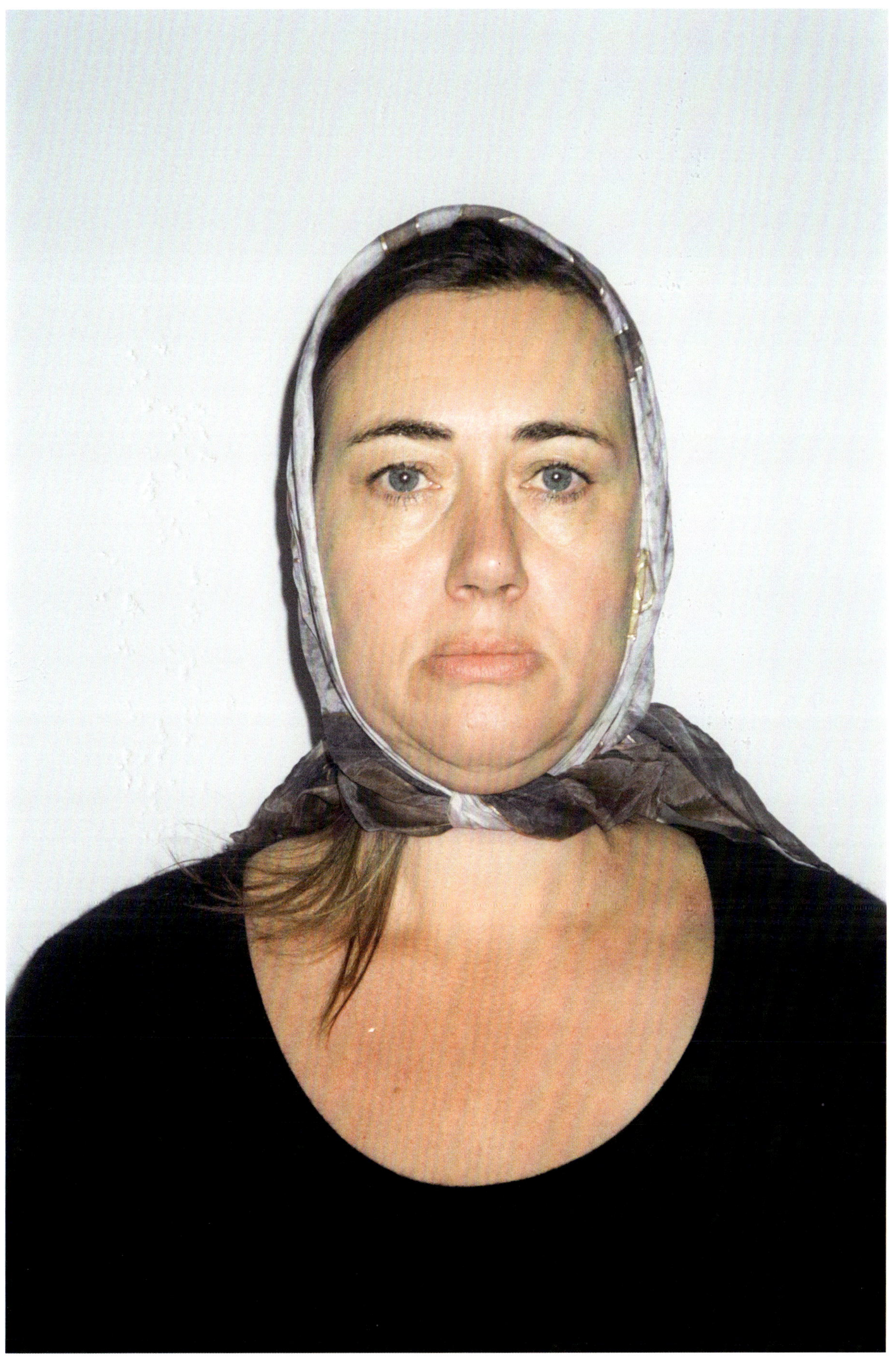

Fig. 73

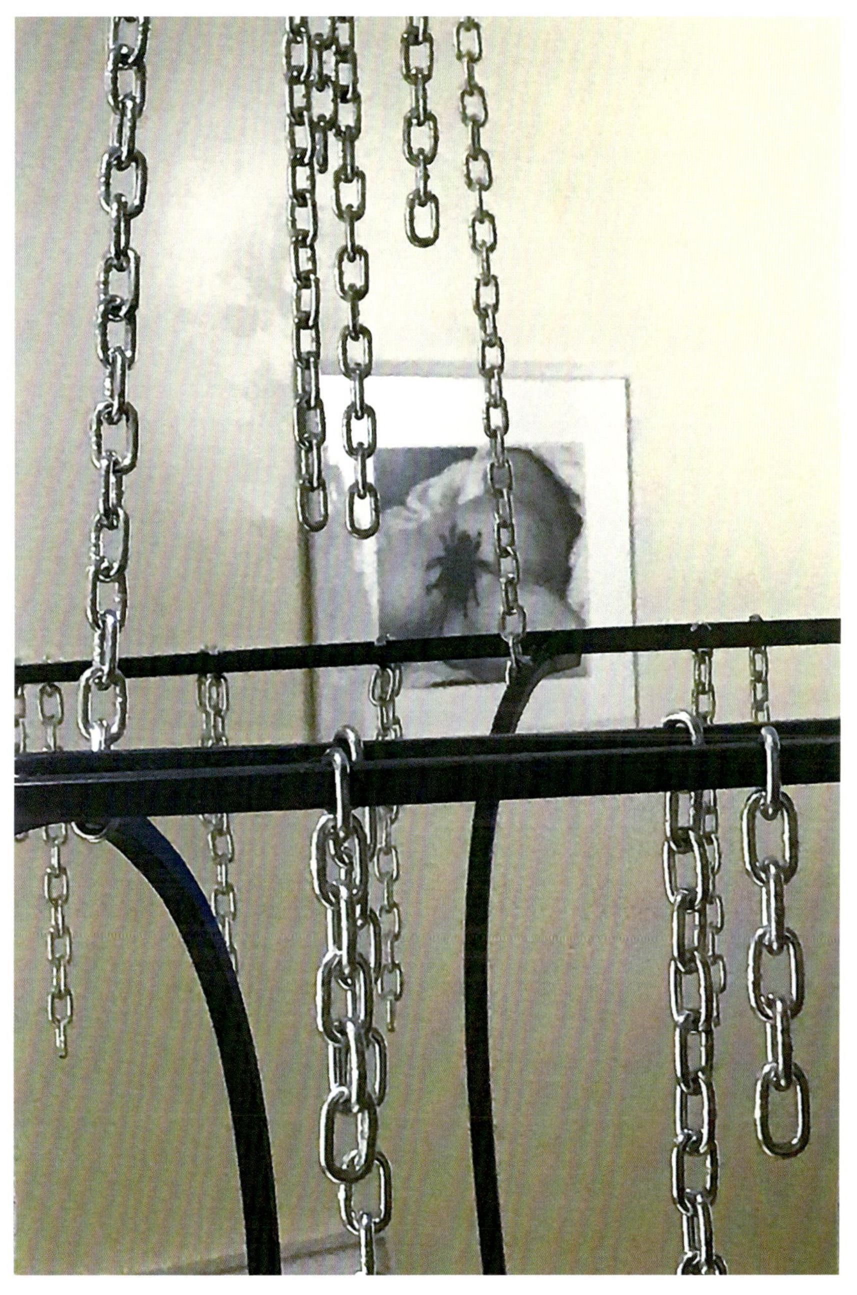

Fig. 74

Fig. 1: Installation view, *life and limbs*,
Swiss Institute, New York, 2019

Fig. 2: Johnny Moke for Adeline André
Egg Heel Shoes, ca. 1986
Satin, leather, and reinforced plaster resin
Courtesy of Northampton Museum
and Art Gallery
Digitized black-and-white photograph
Photograph by Anna Ray

Adeline André is a Paris-based haute couturier, with whom *life and limbs* curator Anna-Sophie Berger apprenticed. Called the "mother of minimalism" by the *New York Times* in 1986, her clothes focus on the essentials of cut, construction, and fabric with conceptual underpinnings. For several years, British self-taught shoe designer Johnny Moke made shoes for André's runway shows. The *Egg Heel* shoes make literal the expression "to walk on eggshells."

Fig. 3: 3D model for *life and limbs*, 2019

Fig. 4: Meret Oppenheim
Untitled, 1936
Paper, ink, pencil, and watercolor
Courtesy of collection Design Museum
Den Bosch/NL

Meret Oppenheim was a Swiss artist, often associated with the Surrealists, who made no distinction between the drawings, paintings, sculptures, writing, furniture, and jewelry she created. The drawings featured in *life and limbs* propose subversive designs for necklaces. This one is a collar necklace formed from a pair of childlike legs dressed in patent leather Mary Jane shoes and high socks, which straddle the contour of a neck. The other is a choker with a large pendant featuring clenched teeth with a gold cigarette protruding from them.

Fig. 5: Kayode Ojo
I'm Fine, 2018
Zikimed 50 m1 revolver syringes,
glass barrel, Luer Lock (animal only),
Master Series Ultimate Male Lockdown
Chastity System, and Howard Elliott 11184
Mirrored Pedestal Table
Courtesy of the artist and Martos Gallery,
New York
Photograph by Charles Benton

Kayode Ojo repositions readymade objects for display, here exhibiting the explicitly listed Zikimed 50 m1 revolver syringes, glass barrel, Luer Lock (animal only), and Master Series Ultimate Male Lockdown Chastity System, which are all shiny and reflective tools for animal husbandry or S&M, on a Howard Elliott 11184 Mirrored Pedestal Table, a mirrored plinth. The materials draw an implicit image of bodies as probed, prodded, or manipulated. The metallic surface of the tools and reflective quality of the table confuse material as utility and as style. Variously violent and kinky, the grotesque is here insinuated with bodies as cavernous, prone to penetration in willful acts of desire and in involuntary deference to aggression. The proximity of these items to the viewer's body places them just within reach of use but cut off from their functioning as things to only be looked at.

Fig. 6: Installation view, *life and limbs*

(left to right)

Walter Pichler
Fingerspanner, 1967
3 photographs
Courtesy of MAK – Museum of Applied
Arts, Vienna

Walter Pichler was an Austrian artist and architect. His *Körperapplikationen* (Body Applications), made in the years 1966–69, imagine different ways of extending the reach and limits of the human body with prosthetics. The photographs here document the wearable *Fingerspanner* (Finger Stretcher) he created as part of a design titled *Standardanzug* (Standard Suit). Other elements of this series included a wearable TV set titled *TV-Helm* (TV Helmet). Pichler says about this series: "We considered clothing as architecture's first layer. Clothing as shell prior to space."

Nathaniel Goldberg / Inge Grognard
Untitled, 1999
Digital print on Epson smooth
bright 300g

This photo was originally published as part of a spread in the "Beauty" section of *purple MAGAZINE* #2 (Winter 1999). In addition to this image, there were photos of three women of different ages, who each had gold, silver, and matte-black threads applied to their faces by makeup artist Inge Grognard, along contour lines and wrinkles. One of the women featured in the shoot and pictured here is artist Annette Messager. Grognard's conceptual approach to makeup played a large part in shaping the runway presentations of many designers in the 1990s, including most famously those by Martin Margiela. Often, her face paints and designs involve the pinning and taping of facial features reminiscent of ritual body modifications or S&M appliances.

Lyle Ashton Harris
Venus Hottentot 2000, 1994
Unique Polaroid
Courtesy of the artist and Salon 94, New York

Lyle Ashton Harris made this photograph in collaboration with artist, activist, and curator Renee Cox, who is pictured in the photograph. Restaging the spectacle of Sara Baartman's exhibition as the "Hottentot Venus" in freak show attractions in nineteenth-century Europe, Harris and Cox's image works to reclaim this canonized Western representation of a Black female body. In its futuristic reinterpretation, Cox's nude form is adorned by metallic breast and posterior plates while her gaze is fixed ahead. Body modification or adornment as part of individual sexual practice is here only formally evoked while actually pointing to the insidious racialized notions of Black bodies as stereotypes.

Fig. 7: Birgit Jürgenssen
Fehlende Glieder (Missing Limbs), 1974
Pencil and colored pencil on handmade paper
Courtesy of the VERBUND COLLECTION, Vienna

Birgit Jürgenssen was a pioneering Austrian artist who made work that often dealt with the female body including through self-portraiture. Her drawings from the 1970s display a detailed cosmology of bodies in transformation. From realistic settings of female household labor to imagined bodily transformation and disintegration, the drawings span from the sociopolitical to the mystical, surreal, and grotesque.

Fehlende Glieder (Missing Limbs) presents a masculine figure dressed in a 1970s-style sports or leisure outfit of white pleated pants and a knit vest over a white shirt. The right side of the figure's body has been transformed into that of a crustacean, likely a lobster. The depiction is very detailed but too flat in dimension to be understood as an anatomically realistic rendering of such a transformation. This quality renders it uncanny or dreamlike.

Fig. 8: Installation view, *life and limbs*

Fig. 9: Ebecho Muslimova
Untitled, 2015
Ink on paper
Courtesy of the artist and Michail Pirgelis

Since 2011, Ebecho Muslimova has made drawings and paintings that feature a corpulent alter ego named "Fatebe," whose pliant naked body contorts to react to whatever impossible situation or context Muslimova places her in. With an attitude of unerring positivity and openness, Fatebe appears to approach her body as though it is a vessel for endless experimentation. Unlike Looney Tunes cartoons, in which extreme violence and bodily harm are frequently cast in an almost candid normalcy but crucially inflicted between adversaries, what happens to Fatebe is at all times based on her volition. Therefore, the penetration of Fatebe's body by various objects is ambiguously violent and self-pleasuring.

Fig. 10: Installation view, *life and limbs*

Fig. 11: Birgit Jürgenssen
Rhinoceros Beetle Battle, 1971
Crayon on Schoellerhammer Bütten cardboard
Courtesy of Galerie Hubert Winter, Vienna

Fig. 12: Birgit Jürgenssen
Ohne Titel (Untitled), 1971
Pencil and colored pencil on handmade paper
Courtesy of the VERBUND COLLECTION, Vienna

In *Ohne Titel* (Untitled), a beetle is depicted with each section of its hard exoskeleton attached together by large stitches, the thread resembling shoelaces and the pierced holes rendered like eyelets.

Fig. 13: Adeline André
défilé Haute Couture Juillet (Couture Runway show), 1999
Color slide photograph, scanned
Photograph by Makiko Kishi

Fig. 14: Walter Pichler
Standardanzug, 1968
Construction drawing, pencil and crayon on paper, dry-mounted on aluminum, foldable
Courtesy of the Generali Foundation Collection–Permanent Loan to the Museum der Moderne Salzburg, © Generali Foundation
Photograph by Werner Kaligofsky

Fig. 15: Manfred Deix
Family Duck Today – Donald and his nephews are starting to show their age, 1989
Watercolor on cardboard
Courtesy of Landessammlungen Niederösterreich
© Manfred Deix / Landessammlungen NÖ

Manfred Deix was an Austrian newspaper caricaturist who gained notoriety for his crude, satirical depictions of members of the Catholic clergy, notably cartoons of priests molesting young choirboys. Though it may seem trivial or unnuanced as subject matter, his practice is firmly linked with the 1980s and '90s in Austria when the country was extremely conservative, alternately swinging between the poles of the right-wing remnants of World War II, and the overbearing influence of the Catholic church. He was particularly critical of the far-right politician Jörg Haider, whom he often depicted as Hannibal Lecter or a tiger. Deix's depictions of Disney characters are therefore not typical of his work but can be read broadly as satire of an America as seen from Europe. Characters like Donald Duck, Mickey Mouse, and Goofy are variously depicted as aged, downtrodden, and devious.

Fig. 16: Helmut Lang
Cow Print Dress, Ready to Wear Spring/Summer, 2001
Photographer unknown

Figs. 17, 18, 19, 20: Heimo Zobernig
Stills from *Nr. 24*, 2007
Video, color, no sound
14 min 22 sec
Courtesy of Petzel Gallery, New York

Heimo Zobernig is an Austrian artist renowned for work in various media from sculpture to painting. Having studied stage design, his post-minimal installations often include architectural interventions into spaces and puns directed at the very structure or setting of a given environment. Early video works feature Zobernig himself, dressed up or nude, walking in a park or telling jokes, in an almost slapstick fashion. In *Nr. 24*, the artist, while naked, fights three colorful figures, red, green, and blue, or the primary colors of video display. Throughout the video, he is tackled and pestered by the colors, who use him as a human stand on which to pack magazines to the point where he falters seemingly underneath the weight of the stacked printed matter and rolls to the ground. Here, too, elements of slapstick prevail. The artist is present, albeit vulnerable and exposed since he is naked. The aggressors are nothing less than primary colors, charging at the "painter." Simultaneously, the male subject performs the deconstruction of the embodied self as authority through the very submission to a scenario of fooling around.

Fig. 21: Installation view, *life and limbs*

(center)

Marija Tavčar
Marquis, 2013
Polymer clay, cotton, silk, pleated fabric, lace, tulle, ribbons, real leather, beads, and embroidered details

Marija Tavčar, who works as a costume designer for the national theater in Belgrade, custom makes her handmade doll puppets from scratch. They are intended to be used as multipurpose characters that can be incorporated into productions or storyboards but also played with and hugged. In 2017 she completed a PhD dissertation entitled "Interactive Costume: Body-Technology-Costume" at the University of Arts in Belgrade. The aim of her dissertation was to define the term *interactive costume* and subsequently utilize it as a conceptual framework for the analyses of the entanglement between technology and contemporary art.

Fig. 22: Kayode Ojo
I wanna see you on your tummy, 2019
Framed archival pigment print

Fig. 23: Marija Tavčar
Velvela, 2015
Photograph by Marko Obradović Edge

Fig. 24: Gina Folly
Research material at Zoo Basel, 2015

Gina Folly
Magic Box IV, 2015
Polycarbonate, screws

Magic Box IV is one of a series of *Magic Box* works that Gina Folly initially produced for an exhibition at SALTS in Birsfelden, Switzerland, in 2015, which replicate occupational tools that she saw in the monkey enclosure in Basel Zoo. The polycarbonate boxes are divided into compartments with several openings and are usually filled with hay and fruits. The boxes act as toys with an educational purpose, simulating a termite mound that the captive monkeys might have found in their natural habitat, and encouraging the animals to develop the logical and cognitive processes that they would have acquired in the wild.

Fig. 25: Manfred Deix
Disney Figuren, 2008
Pencil and watercolor on cardboard
Courtesy of Landessammlungen Niederösterreich
© Manfred Deix / Landessammlungen NÖ

Fig. 26: Installation view, *life and limbs*

(left)

Lucia Elena Průša
blood in blood out, 2017
Cotton, leather, glass, and wood

blood in blood out is composed of pressed clothes between panes of glass in a wooden frame. Though the wearer is absent, a circular hole is cut through the glass and the garment at the point of the torso. The areas of the body that extend it in space such as joints and belly flesh have been cut out to create the sense of a body that exists on a single plane. The clothing in the work was found on the streets of Mexico City while Lucia Elena Průša was living there.

(center left)

Diamond Stingily
Juice Drank, 2018
Trashcan, juice
Courtesy of Christina and Oscar Castellón, Miami

Diamond Stingily describes *Juice Drank* as referencing the joy of social congregation, rather than pertaining to hardship, as often presumed of her work as an African American artist. The readymade consists of colorful juice bottles stacked in an iron gridded waste bin. What would serve as a receptacle for distributing juice at a block party or community gathering, is here for display. Each juice therefore stands in for a person sharing the insinuated commons of a feast or being together outdoors rather than within the confinement of a private home for a moment. Since products such as Little Hug Fruit Barrels are culturally specific and consumed along the logic of class and race, Stingily's sculpture is charged with the precision of her experience.

(center right)

Sarah Charlesworth
Assumption, 1991
Cibachrome with lacquered wood frame
Courtesy of the Estate of Sarah Charlesworth and Paula Cooper Gallery, New York

Assumption is part of a series of works by Sarah Charlesworth called the *Renaissance Paintings*, in which the artist uses fragments taken from Renaissance painting that are collaged and enlarged as photographic prints to explore classic psychoanalytic models such as the Oedipus complex, erotic fantasy, the hero myth, denial of death, and projection. *Assumption* showcases Mary's journey to heaven accompanied by angels, with Mary as the central figure cut out and replaced by the blackness of the background.

Fig. 27: Arakawa and Madeline Gins
Landing Site Study, 1994
Digital rendering
Courtesy of Reversible

Destiny Foundation
© 1997 Estate of Madeline Gins, reproduced with permission of the Estate of Madeline Gins

Fig. 28: Installation view, *life and limbs*

(top, left to right)

Arakawa and Madeline Gins
Reversible Destiny Lofts—Mitaka (In Memory of Helen Keller), 2004
Digital Rendering
Courtesy of Reversible Destiny Foundation
© 2019 Estate of Madeline Gins, reproduced with permission of the Estate of Madeline Gins

Arakawa and Madeline Gins are the founders of the Reversible Destiny Foundation, whose goal is to promote their work and philosophy in the areas of art, architecture, and writing. This rendering shows one of the nine residential units that comprise the *Reversible Destiny Lofts* in Mitaka, a suburb of Tokyo. Arakawa and Gins developed a "procedural architecture" for these residencies, which aimed to challenge and stimulate the senses of its inhabitants and keep the mind and body lively, finding themselves in challenging environments that feel at different times more appropriate to a child or an elderly person. Arakawa and Gins were inspired by Helen Keller, who they perceived as someone who managed to reverse her own destiny, and the lofts are dedicated to her memory. This apartment complex was the first residential work of "procedural architecture" that Reversible Destiny built, and it utilizes three shapes—cubes, spheres, and tubes—which are arranged in stacked forms.

Arakawa and Madeline Gins
Hotel Reversible Destiny—124 West Houston Street, New York, 2006
Digital photomontage
Courtesy of Reversible Destiny Foundation
© 2008 Estate of Madeline Gins, reproduced with permission of the Estate of Madeline Gins

This is a proposal for an unrealized hotel located at the address of Arakawa and Gins's townhouse, which also exhibits their ideas for "procedural architecture," designed to steer residents to examine minutely the actions they take, inducing states of doubt followed by reinvention.

(bottom)

Marc Kokopeli
Untitled, 2019
Framed archival prints, fabric, wood, and steel

These photos are from a photo shoot that Marc Kokopeli's mother, Kathleen, directed for the Committee for Children, a social and emotional learning program for children, between 1990 and 1991. These images were made to be used as teaching aids for depicting ethical scenarios, designed so that students could learn social skills such as empathy, collaboration, and conflict resolution. A number of these staged photographs feature Kokopeli and his sister, as well as their young friends, posing in rooms of their Seattle home, which would be rearranged for the occasion. The images were mounted on a low pedestal covered with fabric, custom fit to the gallery, constructed by Kokopeli.

Fig. 29: Lutz Bacher
Pregnant, 2009
Stuffed fabric, metal, and dirt
Private Collection, New York, courtesy of Greene Naftali
Photograph by Lutz Bacher, April 2010
Photo courtesy of the Estate of Lutz Bacher and Galerie Buchholz, Berlin/Cologne/New York

Pregnant is made up of a mannequin that displays a pregnant belly and a featureless face lying on the ground with its legs bent violently at the knees in the opposite direction that human legs naturally bend in. The sewn figure displays traces of a structure that might have mounted the mannequin on a metal stand. This makes it possible for the piece to be a readymade or a manipulated found object rather than manufactured from design. The soles of the feet that extend vertically in the air are covered with dirt.

Fig. 30: Günter Brus
Meerschweinchen-Experiment 1–4, 1971
Pencil and crayon on paper
Courtesy of Collection Ph.
Konzett, Vienna

Günter Brus is an Austrian artist, performer, filmmaker, and writer, who was part of the Viennese Actionist group alongside Otto Muehl, Hermann Nitsch, and Rudolf Schwarzkogler. The movement became notorious after its 1968 action *Kunst und Revolution* (Art and Revolution), which they staged during student protests at a lecture hall in the University of Vienna. The action, which led to arrests and charges against some of the protagonists, included, among other things, nudity, defecation, masturbation, whipping, self-mutilation, and the smearing of excrement on the body, as well as self-induced vomiting. The drawing series *Meerschweinchen-Experiment* depicts a number of Rube Goldberg–like machines that will slaughter unsuspecting guinea pigs if an attached penis loses its erection. The guinea pig (*Meerschweinchen*) of the title might apply to man, who is as much the subject of the experiment as the rodent.

Fig. 31: Installation view, *life and limbs*

Fig. 32: Tryout for triangular walls, 2019

Fig. 33: Research for exhibition architecture, Google Image result for "animal mouth," 2019

Fig. 34: Anna-Sophie Berger
The Wearer of Clothes, 2019
Nylon, steel, and thread
Courtesy of Cell Project Space, London
Photograph by Rob Harris

Fig. 35: Moyra Davey
Still from *Hell Notes*, 1990/2017
Super 8 film with sound,
transferred to HD video
26 min 16 sec
Courtesy of the artist and Galerie
Buchholz, Berlin/Cologne/New York

In *Hell Notes*, Moyra Davey narrates observations about the city of New York in connection with a visual exploration of different locations, particularly focusing on money, food, and excrement, and their roles in the metropolis. Some are pictured to illustrate the textual explanations, such as the bedrock in Central Park. Others, such as the artist's home or the New York Public Library, serve as a place where the artist appears, works, or writes. Later, Davey explains financial markets to a male friend while seated on a park bench. Her psychoanalytic reading of money is next countered in the video by the depiction of her counterpart's sloppily eating a burger. In the final scene, at her apartment, Davey cooks what appear to be pennies clotted in butter in a frying pan.

Fig. 36: Benjamin Hirte
o.T., 2013
Wick cough syrup, Sinupret drops
Courtesy of the artist and Layr
Gallery, Vienna

Fig. 37: Moyra Davey
Still from *Hell Notes*, 1990/2017
Super 8 film with sound, transferred to
HD video
26 min 16 sec
Courtesy of the artist and Galerie
Buchholz, Berlin/Cologne/New York

Fig. 38: Meret Oppenheim
Untitled, 1937
Paper, pencil, and gouache
Courtesy of collection Design Museum
Den Bosch/Nl

Fig. 39: Installation view, *life and limbs*

(center)

Benjamin Hirte
Ghost, 2019
Steel, zinc-plated steel chains
Courtesy of the artist and Layr
Gallery, Vienna

Ghost is a sculpture modeled after a chandelier at the New York Public Library. It appears here as a ruin or relic. The only commissioned artwork in the exhibition, the piece can be seen to expand a theme present in Moyra Davey's 1991 piece *Hell Notes*, which is partially set in the same library. As a public space, the library figures for both Benjamin Hirte and Davey as a point of reference for civic life in New York. In Hirte's piece, however, the investigation describes a change in the very idealism once ascribed to public institutions. *Ghost*, as opposed to the original it is modeled after, is defined by lack: small chains are all that is left of a structure once adorned with countless light bulbs. The gutting of the public sector is alluded to by this empty shell, although currently the original is still burning brightly at the library, begging the question which chandelier is the ghost.

Fig. 40: Main reading room of the
New York Public Library
Photograph by Bruce Bi via Getty Images

Fig. 41: Installation view, *life and limbs*

(center)

Moschino
Waist of Money Suit, 1991
Acetate, rayon
Courtesy of Claudia Berger

This suit from the 1991 Moschino Couture collection was designed by the iconoclastic Franco Moschino. Claudia Berger, who is the lender of the suit and the mother of *life and limbs* curator Anna-Sophie Berger, wore this suit to Anna-Sophie's first communion. Around the red acetate blazer's waist, the words "Waist of Money" are embroidered in gold filament. "Waist" is split by the front button tab, while "of Money" is displayed on the back of the silhouette.

Fig. 42: Detail view of Lutz Bacher's *Pregnant*
(2009) during installation

Fig. 43: Till Megerle
Untitled, 2017
Ballpoint pen on paper

Fig. 44: Installation view, *life and limbs*

(top right)

Till Megerle
The Hussengut, 2016
Charcoal on paper
Courtesy of Christian Andersen,
Copenhagen

Till Megerle
The Thug Silhouette, 2017
Charcoal on paper
Courtesy of Christian Andersen,
Copenhagen

Combining the styles of Dutch Renaissance painting and satirical cartoons along with contemporary details and personal allusions, Till Megerle's charcoal drawings on paper depict vignettes of people, limbs morphing into pretzels and other twisted forms, in surreal outdoor settings. Employing dense hatching and shading, Megerle confers an erotic corporeality onto tangles of indeterminate matter.

Fig. 45: Anna-Sophie Berger
Tell me what to do, 2013
Performed with Katarina
Šoškić in Madeira
Photograph by Luka Knežević-Strika

Fig. 46: Installation view, *life and limbs*

(left to right)

Birgit Jürgenssen
Schwimmfester Segelschuh (Swimproof
Sailing Shoe), 1972
Pencil and colored pencil on
handmade paper
Courtesy of Galerie Hubert Winter, Vienna

Schwimmfester Segelschuh (Swimproof Sailing Shoe) shows a pink sport or sailing shoe, with its heel transformed into the foot of a duck or other water-based bird species. The nails of the claw yet again link Jürgenssen's detailed style to the fantastical rather than the naturalistic. Jürgenssen went on to create many shoe drawings and sculptures, which married deadpan elements with the surreal while linking these "heel concepts" to the practice of female dressing and social conventions.

Tobias Madison
Coral Larma, 2015
Palladium, steel, paint, and caoutchouc
Courtesy of the artist and
GEMS AND LADDERS

This fetish jewelry impacts the ability of its wearer to form facial expressions by its restrictive metal wires, and superimposes teardrops with its miniature coral hands beneath their eyes. The title, *Coral Larma*, while close to the French word for tears (*larme*), is inspired by a piece of paper that Man Ray gave to Carol Rama with a list of anagrams of her name.

Figs. 47, 48: Upper Rhenish Master
The Little Garden of Paradise, ca. 1410–20
Mixed technique on oak
Courtesy of the Städel Museum, Frankfurt am Main, Permanent Loan from the Historical Museums Frankfurt am Main

From Wikipedia: "*Hortus conclusus* is the Latin for an enclosed garden. The depiction of such a garden in Christian art from the Middle Ages onward is often intended to suggest purity. The garden is frequently shown walled, so implying impenetrability. The image refers to the virginity of Mary, Christ's mother."

Fig. 49: Benjamin Hirte
Still from *Sabeth*, 2009
Looped video, 30 min

Fig. 50: COBRA
The Object - グロリアス -, 2014
Lambda print, clock

COBRA's multimedia work often incorporates his own body via performative gestures to examine strategies for imitating histories of art or behaving in contemporary culture. A photograph of the artist himself is here used as the painted face of a clock, with a plaintive expression.

Fig. 51: Rosemarie Trockel
Replace Me, 2009
Black-and-white digital print
Courtesy of the artist and Sprüth Magers, Berlin/London/Los Angeles

Replace Me takes as its subject matter Gustave Courbet's 1866 painting *L'Origine du monde* (The Origin of the World). In Rosemarie Trockel's black-and-white photograph, the pubic zone of Courbet's female nude is collaged with a black spider that appears to be creeping down between the woman's legs. The generally assumed abjectness of a spider—specifically on naked skin—recalls something akin to torture, while at the same time, iconographically and psychoanalytically, a spider can be associated with female personas and the image of the mother. The title can be read to both refer to the female artist overwriting her canonic predecessor or to the layering of the representational content of black spider atop a woman's anatomy.

Fig. 52: Moyra Davey
Still from *Hell Notes*, 1990/2017
Super 8 film with sound, transferred to HD video
26 min 16 sec
Courtesy of the artist and Galerie Buchholz, Berlin/Cologne/New York

Fig. 53: Alexander Berger
First communion photograph of Anna and Claudia, 1997
Scan from photoprint

Fig. 54: Anna-Sophie Berger
Study for Shutter Speed, 2005
Color photograph, scanned

Fig. 55: Anna-Sophie Berger
Margeriten, 2005
Color photograph, scanned

Fig. 56: Alexander Berger
Flower, 1979
Color slide photograph, scanned

Fig. 57: Anna-Sophie Berger
Untitled, 2015

Fig. 58: Moschino
"No comment," Spring/Summer Trade Press Campaign, 1989
Photograph by Stephano Pandini

Fig. 59: Moschino
Text print shirt, Moschino Cheap and Chic
Photographer unknown

Fig. 60: Moschino
Look 29, Spring 1994 Ready-to-Wear

Fig. 61: Moschino
Look 44: La classe non è ACQUA swimsuit, Spring 1994 Ready-to-Wear

Fig. 62: Anna-Sophie Berger
Still from *Duel*
HD video, 49 min 6 sec

Fig. 63: Guillaume de Lorris, Jean de Meun
Roman de la Rose, ca. 1380
Tempera colors, gold leaf, ink
Courtesy of the Morgan Library & Museum. MS M.132, fol. 71v.
Purchased by J. Pierpont Morgan (1837–1913) in 1902.
Photograph by the Morgan Library & Museum, New York

Fig. 64: Still from *La Prise de pouvoir par Louis XIV*, 1966
Directed by Roberto Rossellini
100 min

Fig. 65: *Workers: The funeral procession for seven unidentified Triangle Shirtwaist fire victims*, 1911
Photographer unknown
Courtesy of Kheel Center for Labor-Management Documentation and Archives, Cornell University, Ithaca, NY

Fig. 66: Still from *The Tin Drum*, 1979
Directed by Volker Schlöndorff
Based on the novel by Günter Grass
144 min

Fig. 67: Johann Christian Brand (design), Johann Ernst Mansfeld (engraver)
Eyerweib (Egg Seller), from the series *Drawings Based on Common People, Especially the Sellers in Vienna*, 1775
Etching on paper
Courtesy of MAK – Museum of Applied Arts, Vienna
Photograph © MAK

Fig. 68: Nicolas de Larmessin II
Page from *Les costumes grotesques et les métiers de Nicolas Larmessin. XVIIe siècle. Habits des métiers et professions*
Éditions Henri Veyrier, 1974

Engraver Nicolas de Larmessin II, whose family had a famous publishing house in Paris, created around 100 of these copperplate engravings over a period of time. In the modern tradition of the adjective *grotesque*, these depictions of the trades as proverbial garments for the workers and craftsmen extrapolate and parody an understanding of work or labor as identity, the defining aspect of a person's milieu and habitus. These prints were made shortly before the onset of the Industrial Revolution in Europe and display both a connotation of rank, pride, and humility connected to the individual crafts, along with satirical elements. Legs become columns in the depiction of the architect, a net is the dress for the fishmonger, and a table features as a skirt worn around the waist for a saleswoman, displaying the goods lying on her lap or festooned across her limbs.

Figs. 69, 70: Andrea Fraser
Stills from *May I Help You?,* 1991
SD video, 20 min
Written and directed by Andrea Fraser
Installation in cooperation with Allan McCollum
Performed by Ledlie Borgerhoff
Produced by American Fine Arts, Co.

Fig. 71: Moschino
Lifesaver Jacket, Spring 1991 Couture

Fig. 72: Moschino
Look 2, Spring 1994 Ready-to-Wear

Fig. 73: Anna-Sophie Berger
Mama, 2012
Color photograph, scanned

Fig. 74: Anna-Sophie Berger
Untitled, 2019

Fig. 75: Jacques Carelman
Detail from *Catalog of Fantastic Things*
Ballantine Books, 1971

Unless otherwise noted, all works courtesy of the artist.

A23 The Human Barrow
Get things moved while testing a friend's loyalty and desire to be of help.

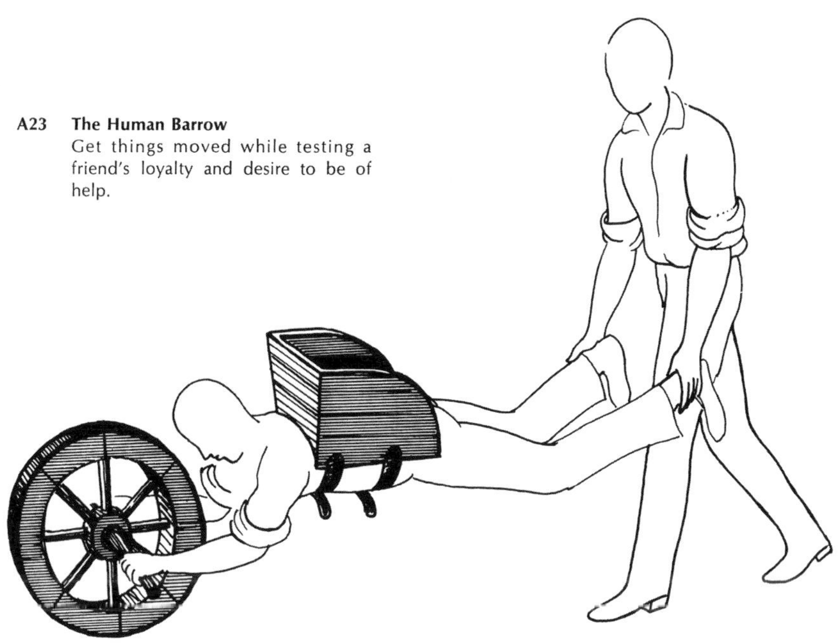

Fig. 75

Anna-Sophie Berger

Anna-Sophie Berger (b. 1989, Vienna, Austria) is an artist living and working in New York and Vienna. She has had solo exhibitions at Bonner Kunstverein, Bonn (2020); Cell Project Space, London (2019); MUMOK, Vienna (2016); Kunsthaus Bregenz (2016); Ludlow 38, New York (2015); White Flag Projects, St. Louis (2015); and Belvedere21, Vienna (2014); among others. She has recently participated in group exhibitions at MACRO, Rome (2021); Huset for Kunst og Design, Holstebro (2021); MAK, Austria (2019); CACBM, Paris (2019); Frans Hals Museum, Haarlem (2018); S.M.A.K., Ghent (2018); Contemporary Art Centre, Vilnius (2018); Kunsthalle Wien, Vienna (2017); Kestnergesellschaft, Hanover (2017); and Kunstverein Munchen, Munich (2017). She is the recipient of the 2017 Ars Viva Fine Arts Prize in Germany; 2016 Kapsch Contemporary Art Prize, Austria; and the 2013 Swiss Textile Award.

Philipp Ekardt

Philipp Ekardt is currently the academic coordinator and a researcher in the NOMIS project "Traveling Forms" at the University of Konstanz, Germany. He studied art history and comparative literature in Berlin, Paris, and at Yale University where he earned his PhD, and previously held a visiting professorship at the Institute for Art and Aesthetics at the University of the Arts/Berlin and worked for several years at the Warburg Institute in London, as well as teaching in smaller capacities in the Department of Classics at University College London and serving as visiting faculty at the University of the Arts/Zurich. He is a former editor-in-chief of the critical art journal *Texte zur Kunst*; the author of two books, *Toward Fewer Images: The Work of Alexander Kluge* (OCTOBER Books/MIT Press, 2018) and *Benjamin on Fashion* (Bloomsbury, 2020); and has published widely in the field of contemporary art, frequently on its processing of the field and phenomena of fashion, such as, recently and upcoming, "Interfacing Paris: Passing by Atelier E.B," in *Atelier E.B: Passer-by* (2020), the catalogue for the eponymous exhibition by Scottish artist and designer Lucy McKenzie and Beca Lipscombe (Serpentine Gallery/Lafayette Anticipations/Garage Moscow), and "The Cheongsam, the French Shirt, and the Puffed Sleeve: Image/Garment Transactions in Evelyn Taocheng Wang's Global Contemporary Artwork," in an artist's monograph dedicated to Wang's work, to be co-published by Dancing Foxes Press and Kunstverein Düsseldorf. Other upcoming articles analyze works by Arthur Jafa and Jeremy Shaw.

Annie Godfrey Larmon

Annie Godfrey Larmon is a writer and editor based in Garrison, New York. Her essays, reviews, and interviews have appeared in *apricota*, *Artforum*, *BBC Culture*, *Bookforum*, *CURA.*, *Even*, *Frieze*, *MAY*, *The Miami Rail*, *Spike*, *Texte zur Kunst*, *Topical Cream*, *Vdrome*, *WdW Review*, and the *White Review*. The recipient of a 2016 Creative Capital | Warhol Foundation Arts Writers Grant for short-form writing, she was the editor of publications for the inaugural Okayama Art Summit and is a former international reviews editor of *Artforum*. As an editor, she has also worked on books for MoMA PS1, Lévy Gorvy, and the Hessel Museum of Art. Godfrey Larmon has been a writer-in-residence at the LUMA Foundation in Arles, France; Mahler & LeWitt Studios in Spoleto, Italy; and Cuttyhunk Island Writers' Residency. She is currently at work on her first novel.

This book before you is the product of artist Anna-Sophie Berger's unrivaled brilliance. *life and limbs* is an adventurous, elegant exhibition and it has been thrilling to see that spirit unfold across these pages. Artist-curated shows are a vital component of Swiss Institute's programming in that they establish links in unexpected places. Placing objects, images, words, and theories together in novel configurations is a strong suit of Berger's and, entrusted with her vision, we are proud to publish her groundbreaking essay.

Both Phillip Ekardt and Annie Godfrey Larmon contributed stimulating, moving, and perceptive texts that reflect on Anna-Sophie's exhibition. For their intellectual rigor, emotional perceptiveness, and original thought, I am truly thankful.

For their commitment to editorial excellence, I am deeply grateful to SI's curator-at-large Laura McLean-Ferris and SI Senior Curator Alison Coplan. Their sharp insights, boundless imaginations, and diligent efforts shape SI's publications into treasures. Many thanks go to Vela Arbutina for establishing a beautiful layout for SI's book series. I am also immensely proud to initiate our collaboration with Elizabeth Karp-Evans and Adam Turnbull of Pacific, who have lent their abundant talents to designing this exquisite book. For his work on the catalog, I am also grateful to SI Curator Daniel Merritt.

For support of this publication, I would like to heartily thank the Austrian Consulate. Because of the organization's generosity, *life and limbs* will live on in this remarkable and inventive publication.

We gratefully acknowledge the support of the Vienna Tourist Board as the Presenting Partner of *life and limbs*. For their generous support of the exhibition, we are grateful to the Federal Chancellery Republic of Austria, the Austrian Cultural Forum New York, the SI Architecture & Design Council, and Sister City, our then hotel sponsor. We also extend our deepest gratitude to the artists and the lenders to the exhibition: Claudia Berger; Christina and Oscar Castellón; collection Design Museum Den Bosch/NL; Collection Ph. Konzett, Vienna; Estate of Madeline Gins; The Estate of Sarah Charlesworth and Paula Cooper Gallery, New York; Galerie Buchholz, Berlin/Cologne/New York; Galerie Hubert Winter; GEMS AND LADDERS; Greene Naftali; Birgit Jürgenssen Estate; Landessammlungen Niederösterreich; MAK – Museum of Applied Arts, Vienna; Martos Gallery, New York; Northampton Museum and Art Gallery, Northampton; Petzel Gallery, New York; Michail Pirgelis; Reversible Destiny Foundation; Salon 94, New York; Sprüth Magers; The VERBUND COLLECTION, Vienna.

Lastly, as always, I wish to express my sincere gratitude to SI's Board of Trustees and its dedicated, unparalleled staff. Your unyielding belief in art's immense power is an endless source of inspiration and energy.

Simon Castets

Founded in 1986, SI is an independent nonprofit contemporary art institution dedicated to promoting forward-thinking and experimental art making through innovative exhibitions and programs.

SI Programming is made possible in part with public funds from Pro Helvetia, Swiss Arts Council; the New York State Council on the Arts, with the support of Governor Kathy Hochul and the New York State Legislature; and the New York City Department of Cultural Affairs in partnership with the City Council. Main sponsors include LUMA Foundation, Friends of SI, the Andy Warhol Foundation for Visual Arts, and the Horace W. Goldsmith Foundation. Exhibitions are made possible in part by the SI Annual Exhibition Fund with leadership support provided by the LUMA Foundation, Michael Ringier, Olivier Audemars, Philippe Bertherat, Max and Monique Burger, the Garcia Family Foundation, Florian Gutzwiller, Dominique Lévy, Susanne von Meiss, Iwan Wirth, Ghislaine Brenninkmeijer, the Kevin Wendle Foundation, and the Freedman Family Foundation. SI gratefully acknowledges Swiss Re as SI ONSITE Partner, Vitra as Design Partner, Crozier Fine Arts as Preferred Shipping Art Logistics Partner, and SWISS as Travel Partner.

Critical operating support has been provided to SI in 2020–22 as part of a collective fundraising effort. We thank the following supporters: Teiger Foundation, The Willem de Kooning Foundation, Helen Frankenthaler Foundation, The Destina Foundation, Stavros Niarchos Foundation, Cy Twombly Foundation, Henry Luce Foundation, The Fox Aarons Foundation, David Rockefeller Fund, Arison Arts Foundation, Blavatnik Family Foundation, Jacques & Natasha Gelman Foundation, The Robert Lehman Foundation, The Jill and Peter Kraus Foundation, The Milton and Sally Avery Arts Foundation, and the Richard Pousette-Dart Foundation.

Board of Trustees

Staff

Published for the exhibition *life and limbs,* curated by Anna-Sophie Berger at Swiss Institute, New York, September 25–December 29, 2019

Editors: Alison Coplan, Laura McLean-Ferris
Copy Editor and Proofreader: Miles Champion
SI Series Visual Identity: Vela Arbutina
Design: Adam Turnbull and
Elizabeth Karp-Evans, Pacific
Installation Photography: Daniel Pérez

Swiss Institute staff for *life and limbs*:
Simon Castets, Katherine Ahn, Andrew Alexander, Alison Coplan, Sadik Grice, Scott Kiernan, Laura McLean-Ferris, Daniel Merritt, Lou Neyland, Mojdeh Pishyar, Mary Provenzano, Kristen Wawruck
Volunteers: Danielle Bruce, Anna Cloarec

SI gratefully acknowledges the support of the Vienna Tourist Board as Presenting Partner of *life and limbs*. Generous support is provided by the Federal Chancellery Republic of Austria, the Austrian Cultural Forum New York, the SI Architecture & Design Council.

Bundesministerium
Kunst, Kultur,
öffentlicher Dienst und Sport

First published by: Swiss Institute, New York; Lenz, Milan

Swiss Institute
38 St Marks Pl
New York, NY 10003
www.swissinstitute.net

Lenz
Via Adige 17
20135 Milan, Italy
www.lenz.press

Printed by OGM Printing, Padova, Italy

ISBN 979-12-80579-09-6

Distributed in Europe by:

Les presses du réel
35 rue Coslon, 21000 Dijon, France
www.lespressesdureel.com

Idea Books
Nieuwe Hemweg 6R, 1013 BG
Amsterdam, The Netherlands
www.ideabooks.nl

Distributed in the UK, Americas, RoW by:

ARTBOOK | D.A.P.
75 Broad Street, Suite 630
New York, NY 10004
www.artbook.com